EAST–WEST REFLECTIONS ON DEMONIZATION

NIAS–Nordic Institute of Asian Studies
NIAS Studies in Asian Topics

NIAS Press is the autonomous publishing arm of NIAS – Nordic Institute of Asian Studies, a research institute located at the University of Copenhagen. NIAS is partially funded by the governments of Denmark, Finland, Iceland, Norway and Sweden via the Nordic Council of Ministers, and works to encourage and support Asian studies in the Nordic countries. In so doing, NIAS has been publishing books since 1969, with more than two hundred titles produced in the past few years.

UNIVERSITY OF COPENHAGEN

Nordic Council of Ministers

East-West
Reflections on
Demonization

North Korea Now, China Next?

edited by
Geir Helgesen and Rachel Harrison

 **niaS**PRESS

EAST–WEST REFLECTIONS ON DEMONIZATION
North Korea Now, China Next?
Edited by Geir Helgesen and Rachel Harrison

Nordic Institute of Asian Studies
Studies in Asian Topics, no. 73

First published in 2020 by NIAS Press
NIAS – Nordic Institute of Asian Studies
Øster Farimagsgade 5, 1353 Copenhagen K, Denmark
Tel: +45 3532 9503 • Fax: +45 3532 9549
E-mail: books@nias.ku.dk • Online: www.niaspress.dk

A CIP catalogue record for this book is available from the British Library

ISBN: 978-87-7694-288-5 (hbk)
ISBN: 978-87-7694-289-2 (pbk)

Typeset in Minion 13/15.6
Typesetting by NIAS Press
Cover design by Jonathan Foran

Back cover text by Professor Moon Chung-in, quoted from
'The US' "3 demons" and how they're misguiding foreign policy
into a new cold war', *Hankyoreh*, 10 August 2020.

Printed and bound in the United States
by Maple Press, York, PA

Contents

A Message of Hope

*T*here is one thing that we all do, to a greater or lesser extent, perhaps out of laziness, thoughtlessness or ignorance; or mainly just to keep things simple in everyday life. That is, we generalize.

As a child, I often heard people talk about different people – 'the Swede', 'the American', 'the German' and 'the Russian' – as stereotypes. The Swede was stingy, so they said; the American was rich; the German effective; and the Russian persevering. These were not references to any one particular Swede or Russian, but rather to Swedes and Russians in general. That was just the way they were. And I believed it. That was, until I met a real-life Swede, who had married an aunt of mine. He was certainly not stingy, but was instead friendly and generous. He was therefore probably the exception that proved the rule.

The problem is that when we generalize, we tend to overlook nuance. The range of colours disappears and the world turns black and white. We become one-dimensional and self-righteous, convincing ourselves that, 'He who is not with me is against me.' Or that Others belong to an 'Axis of Evil.'

There is one word in the language that I use, as a teacher, to inoculate my students against the debilitating effects of generalization. And that word is 'some', not others. When some (and there the word is!) claim that immigrants – Muslims, Americans, Chinese or North Koreans – are this way or that way, then I wish an alarm bell would ring and that the word 'some' would pop up as an alert. For then the statements can sound very different. Some immigrants commit crimes. But most do not. Some Muslims are fundamentalists. But most are not. Some North Koreans are brainwashed. Others are not.

The first stage on the road to creating enemy images is characterized by the notion that Others are somehow different: they behave differently; they have a different culture. In short, they are strange. They are strangers.

The second stage on that road is one of downgrading the Other. At this point, strangers are not only seen as different from ourselves, but that difference implies that their morals and their culture is also questionable. While 'we' see 'ourselves' as responsible, 'we' see 'them' as irresponsible. While 'we' are honest, decent and hardworking, 'they' are the opposite. While 'we' are Christian/Muslim/Jewish or other kinds of religious believers, 'they', by contrast, are idolaters. In short, 'they' are everything that 'we' are not, nor would ever want to be.

On the third stage of the road, the threat posed by the Other becomes yet clearer. Not only are Others obscene and immoral, but also menacing. (The threat they pose can be real or imagined.) They slander us and aim to hurt us. They want to take our jobs, drive us out of the places we live, shut down our places of worship and our schools, destroy our homes, and perhaps even to kill us. At this stage, 'we' and 'they' have become two, distinct, close-knit and fixed-minded groups, each having little or no contact with the other and even fewer opportunities to develop any sense of mutual understanding. All the problems 'we' experience are the result of Others – for someone else must be to blame for our misery. And thus the hunt for scapegoats begins.

If the situation is further aggravated, then it becomes a question of them or us, at which point it is best to pre-empt 'them', using attack as the best form of defence. After all, we should not simply sit around idly waiting to be destroyed when killing a deadly enemy is not a crime but rather both sensible and legitimate.

But how can we be sure that enemies only come from out-side? Can they not also be found amidst our very own ranks? And are they not even more insidious because they reside among us? The only way to protect 'us' is to pull the weeds up by the root. When Hutus killed at least 800,000 Tutsis and moderate Hutus over a period of a hundred days in Rwanda in 1994, cries rang out around the houses: 'Kill the cock-roaches, kill the cockroaches!' An article in *Kangura* magazine (February 1993) read:

> A Tutsi is one who has a sweet tongue but is indescribably mali-cious. A Tutsi is one who has an insatiable need for revenge; one who is unpredictable, one who laughs when he suffers. In our language, a Tutsi is called a cockroach because he uses the night to achieve his goals.

The Balkans in the 1990s also provide a telling example of how good neighbours were turned into deadly enemies. It was not ethnic differences that caused the war in Bosnia Herzegovina but rather the war that created a greater distance between certain groups of people. In *The Myth of Ethnic War: Serbia and Croatia in the 1990s* (2004), Valère Philip Gagnon argues that it was members of the political and military elites in Belgrade and Zagreb who mobilized the population along ethnic lines to protect their own economic and political power interests. The war became so brutal and bloody pre-cisely because of the closeness and similarity between people. The social fabric had to be torn apart in order for nationalist politicians to secure their own positions.[1]

There are many ways to fight against perceiving the Other through the lens of enemy images. Most important is face-to-face human encounter. Dialogue is a meeting between peo-ple, where the purpose is to learn from each other. Whereas propaganda seeks to persuade, we try to understand each

---

1. Valère Philip Gagnon, *The Myth of Ethnic War. Serbia and Croatia in the 1990s*. Ithaca: Cornell University Press (2004).

other through dialogue. Whereas debate is aimed at winning over the other, dialogue provides an opportunity to overcome our own prejudices. While we try to reach agreement through negotiations, we try to understand the causes of the disagreement through dialogue.

This is not the same thing as simple relativism; nor is it a question of disregarding our own core values. It does not mean that we should walk around disguised as one another so as not to offend, or that we should self-indulgently peddle our own beliefs. The fact that we are willing to enter into dialogue with the 'Other' means that we realize our experiences to be our own, and that others have experiences of *their* own as well. Had I been in their place, I might probably have thought and acted just like them. So, I make every effort to understand their way of thinking. Not to make it mine, but to develop a more nuanced and more accurate picture of the world.

As part of this process, we need to practice what some refer to as 'methodical empathy'. That is, we need to try to empathise with and understand the situation of others, as they perceive – or have perceived – themselves. Here it is important to stress that understanding is not the same as accepting. How could German youths in their hundreds of thousands shout out 'Heil Hitler!' in the rapture of excitement and want to follow him? Could I have been one of them? Yes, perhaps I could. I think many of us can commit the most terrible acts on others, if the external environment becomes sufficiently extreme.

After a war in which powerful images of the enemy have dominated, there comes a period of reconciliation. It is our capacity to reconcile that has enabled us to survive as a species. Without this, we would long since have eradicated each other in cycle after retaliatory cycle of bloody revenge.

In Korea, reconciliation after the war that ended in 1953 has yet to be reached. A precondition for reconciliation is at least some level of trust. This was reaffirmed by all parties concerned in the Six-Party Talks[2] held in Beijing in 2007, when they stated that they would 'take positive steps to increase mutual trust' and 'make joint efforts for lasting peace and stability in Northeast Asia.'[3] That this has not been reached 13 years later is a disturbing fact.

The Truth and Reconciliation Commission in South Africa, adopted in 1995 through the 'National Unity and Reconciliation Act', has shown one way in which we can move forward. In the preface to the Commission's final report, which was handed over to President Nelson Mandela on 29 October 1998, the chairman, Archbishop Desmond Tutu, wrote:

> Having looked at the bestiality of the past, having prayed and received forgiveness and given redemption, let us close the door to the past – not to forget it, but not to allow it to take us captive. Let's start moving toward the wonderful future of a new society where people count – not because of biological coincidence or external characteristics, but because they are people of infinite value created in God's image ...[4]

The Commission's report stated that reconciliation needs something over and above remorse and respectful remembrance. Rather, it requires justice and redress, not only individually but also socially: 'Only if the truth triggers a social dynamic that alleviates victims' suffering will it respond to the demand for restorative justice.'[5] It was therefore incumbent on those who had benefitted from apartheid in terms of educational privilege or a monopoly on land, buildings and commerce, to make a specific contribution to the reconstruction of society.

---

2. The six parties were: China, the USA, Russia, Japan, North Korea and South Korea.

3. 'North Korea – Denuclearization Action Plan'. https://worldview.stratfor.com/article/text-feb-13-2007-six-party-agreement.

4. Vol. I, Ch. I, §91.

5. *Ibid.*, Ch. V, §100.

On the many occasions that I have worked on reconciliation over the years, I have experienced what can happen when we meet face-to-face. In an atmosphere of suspicion, participants tell their stories. Everyone listens. That's how it was to be me, such was my family's situation. Do you understand why I acted the way I did and think the way I think? No? Then the stories have to be repeated, and the conversations continue. After a week or a month, a new question begins to take shape: What if I were in the Other's position? Would I then have thought and acted the way they did? Maybe I would.

Nelson Mandela has become the foremost champion of justice and reconciliation of our time. After 27 years in captivity on Robben Island, he was still able to see the human being in the system and the face behind the actions. In his autobiography *The Road to Freedom* (1994) he writes:

> I have always known that in the heart of every human being there is compassion and generosity. No one is born with hatred for another human being because of their skin color, background or religion. People must learn to hate, and if they can learn to hate, they can also learn to love. For love is more natural to the human heart than the opposite. Even in the gloomiest time in prison, when my comrades and I were pushed to the limit of what we could endure, I could see a glimpse of human love in one of the guards, maybe just for a second. But it was enough to comfort me and keep me going. The goodness of man is a flame that can be hidden, but never extinguished.

Mandela's example shows that even the darkest of enemy images can change its colour when held up close to the flame of human goodness.

My hope for the future is connected to human encounters and to the understanding they can generate. We must create societies where we prioritize meeting face-to-face – at the local, the national and the international level. Young and old, women and men, Christians and Muslims, Hutus and Tutsis, Americans and Chinese, as well as the North Koreans. It is through these encounters that we discover just how different we are – and that such differences are enriching. We are given the opportunity to learn something from the Other, and for them to learn something from us. For just as a rainbow consists of many colours, so too does the society of humankind. As a wise man once said to me, 'It takes all kinds of people to make a world.' To invite strangers into a community by saying, 'Come as you are and become like us!' is coercive – and should be named as such.

When we meet in mutual respect across cultural and political divides, we also discover how equal we are and that there is more that unites us than divides. Everyone eats and sleeps, works and loves. When we burn ourselves, we feel pain; when someone dies, we grieve. We share the experience of having been children, adolescents, siblings, pupils, and so forth. We yearn for security and love, to be seen and to be valued. We are the same, and yet different, like *yin* and *yang*. And we are both blessed and doomed to live together on this small globe, the home of humanity.

In the age of nuclear weapons and the crisis of climate change, we have a choice to make: what the Danish artist and poet Piet Hein refers to as the choice between 'co-existence or no existence'. War is the most primitive of all ways to resolve conflict. In the 21st century, we must realize the UN Charter's vision of 'rescuing the forthcoming generations from the scourge of war ... and uniting our forces to maintain international peace and security.' A prerequisite for that is we learn to see through the seductive mechanisms of enemy images and the tragedies that they have caused. The fact that someone is different from us does not mean that they are worth less as human beings, much less that they are a threat. And, as Nelson Mandela said, 'No one is born with hatred for another human being because of their skin colour, background or religion. People must learn to hate, and if they can learn to hate, they can also learn to love.' This message gives us hope.

And it is the message of hope that this book conveys.

Inge Eidsvåg

About the Author Inge Eidsvåg is a writer and former director of The Fridtjof Nansen Academy in Lillehammer, Norway. He was among the initiators of the Nansen Peace Centre and took active part in the Nansen dialogue projects in the aftermath of the wars in former Yugoslavia. He is the author of several books, and has been awarded prizes for his work on dialogue and reconciliation, both in Norway and in the Balkans.

Acknowledgments

*T*his book is the outcome of a very much collective effort by eighteen writers from seven countries, all of whom are engaged in promoting international understanding. As editors we would like, first and foremost, to recognize the contribution made by each of the authors as an important and invaluable constituent of the resulting volume. Each represents an integral part of the whole.

There are several experts besides those contributing to this volume who should be acknowledged, as they have contributed with lifelong struggles for peace and mutual understanding. We will mention only one here, someone who has particularly inspired many of us – and many others – to maintain a positive and optimistic approach, even when dark clouds covered the sky and 'realists' advised us to start preparing for war. Professor Moon Chung-in has been unshakeable in his struggle for peace and was rightly seen as one of the chief architects behind the Sunshine Policy. A column of his – entitled 'If you want peace, prepare for peace' – recently appeared in the *Hankyoreh* newspaper. We bring extracts from it on page 254.

The overall arguments made in this volume were addressed and rehearsed with the specific support of NIAS, the University of Copenhagen; the Fudan Development Institute, Fudan University, Shanghai; and SOAS University of London as venues for discussion. The opportunity to further develop the ideas was supported by a seedcorn grant from SOAS and by funding from the Arts and Humanities Research Council in the UK. At the Nansen Academy in Norway, central themes of this book were presented and discussed at the *Understanding Asia* course and during the Nansen East–West Dialogue Academy (NEWDAY), an international summer school for university students from East Asia and the Nordic countries.

We would also like to acknowledge the contribution made by Nicol Foulkes Savinetti for her important role as assistant editor in the early stages of the production of the work; by David Stuligross for his tenacious editing, proofing and indexing of a highly diverse text; and by Jonathan Foran for the design of a book jacket that reflects the key ideas represented in this volume. Last but not least, two colleagues from NIAS deserve a special recognition. Liu Chunrong's personal engagement with this project as well as his scholarly contribution has been particularly encouraging, and we warmly thank the Fudan-European Centre for China Studies, University of Copenhagen, for a financial contribution that was needed but unexpected. This volume could not have come to fruition, of course, without the professional and creative input offered by the editor-in-chief at NIAS Press, Gerald Jackson, throughout the process of its production, from inception to finalization.

Geir Helgesen and Rachel Harrison

Fifteen Essays on Demonization, and Why to Avoid It

*T*his collection of fifteen essays deals with the act of *demonization* in international affairs, by which we mean the process of cultivating a fundamentally negative perspective on an international 'Other'. In this volume, the Other refers largely to two neighbouring countries in East Asia: North Korea is our primary focus, China our second. This seemingly illogical choice of emphasizing the smaller and less significant of the two countries is because North Korea is the prime example of a country demonized by the West. It is hoped that China will not come to be treated with the same one-sidedness that North Korea has so long suffered: were that to become the case, then the geopolitical tremors that the treatment of North Korea, and its reactions, have caused might be replaced by earthquakes. China and North Korea share cultural similarities, and are also formally related in political terms, since both are seen as practising a similar non-Western governing system, albeit with important differences. What is obvious is that bigger, more significant and more numerous differences exist between these two East Asian nations, on the one hand, and 'the West' on the other. Far less obvious, however, is how we relate to these differences, whether cultural or political, or rather a mix of the two.

This volume therefore engages with what we see as a persisting East–West divide, one that is both cultural and political. In the case of North Korea, ongoing demonization does not distinguish between what is cultural and what is political; worse still, it fails to acknowledge that the one very often strongly affects the other. It is therefore important to make clear from the very beginning that we offer a different perspective here. The contributors to this book – all of us scholars and professional writers – share a serious concern regarding the extensive, one-sided and negative representation of the Other, no matter whether that Other is labelled an enemy or not. In principle, we are politically 'colour-blind', and, more important, open to other ways of living and organizing societies.

As emphasized in the Foreword by the acclaimed Norwegian writer and mediator, Inge Eidsvåg, a premise for reconciliation and peace is that the parties concerned are able to empathize with the Other. The current state of East–West relations, in particular those between China and the USA, which influence or even dominate global international affairs, shows alarming tendencies towards the opposite direction. In our view, it is therefore of urgent importance to disclose demonization and its consequences, and to warn against the creation of generalized enemy images, since this opens doors for generalized violence, fuelling the scourge of war.

Korea, a divided country

Korea is one, and yet divided. Historically the country was a kingdom between China and Japan, the bridge from China to Japan, as some say; a shrimp between whales, say others. In any case, Korea was an independent kingdom situated between two East Asian rivals. All three of them were socially and politically shaped by different but often coexisting religions and moral systems, the most important of which were Confucianism, Buddhism and Shamanism. The three countries (which, due to Korea's division now count as four) are characterized by a common political culture. Though not identical, they are clearly characterized by shared common features that are significant enough to separate East Asia, on the one hand, from Europe and the United States on the other. Hence the concept couples *East–West*, two regions, each of which comprises relatively large differences, but which appear as 'the Other' in relation to one another: the differences are more conspicuous than the similarities.

Korea, colonized by Japan from 1910 to 1945, was then divided as a result of World War II. The southern half became a western-oriented zone connected to the United States and, via this connection, with its archenemy, Japan. The northern half associated with the Soviet Union and China but, largely as a result of the rivalry between these two communist giants, it placed a strong emphasis on 'national independence'. The division of Korea into two thus produced one zone that was western-oriented, albeit initially more in name than through any benefit, and another that was communist, though nevertheless more Korean than communist. Such was the beginning of a long and, to date, ongoing tragedy.

Since then, Korea has been divided into two almost opposing economic and political systems, as a result of which the people in each camp have been barred from contacting those in the other. At the same time, the two countries have failed to establish normal international relations, seeing the other as the enemy. And in both countries – via comprehensive political-ideological propaganda dispensed through upbringing and education, and through various forms of mass media – a picture of the Other as inferior, inhuman, sinister and aggressive, among other similarly negative characteristics, has been clearly drawn. That such pictures are caricatures that of course cannot encompass the traits of an entire population, be they the 25 million people living in the north or the 50 million in the south, has done nothing to prevent the ongoing process of mutual defamation.

Within Europe, a similar division between East and West was experienced until 1989 and the subsequent collapse of the Soviet Union. The European divide, however (or for that matter the division of Germany), was not as absolute as the Korean one. The military situation was not constantly tense, although there were periods when it looked bleak, not least in divided Germany. Crossing borders and meeting the Other was difficult at times, but never impossible. In most countries, some people, organizations and political parties sympathized with the Other. Although not widely popular and in the minority, their opinions were not illegal. At times, this position of sympathizing with the other side proved difficult, in the West as in the East, and at times almost criminal, particularly in the East. Still, there was a slow, positive development towards normalization on both sides of the ideological divide.

In the two Koreas, opposition to the other has taken first priority, as the primary rationale for what one can and cannot do, say and think. It was a main theme in upbringing and in education, in art and literature, and of course in the news. Yet while relations with the other were marked by fear and anxiety, this did not equate with hatred, since each has always fundamentally seen the other as 'like us', as brothers and sisters. Many had family members on the other side, but few had contact. For the individual, this separation was a forced condition, viewed of course as most or solely caused by the Other. To think otherwise was taboo, and to give voice to such thoughts extremely risky.

The fact that the division of the Korean peninsula has adversely affected both countries for 75 years is not often included in the news flow from and about conditions on the peninsula. The light of common cultural traits has also been dimmed, in contrast to the sharp differences that have been highlighted. From the perspective of the Western and South Korean news media, there is only one perpetrator and one victim, one aggressive party and one who must be alert and on guard, one unfree and one free. The North is the enemy, and the South is the normal country. In such a story, there is no room for nuance. But are there not nuances in Korean history, and in the Korean present? Of course there are: not everyone in the North today is a monster, nor everyone in the South an angel. The North Korean government is not *only* bad, and the South Korean government is not *only* caring, humane and democratic.

In the current phase of globalization, 30 years after the official end of the old 'East–West' Cold War, international relations have again reached a precarious state. The practice of *demonizing* the enemy Other has had the effect of reigniting tensions, reminding us of the period from the 1950s to the 1990s, when contending political ideologies spawned animosities, enmities and physical conflict between opponents, and when fear of a Third World War breaking out was at times widespread.

There was a brief moment, just before the turn of the millennium, when a number of opinion shapers in the Western world celebrated – in advance – 'the end of history'. This 'end' was understood as the victory of Western liberal democracy over all other political systems and was linked with the affirmation of a thriving global, capitalist economy. Such simplified and self-righteous 'optimism' became widespread in the West. Since that time, and at an accelerated pace, *social*, *cultural* and *economic* development have proved belief in an imminent 'end of history' to be premature. And of the three societal factors, culture appears the most resilient.

A clash of civilizations?

East–West ideological warfare may have ended after 1990 but continued international animosities between East and West often seem to run even deeper than before, now shaped by a depiction of the Other focusing on particular geographical, cultural and ethnic characteristics. In more learned and sophisticated presentations, it may have been different, the target of criticism, hatred or fear being the authorities of the Other: its political system and its main actors. Information for the broader public, however, has generalized and lumped together the entire population of that nation. This was, and still is, particularly the case with North Korea and partly also with China, to mention the two examples that we deal with most closely in this book.

North Korea shares a Confucian-based political culture – as does the southern half of the peninsula, and so too its immediate neighbours, China and Japan. It is important to state, and to bear in mind while dealing with East Asia and its relations with the Western world, that cultural traditions persist, not least in political practices. Therefore, to measure East Asia and the West with exactly the same yardstick is, and will remain, inaccurate and problematic, to say the least. It goes without saying that we also acknowledge the persistence of Western cultural traditions. Therefore, it is the significant differences between Eastern and Western ideas, values and norms, particularly in relation to power and authority, which necessitate an urgent reappraisal.

This is not to argue that culture remains a static power *determining* people's ideas, attitudes and actions. Neither economy nor politics nor culture are determining forces; but the relations between culture (values), economics and politics clearly seem to be reciprocal. This is supported by the lead researcher of the World Values Surveys, who also adds: 'Nevertheless, there is some truth in the idea that culture *itself* tends to be a conservative influence.'[1] While cultural differences remain a fact to be accepted and respected, it is our common and shared human capacities that make cross-cultural understanding possible, de-

---

1. Ronald Inglehart, *Modernization and Postmodernization. Cultural, Economic, and Political Change in 43 Societies*, Princeton University Press (1997), pp. 4, 18.

sirable, and in this era of globalization, utterly necessary in order to preserve peace and to promote international cooperation.

North Korea has been with us as a difficult, strange and frightening entity since its establishment as a part, although never fully a member, of the communist bloc after the end of World War II. For many years it was portrayed as the last Stalinist dictatorship. The label never made much sense but the term 'Stalinism' was nevertheless used to stress that this was an example of the most inhumane society imaginable. North Korea is probably also, however, the clearest example available of the complete, wholesale *demonization* of a nation.

> **North Korea is probably also ... the clearest example available of the complete, wholesale *demonization* of a nation.**

Over the last 30 years, the country has occupied a disproportionate amount of space in Western media and has been more thoroughly vilified in those media outlets than any other state of a similar size and importance.

China has also, in the past, shared this experience of being demonized: long referred to as the *Yellow Peril*; then later as a communist dictatorship known for its excesses during the 'cultural revolution'; for its crackdown on a student-led uprising in 1989; and most recently as the source of the Covid-19 pandemic, provocatively labelled by US President Trump as the 'China Virus'. Now, however, things are different. While North Korea has survived as a nation – something that few expert observers had thought possible, and with a government still headed by a representative of the same family as the state's founding father – China has undergone great change. From being a huge yet poor developing country it has transitioned to its current position as a huge, rich, powerful and self-confident nation ready to challenge the economic and political hegemony of the West. By contrast, the hitherto leading great power, the USA, is waging an uphill struggle to maintain its global economic dominance.

This 'tectonic' change might be the reason why North Korea plays such a significant role for the larger emerging East–West animosities. USA might well find North Korea useful as a pretext for maintaining a massive military presence in the region – a presence China cannot possibly ignore, and a rationale they cannot accept.

The struggle that is unfolding between one current leading global power and another upcoming one will not necessarily alter the entire global order, although it might. What is currently happening, however, is that China, with its sheer size and fast pace of growth, is already a world-changing phenomenon. Relations between the USA and China affect us all. It is this very struggle that makes demonization not only a problematic activity, but an incredibly dangerous one. Concerned scholars in the social sciences and the humanities need to engage with and share their insights and experience about this situation.

Religious and ideological demonization, East and West

The concept of the 'demon' has been used mainly in religious contexts. In Buddhism, for instance, it refers to an evil spirit, while in Christian mythology it is another word for the devil – the antithesis of God. In the West, the word demon can also be used to characterize a human who has an evil agenda, one considered extremely wicked or cruel. In the field of politics – coloured as it is by religious sentiment – the demonic epithet could easily be applied to a wicked and cruel political leader, a dictator.

To be demonized, then, is to be portrayed as falling under the influence of such a leader and the evil passion he propagates. Demonized people are seen as having been hypnotized, acting as faceless victims under the spell of evil, having lost their human dignity and their ability to think independently.

In East Asia, however, this usage of absolutes – of good versus evil – has no place in traditional moral thinking, and is also currently unfamiliar to people at large. In 2002, when US President George W. Bush's State of the Union Address included North Korea in an 'Axis of Evil', Koreans were alarmed, in the South as well as the North. After all, from the southern perspective, people in the North were also Koreans so they asked themselves how he could generalize in such a way. Three years earlier, another North American, political scientist Fred Alford, interviewed hundreds of people all over South Korea. Nobody could accept that the label *evil* was attached to their Northern brethren, not even to their leader.[2]

For this 'cultural' reason alone, the demonization of this particular *Asian Other* is a grave mistake and, as such, an outrage to Koreans. Despite this, President Bush nevertheless continued to use this derogatory term to characterize North Korea, a country that the media had already denigrated as the worst thinkable place on earth, with a cruel system on the verge of collapse and a leader about whom words were inadequate to describe all his negative traits and brutalities. Mr Bush claimed he was disgusted and felt like vomiting when he saw an image of this person, to which Mr Kim retorted that this feeling likely was caused by the intake of too much alcohol.

The absence of normal relations between North Korea and the outside world, partly due to the country's self-imposed isolation based on the ideological aim of being independent and self-reliant, and partly due to the ever-tightening embargo imposed by the US/UN, make it an easy target for media criticism – some of it justified, some not. The problem has grown over time. With the scarcity of trustworthy information and the abundance of speculations and stories based on rumour, or facilitated by hostile foreign agencies, it is not an exaggeration to state that North Korea is presently totally demonized.

---

2. C. Fred Alford, *Think No Evil. Korean Values in the Age of Globalization.* Ithaca: Cornell University Press (1999), pp. 104–105.

What we maintain throughout this book is that, despite obvious regime deficiencies, it is unfair and counterproductive to depict political and cultural systems in their entirety as demonic; just as it is unacceptable, also from a Western Christian or humanistic moral perspective, to portray whole populations under a generalized enemy image. To do so is also literally dangerous. Historically, the act of demonization has been used on numerous occasions to promote and justify wars already long-planned.

How does demonization work?

The following example shows how a generally negative view of a region and its people promoted by mass media in the West has a negative effect on something totally unrelated. Recently, a survey institute in the USA asked 3,200 citizens if American children should use Arabic numerals at school.[3] The survey dealt with mathematics in general and its place in the school curriculum. Fifty-six per cent of the participants responded *no* to this question, while fifteen per cent said they did not know. Apparently, the respondents were unaware of the real meaning of the term Arabic numerals or the fact that they had been using them all along. What seems clear from this is that the respondents harboured a general animosity towards anything linked to the Arab world. This animosity comes as a consequence of the long-standing difficult relationship between the West and the Middle East, further fuelled by strongly biased media coverage of the Arab world after 9/11.

Then there are the more ordinary or banal examples of people who are demonized, those with seemingly sane and positive traits, but who are still considered different and strange in some sense. In the West – Europe and the USA – during and also after the period of the Cold War, the people it was seen one should be wary of were often those on the political Left:

---

3. Iflscience.com/editors blog/56-percent-of-americans.

the socialists and the communists. They were usually normal individuals – even, now and then, gentle people with noble characters – but nevertheless, dominant belief systems warned 'good' citizens to beware! These people were the carriers of a dreadful ideology, a creed promoting all those things that 'normal', non-political and civilized citizens should detest and fear.

Currently, 30 years after the collapse of the Soviet Union and with it the communist-ruled states in Europe, fear of the Reds and their ideologies (there were several) remains strong; this fear governs many people's understanding of and reaction to such ideologies. Soviet-style communist ideology and practice is seen, without doubt, as a complete disaster. The Soviet leadership ruined whatever was left of reasonable ideas in the ideology; today, no sensible person would stand up for Soviet-style communism, let alone speak of exporting it to other parts of the world. Actually, very few in the West wanted that even when the Soviet Union seemingly performed well as a state.

Contemporary leftist political parties and their leaders do not lean towards this Soviet past: they find no inspiration in what was mis-termed 'realized socialism', nor do they want to undermine democracy or belittle the importance of human rights. And yet, a majority in the Western world still tend to believe that they do. This fear of 'the reds' has been created, developed and transmitted via the media, directly and indirectly, for so long that it has become an 'indisputable truth'. As a result, whatever representatives from the political left claim about their political goals and their ideological backgrounds, the dominant and mainstream response to their claims remains one of scepticism and it fuels gut reactions that such persons are not to be trusted.

In the contemporary West, centre-left politicians do not have an easy path to political power, not because they want to replicate the Soviet model, but because that is what the majority of the European electorate have been trained to believe. Jeremy

Corbyn in the UK and Bernie Sanders in the USA provide clear examples of political leaders with a 'socialist bias' who faced extreme difficulties as they tried to be heard and understood beyond their not-insignificant number of supporters. When Corbyn was first elected leader of the Labour Party in 2015 and was accused by the mainstream media of being the ultimate symbol of Britain's 'Loony Left', the observation was also made that, had he been a politician in Norway, he would have been considered nothing more demonic than an ordinary, harmless, even well-meaning, socialist or social democrat. It is more than ironic that, in the wake of the coronavirus pandemic, the UK Tory government – resoundingly elected to power in December 2019 to 'Get Brexit Done' – has adopted a large part of the Labour Party manifesto on which Corbyn himself was roundly defeated in that very same election.

It is possible to infer, then, that politicians such as Sanders and Corbyn would encounter far fewer problems in reaching a broader and attentive audience in the Nordic region. Still, even in this part of Europe, as in the rest of the West, East European experiences have undermined the notion that any idea of socialism could be a reasonable alternative to conservative, nationalist governance. Nevertheless, socialist political parties including the social democrats have remained equal competitors for political power. Perhaps this is something that the tiny Nordic region could bring to the international scene by way of inspiration for a more democratic public political sphere. Our earlier findings in comparative projects on East–West political cultures clearly indicate that Nordic/Scandinavian ways have a positive connotation in both China and South Korea, and, from personal experience, we know that even North Korea has expressed a positive interest.[4]

---

4. Personal conversation with members of the DPRK State Planning Committee, Pyongyang 2004.

If not fighting the enemy Other, then what?

This book has a mission: it aims to both explore and explain the phenomenon of demonization of *the enemy Other* by presenting examples from the personal experiences of the authors, as well as by highlighting instances from the news media and from the scholarly literature. We share the fear that a general lack of understanding of the cultures of others, their values, their norms, and thus their world outlook, constitutes a growing danger in world affairs. Our capacity to understand, not to mention appreciate, differences in thoughts, ideas and behaviours has not kept up with the pace of globalization. From our perspective, this deficiency represents an almost un-noticed challenge: one with potentially deadly consequences.

Our mission can be seen, therefore, as an effort to contribute to the humanization of international relations. Taking a broad look at the globe in its present state, self evidently the survival of human civilization demands that several urgent issues are addressed. It is impossible to ignore just how the coronavirus pandemic has revealed the need for common global monitoring and collaboration to combat this and similar diseases, present and future. Climate change requires immediate and united action. Poverty and inequality must be seriously addressed. So, too, the preservation of peace, at all costs. In order to confront these gigantic tasks with the aim of finding sustainable, effective and common solutions, however, something very fundamental is required as a precondition: and that something is *mutual trust.*

The incipient frictions between the USA and China, and the hostile relations that persist between the USA and countries that used to belong to the so-called 'Axis of Evil' have brought back war as a tangible threat in international affairs. Therefore, trust (or lack thereof) has become a central issue globally.

Perhaps no one formulated this need for trust more clearly than the German philosopher Immanuel Kant (1724–1804) when he stated:

> [N]o nation at war with another shall permit such acts of war as shall make mutual trust impossible during some future time of peace. … Some level of trust in the enemy's way of thinking must be preserved even in the midst of war, for otherwise no peace can ever be concluded and the hostilities would become a war of extermination.[5]

Although proposed over 200 years ago, Kant's dictum is particularly relevant for nations perceiving each other as enemies. Globalization has made his statement ever more important, even during periods of peace. Communication between countries, and the ways in which the mass media covers these activities, has implications for how such relations develop.

North Korea's Kim Jong Un is perhaps the best example of a leader who is utterly demonized outside his own country. Other leaders to the east of Europe are, interestingly, also tarred with the brush of demonization, albeit to a slightly lesser extent – Russia's Vladimir Putin being one, and the Chinese president Xi Jinping another who is portrayed and described as being 'a cause for serious concern'. This is despite the fact that the systems and their ideologies differ, and that in their own countries, the three leaders mentioned here command authority and enjoy popularity among a strong majority of the people. However, since these leaders are certainly not representatives of liberal democracies, they are clearly unacceptable to the West. Unfortunately, this is the measurement used by the West: 'our' systems are universally valid, and the end station of development for *all* humanity. Any non-Western disagreement with this cannot be taken seriously.

Thus, relations between the USA and North Korea demonstrate just how a lack of trust can be so dangerous; increasingly, relations between the USA and China may also be

---

5. Quoted from Immanuel Kant's 1795 essay 'Perpetual Peace: A Philosophic Sketch'

moving in a similar direction. To have some degree of trust in the 'enemy's' ways of thinking might, however, be extremely difficult, as these ways have so often been negatively defined in propaganda to condemn the enemy. A pre-condition for overcoming this difficulty would be to approach the Other open-mindedly, to achieve knowledge about and insights into even an enemy's cultural habits and beliefs, and to acknowledge their right to be different, and to remain so.

The ambition of this collective work, then, is to show how unjust and counterproductive demonization is, no matter the target of that demonization. In doing so, however, many different approaches to the topic are entertained, including how to describe the phenomenon of demonizing, and how to explain the negative consequences of this practice. This diversity characterizes the present volume, where each chapter tells an independent story about the given topic, based on the author's deep knowledge and personal experience. Another aspect that adds to the diversity is the professional background of the contributors, comprising scholars with a humanities and social science background from different disciplines, different generations and different regions of the world. In each case we made the editorial request that the chapters be written in the most straightforward language and form possible, not to oversimplify the content but to make it as accessible to as wide a readership as possible, beyond the immediate confines of academia. This because we believe that the topics of international affairs and global politics to be simply too important to leave to specialists, given that the result of misunderstandings and wrong decisions may have deadly results not only for those who should know, but for each and every one of us.

A brief overview of the book

In the first chapter, Rachel Harrison, a British scholar specializing on Thai society and culture, deals with demonization in a variety of circumstances. She shares her own early personal experiences of living in a conflict-ridden social environment and divided population in Northern Ireland and then links this to her work on Southeast Asia, where nominally Buddhist nations considered largely peaceful and compassionate also manifest forms of demonization. This serves to suggest that nowhere are people protected against the poison of fear and hatred, which underscores the importance of addressing and dealing with it.

The following chapter is a travelogue from North Korea. Kåre Bluitgen, a professional writer from Denmark, gives a rare glimpse into some aspects of daily life in the North, not often experienced by foreigners, and even more seldom shared in writing. Via his entourage – the guide, translator and driver – the author provides us with more than a glimpse of the country and its people. Despite sharing his frustrations, however, he never writes with anger, and never does he demonize.

In the third chapter James Hoare, a UK scholar-diplomat portrays his life and work as a Western diplomat in Pyongyang. This was a trial and error process, often with error as the ultimate outcome. His story gives us a clear insight into the ways North Korea deals with the outside world. His critical pen does not spare any of the actively engaged parties on the conflict-ridden peninsula, while his own position is evident: dialogue is possible and preferable.

In the fourth chapter, Scandinavian scholar Geir Helgesen suggests that the demonization of North Korea by the West is based on a Western inability – or unwillingness – to try to understand East Asian political culture, more than the fact that North Korea is seen as a 'communist threat'. The international dimension of the conflict is considered highly disturbing and problematic. For the USA, a 'military solution' constitutes part of the diplomatic menu, which for the Chinese is an anti-solution: totally unacceptable and perceived as a threat directed against them.

This is followed by the insights of Han S. Park, an American scholar with roots in Korea. Park maintains the importance of avoiding the view of North Korea as an isolated entity, since both Koreas are strongly affected by a common traditional political culture. This common basis has been neglected and distorted, proving detrimental to both halves of the peninsula. Taking these wider geopolitical interests into consideration, Park shows us that there are good reasons to take North Korea seriously.

This perspective is further developed by Hazel Smith, a British scholar who has conducted extensive fieldwork in North Korea. Her focus is on national sovereignty as a basis for a well-functioning international system. This is certainly an important argument for taking North Korea seriously, demonstrating that the ongoing demonization of the North is highly counterproductive to any sustainable solution.

In the following chapter, Italian scholar Gianluca Spezza argues that demonization has created an abnormal image of North Korea, and maintains that it is this false image that dominates people's view of North Korea worldwide, including that of politicians. Dealing with a caricature, however, is not conducive to any political solution, demonstrating just why studies that take the country seriously, including its government and official material, are in such great need.

The three chapters that follow are penned by authors from South Korea. Gyuseog Han deals with what he terms the *Red-complex* in South Korea. He reviews how demonization has fundamentally affected people's view of the North, colouring the entire political scene in South Korea. The author argues that the overall negative consequences of demonizing the Other are that it prevents dialogue, which is why it negatively affects both the demonized and the demonizers.

Myungkoo Kang directs his critical eye toward the ways the South Korean media depicted the Northern athletes and officials who took part in the 2018 Winter Olympics in South Korea. This 'sports diplomacy' failed, because this act of good will from the North Korean authorities and the incumbent South Korean government, supported by the Olympic committee, was presented in the mainstream media as a North Korean propaganda show. Kang clearly demonstrates how a free press can be as one-sided and politicizing as if the guidelines on reporting came directly from the political authorities in a dictatorship.

Sungju Park-Kang challenges conventional wisdom by asking unconventional questions about the disappearance of a South Korean civilian airliner over the Indian Ocean in November 1987. Although the truth about this tragedy remains in doubt, the obviously tempting opportunity of using the tragedy for political ends was adopted all too quickly. Who would not blame a demon? The author reminds us that reality, as usual, might be more complex.

James Wertsch and Jacob Finke, both US political scientists, jointly present a North American perspective. One of their main messages is that a military solution has little or no support among those who are in the know, but strong support from those who elected the incumbent US President Donald Trump. They point to the media as a root-case of the problem, and emphasize the negative role that the corporate media and (so-called) social media play, by demonizing North Korea, instigating hatred and proposing violent 'solutions' to the North Korean issue.

Reviewing Southeast Asia's approach to North Korea, Erik Mobrand, an American scholar working in Seoul, and Hyejin Kim, a South Korean scholar working in Singapore, jointly argue that the views promoted by the USA and supported by Western countries have only weak support in Southeast

Asia, where the common principle is that dialogue does not presuppose agreement. These countries also remain less convinced that what is termed 'universal values' by the West are truly universal. A more culture-sensitive Western approach to Korea, and to Asia in general, is therefore called for.

China next?

Up until now, the focus of the book has been on Korea, and how the northern half of the peninsula has been demonized over the years. At present, however, we further experience extensive criticism – or uneducated critique – directed towards other countries and systems as well. One recent case in point is China. The following two chapters deal with the Chinese case.

Chunrong Liu, a Chinese political scientist based in Copenhagen, asks whether China is a strategic partner or a systemic rival. He points to three difficulties faced in deciding this from a Western perspective. The first is to place this newly arrived great power on the global scene. The second, is how to deal with a political system that is not readily accepted by the West. Thirdly, the political culture of China seems difficult to comprehend by people who are unwilling to be open to the possibility that non-Western ways of organizing societies might have 'local' legitimacy. Liu suggests that both China and the West have homework to do in the sphere of cross-cultural relations in order to reach a better and mutually normative resonance.

Daniel A. Bell, a Canadian scholar working and living in China, points to the general absurdity of demonizing large groups of people, maintaining that this might in part be motivated by racism. Reminding us that China is a major global power, Bell claims that the effect of this activity may be worse for the demonizer than for the demonized, such as for instance, in cases where positive high-tech achievements are seen to be part of an aggressive Chinese global strategy. Or, when 'green' developments in China go almost unmentioned by the Western media. Both approaches hamper the global cooperation necessary to tackle major current challenges. Demonization may thus be nothing less than a serious threat to our common future.

In the final chapter of this volume, Norwegian professional peace mediator Steinar Bryn deals in general terms with the role of enemy images in peacebuilding processes. This, he writes, has been a largely neglected theme in the field despite the fact that the act of demonizing the enemy Other obviously promotes reasons for conflict and further complicates dialogue and mutual understanding. What might be a universally valid statement is that dialogue is necessary in order to avoid a conflict from erupting, as well as to build trust in the aftermath of a such a conflict. Above all else, what matters are people, relationships, empathy and mutual understanding. To demonize is to pour poison in the water that both parties to a conflict need to sustain them.

Although primarily focussed on the cases of North Korea and China, this volume both opens and concludes with the words of two veteran Norwegian peace campaigners – Inge Eidsvåg and Steinar Bryn. Associated with the Center for Peace and Dialogue at the Nansen Academy in Lillehammer, and former Nobel Peace Prize nominees for their groundbreaking contribution on reconciliation in former Yugoslavia, these two authors have dedicated much of their working lives to the thorny task of fostering dialogue in the most challenging of situations. As editors, we have drawn inspiration from their efforts in the continued hope of prioritizing dialogue as one of the applied benefits of academic research. We have, like them, taken motivation from the visionary work of Fridtjof Nansen (1861–1930), after whom the Academy in Lillehammer is named, in his capacity as explorer, scientist, diplomat and humanitarian. Writing at the time of the First World War, Nansen expressed the view:

> If nations could overcome the mutual fear and distrust whose sombre shadow is now thrown over the world, and could meet with confidence and good will to settle their possible differences, they would easily be able to establish a lasting peace.

Now, a century later, the Doomsday clock stands closer than it has ever been, at under 2 minutes to midnight. We must take heed, more than ever, of Nansen's call for an end to human conflict:

> The history of the human race is a continual struggle from darkness into light. It is, therefore, to no purpose to discuss the use of knowledge; man wants to know, and when he ceases to do so, is no longer a man.

Thus, we are committed to the belief that scholarship has a role to play in promoting the value of intercultural understanding, serving as a necessary tool to avert the dangers that come from an increasingly antagonistic world. Within this context, we argue that a key element of that understanding can only be achieved through the erasure of demonization. This volume argues, therefore, that demonization is wrong not only because it is dangerous, unjust and even counterproductive, but ultimately also because it prevents us from understanding, from using our intellectual and emotional capacities. Demonization forces us to accept what we would surely reject if we were able to deploy our senses to the fullest. As scholars, we question any act of demonization, keep the spirit of an open mind, and make every effort not to demonize the demonizers themselves. In so doing, we take heed of Nansen's shrewd and pithy observation: 'The difficult is what takes a little time; the impossible is what takes a little longer.'

Geir Helgesen and Rachel Harrison

21

Demonizing West and East

IT IS NOT ENOUGH TO DEFINE THE WORD in order to understand what demonization is, and what it does to people; that is actually seldom sufficient. More important is to place it in a relevant and well-known context. Harrison's way of doing this is by referring to how we might encounter this particularly frightening phenomenon at different stages in our lives, when we were likely to hear about and thus, in our imaginations, to meet demons and demonization. During childhood, most of us heard of demons in fairy tales, bedtime stories and literature. Beyond the confines of family and home, there may have been demons in our daily lives. In a book predominantly focusing on the processes of demonization in Asia, it is important to turn our attention to demons and demonizing in other parts of the world. The author's early experiences of a conflict-ridden social environment and a divided population took place in Northern Ireland during the 1960s. Then and there, one could say that she experienced a school for developing notions of the enemy Other, (or became vaccinated against the act of demonization). Later, as a scholar in Asian Studies, she experienced demonization in Thailand, a country considered peaceful and populated by an extraordinarily kind people. However, nowhere are we protected against the poison of fear and hatred, hence the importance of dealing with it.

About the Author: Rachel Harrison is Professor of Thai Cultural Studies at SOAS University of London, where she also earned her undergraduate degree and PhD and where she has taught since 1989. Her research focuses on a range of issues in connection with contemporary mainland Southeast Asia in general, and with Thailand in particular. Her interest in Thai literature, film and culture has led to a wider engagement with public health, well-being, social cohesion and intercultural communication, and the relationship of all these fields to Area Studies. She is a strong believer in the benefits of interdisciplinary research and multidisciplinary teamwork, with all the challenges and rewards of differences that it entails. She is also editor of the quarterly journal *South East Asia Research*.

CHAPTER ONE

"Tis No Sin to Cheat the Devil': Demonization as Dehumanization

*I*n his introduction to *The History of the Devil*, first published in 1726, the English author Daniel Defoe pokes gentle fun at the 'over-demonization' of Satan himself:

> *Children and old women have told themselves so many frightful things of the Devil, and have form'd ideas of him in their minds, in so many horrible and monstrous shapes, that really it were enough to fright the Devil himself, to meet himself in the dark, dress'd up in the several figures which imagination has form'd for him in the minds of men; and as for themselves, I cannot think by any means that the Devil would terrify them half so much, if they were to converse face to face with him.*

Here Defoe makes an important point that is central to the psychological process of demonization as it continues to operate in the present day: that **fear**, fuelled by the fantasies of the human imagination, far outstrips the reality of an actual encounter with the Devil himself. Writing from a specifically Western and Christian perspective, Defoe also envisages the Devil as a genuine political force. The cultural characteristics and perspectives that he brings to this short political treatise are the ones that continue to characterize Western forms of the demonization of Others in the contemporary world. But they are often also shared outside the West as well, as I relate in this chapter through a personal, comparative account of demonizing processes in Northern Ireland, where I grew up; and in Thailand, which has been the focus of much of my research career.

Better known as the author of *Robinson Crusoe,* Defoe's story of the Devil is a reminder that our earliest encounter with the Devil comes in religious teachings, and our awareness of demons, monsters and ogres from fairy tales, nursery rhymes and mythical beliefs. Such stories exist across all cultures, no matter where in the world, from Latin America to Scandinavia and from China to Mozambique.

Most Western children can probably recall the terror they felt on hearing the cautionary tale, for example, of Hans Christian Anderson's *The Tinderbox* with its three monstrous, giant-eyed dogs guarding vaults full of copper, silver and gold; or the plight of Little Red Riding Hood when she suddenly discovers her dear, bed-ridden grandmother to be a ravenous, predatory wolf in disguise. Usually told at bedtime, such stories were the stuff of nightmares! By way of comparison, in South Africa, for example, children are goaded into timely sleep by tales of the Tokoloshe, a monstrous dwarf from Zulu mythology with a demonic face who might grab them in the night. In Thailand, Laos and Cambodia, night terrors

Courtesy: British Library, Or.16102, f.12"

Image of Rahu, the demon of eclipses, from a 19th-century Thai paper folding book of poetry.

also abound: grown men go to bed fearing they will be raped and murdered by lustful 'widow ghosts'; and the paddy fields and the forests run riot with spirits and mythical creatures who have the potential to wreak havoc if not sufficiently appeased by human beings. Influenced by early waves of Indianization, Southeast Asians also follow the practice of beating sticks to ward off the darkness that falls during a solar eclipse, to prevent the Hindu ogre Rahu from swallowing the sun and not spitting it back out again.

Following the theme of demonic transformation, these tales and folk beliefs warn their audiences to beware! Beware of the danger of the Other, lurking in every corner of our lives, threatening to do us harm, indeed to kill and even to consume us!

> **Beware of the danger of the Other, lurking in every corner of our lives, threatening to do us harm ...**

I recall my father telling me that European fairy stories traditionally had reason to be brutal, to instil in children the necessary sense of fear that would prevent them from taking undue risks in life: Little Red Riding Hood needed to know that the forest harboured dangerous predators and that not everything that seemed familiar could really be trusted. Instead, she needed to be vigilant and to keep her wits about her. With the ever-present threat of a demonic enemy Other implanted into the imagination of most human beings from an early age, it is hardly surprising that children learn to nurture a sense of fear, anxiety and repugnance in relation to the question of difference that can in turn lead to bullying and aggression in the face of the Other.

This was certainly the context I recall from my own early childhood, growing up amidst the sectarian divide of late 1960s Belfast in the lead-up to the notorious 'Troubles' (a misnomer, in my view, for what was in fact a low-key civil war that raged for decades in the British Isles). As UK negotiations over Brexit, and post-Brexit, repeatedly flounder at the time of writing this piece, it is evident how little most English voters know or care about the 1998 Good Friday Agreement, which effectively brought a halt to Catholic/Protestant violence in

Northern Ireland through a carefully crafted power-sharing arrangement between the two warring sides.

When my devoutly atheist parents moved to Belfast in 1964, they were ill-prepared for the corrosive religious divide that marked out the distinct and polarised territories of the city. They were shocked to go in search of accommodation in the sprawling housing estates of Catholic Andersonstown, only to find statues of the Virgin Mary peeping from behind the curtains of every home. Opting for the rather more middle-class confines of Protestant East Belfast, we settled, after a fashion, into a tiny house with tell-tale fleur-de-lys insignia on the small iron front gate. Although it lacked the crude conviction of the inner-city streets, with their Loyalist red, white and blue-painted kerbstones and their end-of-terrace murals daubed with the victorious William of Orange – 'King Billy' – and the Red Hand of Ulster, it was still clearly marked by Protestant mores. On Sundays everyone went to church, and children were strictly forbidden from partaking in the innocent indulgences of blowing bubble gum or playing on the garden swing: to ensure they were free from the slightest temptation of pleasure, swings were duly chained to their frames. In the midst of this grey and cheerless setting, as Unionist and Republican paramilitary organisations shot and bombed each other with reckless abandon (the total number of dead in the 'Troubles' reached over 3600, with many thousands more maimed and injured) their children replicated the division and the hatred. Schools – strictly aligned to one and only one version of Christianity – peddled fear and distrust of the Other. At my own Protestant primary school, we regularly chimed out not only God-fearing hymns and prayers, but also the Loyalist Orangemen's marching anthem – *The Sash My Father Wore*. I can still hum the tune today, some fifty years later; and my childish dream of being accepted by my peers took the form of longing to become a drum majorette at the head of one of those dour processions of elderly men in orange sashes and bowler hats, together with teenage boys beating drums and playing pipes.

I have a lasting image of one of my primary school class-mates – the eight-year-old daughter of a local Presbyterian minister, doubtless pals with the ever-vocal Reverend Dr Ian Paisley. The memory comes from the annual fancy dress parade where she appeared in the ultimate costume of the times. I can hardly believe it was permitted but, in a tribute to her favourite paramilitary organisation – the UDA (Ulster Defence Association) – she had donned a swimming costume, dark glasses, a handkerchief disguise over her mouth and nose, and a sash inscribed 'Miss UDA'!

At school 'we' were always at war with the enemy Other – the Fenian bastards, the *taigs*, the 'left footers', the Provos, the IRA, the Papists, and a host of other derogatory terms that categorized 'them'. This was the daily language of demoniza-tion, which was in some ways – though not all – dissolved by the Good Friday Agreement. But while politics moved on (and Ian Paisley even struck up a friendship of sorts with his Sinn Fein arch-rival, Martin McGuiness) cultural prac-tice changed much more slowly. The events in 2001 at the Catholic primary school of Holy Cross, located in a part of Belfast demarcated as Protestant, was a tragic indictment of the persistence of demonization and dehumanization. For several months of that year, the young pupils of Holy Cross were bombarded with abuse, and worse, plastic bags filled with urine and faeces as they ran the gauntlet of the jeering Protestant crowds en route to school across enemy lines. This was the (dis)United Kingdom of the new millennium, with demonization of the Other alive and kicking, aimed this time at little children who were, as a result, so traumatized that it took years of professional counselling to aid them in their recovery.

If demonization becomes embedded in our cultural, social and political practices from such an early age, it is inevitably well-rooted by our adult years. Nor is this limited to any one particular cultural, religious or political milieu. Although the process in Northern Ireland emerges from a specifically Christian schism, the more widely divisive repercussions of demonization and dehumanization cross centuries, continents and cultures. While evidence in the tensions between groups whose religious beliefs support and perhaps even encourage recourse to violence against the religious Other, they are nonetheless also to be found amongst peoples who are nominally committed to pacifism, such as, for example, practising Buddhists. Yet in the recent attacks against the Muslim minority Rohingya in Myanmar's Rakhine State, Burmese Buddhist monks were often at the forefront of hate speech and calls for violent retribution. The hard-line Buddhist nationalist group *Ma Ba Tha* – the Association for the Protection of Race and Religion – believe, much as the divided Catholics and Protestants of Northern Ireland, that the existence of the one religious faith represents an attack on another; and that the two cannot simply co-exist, in peaceful appreciation of the difference of the Other.

Further back in time, and in a neighbouring nation, the Theravada Buddhist monk Kittiwuttho achieved notoriety for expressing a similar antipathy to the then-perceived dangerous Other – those suspected of being Communists in the Thailand of the 1970s. Heavily influenced by the Cold War concerns of the US, the Thai nation, with state Buddhism as its moral arm, nurtured an increasing antipathy to both Communism and Socialism. In such a fevered environment it became possible for the ideally compassionate and peace-loving doctrines of Theravada Buddhist thought to be reshaped in service to the nation in crisis: killing Communists could not be considered a Buddhist sin. On the contrary, in the Venerable Kittiwuttho's influential reflections, it was in fact a moral duty to kill them, 'because whoever destroys the nation, the religion, or the monarchy, such bestial types are not complete persons. Thus, we must intend not to kill people but to kill the Devil (*Mara*); this is the duty of all Thai.' Here, dehumanization and demonization go hand-in-hand, both encouraging an act of violence in the name of a greater moral and national good. 'It is just like,' as Kittiwuttho expanded, 'when we kill a fish to make a stew to place in the alms bowl for a monk. There is certainly demerit in killing the fish, but we place it in the alms bowl of a monk and gain much greater merit' (quoted in Keyes, 1978).

Months of unrest during this troubled recent period of Thailand's history signalled a growing polarisation of Leftist and Rightist sentiments in which expressions of hatred and dehumanization culminated, on 6 October 1976, in violent and sadistic attacks on student demonstrators suspected of being communist sympathizers. Official figures suggest there were 46 deaths on the campus of one of Bangkok's largest universities – Thammasat – though the total number likely far exceeded that, and will probably never be known. The assassination of these student protestors was made possible – culturally, morally and politically acceptable – due to a constant stream of propaganda and hate speech pitching Right against Left and encapsulated in the dehumunanizing words of popular, military-backed songs such as *Nak Phaen Din* (*Scum of the Earth*). Its chilling words read as follows:

> *Anyone who calls themselves a Thai, and who looks like a Thai*
> *Who lives in the Buddhist land of the King, but who thinks to destroy it.*
> *Anyone who thinks the Thais are enslaved, and looks down upon the Thai nation,*
> *But still lives off its provisions, while despising Thais as its slaves.*
> *They are the scum of the earth.*
> *They are the scum of the earth.*

These people are the scum of the earth!

*Anyone who agitates for Thais to fight among themselves and
    disunite them*
*Who rouses the mob to cause confusion to pitch Thais against
    each other*
Anyone who extols other nations, yet threatens their own
*Seizing our assets to slaughter fellow Thais, while respecting
    foreigners as their own.*

They are the scum of the earth.
They are the scum of the earth.
These people are the scum of the earth!

In 2008, when it was still possible in the UK university system to teach small classes in specialist subjects such as Thai cultural studies, I taught my final-year Thai language students the words to this song, in the context of analysing an anti-communist propaganda action movie of the same name. A year later, several of those same students had graduated and gone to live and work in Thailand. Two of them wrote to me from Bangkok to say how useful it had turned out to be to have learned the words of *Scum of the Earth*, despite the threat of Communism to Thailand having long disappeared. The song had instead resurfaced as a popular form of accusation against Red-Shirt demonstrators on the streets of the capital. Formerly played on a daily basis by the Thai military after its release in 1975 and adopted as the anthem of vigilante groups such as the Village Scouts and the Red Gaurs, it re-emerged in the protests against former Thai Prime Minister Thaksin Shinawatra, who was ousted from power in a coup in 2006.

Thaksin's supporters, the so-called Red-Shirts, inherited in many senses the demonic red mantle that had been worn by the Leftist students and intellectuals of the 1970s. They were the new Red Peril, and their demonization took the form of dehumanizing them as Red 'germs' that had infected the capital with their presence and spread a pernicious disease throughout its streets. When Red-Shirt demonstrators, largely from the rural heartlands of the North and the North East occupied the main thoroughfares of the city centre they were ridiculed by the common moniker reserved for 'hicks' from the countryside – as buffaloes, a synonym for their blind obedience and stupidity as well as their rural backwardness. One popular cartoon in a mainstream daily newspaper compared the old problems of Bangkok's traffic jams to the new one of streets blocked by dense buffalo herds. In May 2010 the 'sophisticated' urban-elite Prime Minister, Eton and Oxford-educated Abhisit Vejjajiva, gave the orders for a military crackdown on the Red-Shirt occupation of the capital's central business district that resulted in just under 100 deaths. Interviewed shortly afterwards by the BBC, Abhisit explained the outcome with the causal – and now infamous – phrase: 'Unfortunately some people died.'

Almost a decade later – time passes so quickly and yet we learn so little from the experience of the years! – the fallout of the Red-Shirt/Yellow-Shirt divide persists to some degree in Thailand, even though the colours themselves may have shifted. At the time of writing this piece, the elections held in March 2019 have reinstalled a military-style government, with an opposition led by the Future Forward party, symbolized by the colour orange. A far cry from the Orangemen of Ulster, or indeed the orange-robed Theravada Buddhist clergy, Future Forward represents mostly the younger generation of Thais, calling for changes to tradition and new ways of doing politics in Thailand. A newspaper article in the English-language daily *The Bangkok Post* (17 June 2019) by Thai academic Pirongrong Ramasoota declares in its headline that a new 'chill' is coming to Thailand. She refers to the latest condemnation of Future Forward spokeswoman and MP Pannika Wanich (nicknamed Chor), who stands accused of one of Thailand's most serious crimes – that of *lèse majesté*. As Ramasoota writes, within 24 hours of the resurfacing of nine-year-old Facebook photos now deemed to be offensive to the former king, Thai netizens fell into a frenzy. #ChorScumofEarth became a trending topic on Twitter and scores of comments on social media made it clear that she should no longer lay claim to Thai citizenship. She and her fellow party members have taken on the mantle of the newly demonized enemy Other – for now. The result of this came in the Thai constitutional court's dissolution of the Future Forward party in its entirety, in February 2020. The rhetoric remains unchanged, even as its victims come and go in colour and in ideology: but the demonized Other is always the 'Scum of the Earth', disloyal to the symbols of the Nation, and hence disenfranchised from the claim to be a rightful citizen of that land. And so, the witch hunts continue.

As the victims of demonization and dehumanization come and go, so too do the methods by which they are demonized. The last decade has seen the rise of the role of social media in this pernicious process. We now live, for the most part, in a world of disinformation, 'fake news', images easily doctored by photoshop and film enhanced by the smart effects of computer graphics. These are the newest and most effective tools with which we now mould and disfigure our contemporary demons. While the mechanisms of demonization may have shifted over the centuries, the thrust, the purpose and the outcome remain largely unchanged. When we demonize the Other, we engage in an act of violence against fellow humanity. We dull our senses, closing down our abilities to look, listen, see, hear, speak, touch, communicate and feel as human beings – as if our own survival can only come as the result of the extinction of an imagined demonic Other.

The precarious state of the world as it stands today requires nothing less than a rejection of this fundamental human inclination towards the demonization of Other ethnicities, religions and nations. To recognize our shared future as a community of human beings is to set foot on the only path to our survival.

Rachel Harrison

Reference

Keyes, Charles. 1978. "Political Crisis and Militant Buddhism in Contemporary Thailand". In B. Smith (ed.) *Religion and Legitimation of Power in Thailand, Burma and Laos*. Chambersburg, PA: Anima Books, pp. 147–64.

North Korea, a literary writer's account

IN 2015 KÅRE BLUITGEN SPENT A MONTH in North Korea to conduct research for a book about the country and its people. This was not to be a hidden notebook or an exposé: Bluitgen had been invited by the country's Writers Union. As such, this chapter represents an incredible achievement. People's daily lives are observed at a distance, and the author undoubtedly aims to move closer to people in the fields, in offices and factories. All serious observers of North Korea share a similar wish, but, unlike Bluitgen, few have the stamina and patience to expand the boundaries of the possible. Bluitgen's travelogue gives a rare glimpse into several aspects of daily life in North Korea not normally experienced by foreigners, and even more seldom shared in writing. The guide, the interpreter and the driver are all part of the official North Korea, as are the people Bluitgen meets on his one-month tour of the country. It is their daily work and life that we encounter in this text. The author contextualizes this encounter, providing historical facts that help us to understand the story. In addition, he shares his own opinions, which often contrast with what we believe we know about North Korea. He reports what he sees and shares his frustrations, but never does he write in anger; and never does he demonize.

This text is a revised version of a chapter in Kåre Bluitgen: *Jeg vil gerne klippes ligesom Kim Jong Un. Indtryk fra Nordkorea* [I want a haircut like Kim Jong Un's. Impressions from North Korea]. Tøkk Publishers, Copenhagen, 2016.

About the Author: Kåre Bluitgen, b. 1959, is a Danish author. He was educated as a journalist and visited North Korea for the first time back in 1984. In 2015 he spent a month travelling in the demonized country writing a comprehensive work of his travel and of Korean history and society.

Bluitgen has a varied list of publications, including children's and youth books, adult novels, short stories, retellings, photo documentaries, biographies, essays, film and theatre manuscripts and non-fiction. Bluitgen's books have been translated into many languages, and he has received several awards. Both novels and nonfiction often originate in international environments ranging from Eritrea, South Africa, Mexico, Kurdistan and Burma to Haiti, Liberia and Nepal – and North Korea.

CHAPTER TWO

The Night is Dark in
North Korea

*T*he night is dark in North Korea. Pitch-dark. As the sun hastily disappears into the West Sea of Korea (the Yellow Sea) the last thing I see from the car's rear window are two very long-barrelled anti-aircraft guns perched on the nearest hilltop.

There are three others accompanying me on my month-long road tour of North Korea in the autumn of 2015: a driver, a guide and my young interpreter, Ms Ok. She is 23 years old, the same age as my daughter, and is also studying the same subject at university – Arabic language and Middle-Eastern affairs.

When we are not talking to each other, Ms Ok communicates with her friends in endless chats and picture exchanges. The screensaver page on her smartphone shows a photograph of her little sister, who suffered from severe anxiety because, as Ok herself revealed to me, Ok had pressured her too much about her homework.

Though barely past 7pm, it is already very dark, and the working day is coming to an end. We are heading for Haeju, and we are literally the only car on this main road, while hundreds of people are walking along the roadside. Children walk alone, some carrying wood on their heads; there are even more cyclists, most of them without lights. Several of the bicycles are so heavily loaded that the older women have to get off and walk as soon as there is the slightest incline.

Holes in the road are repaired with asphalt heated in a kettle over a glowing fire. But the road is still so rugged and bumpy that we are constantly thrown about in the car. When the main road deteriorates into a gravel track we kick dust up at the people and animals as we roar past them in the car. We are driving for hours, and still people are walking or cycling along the roadside. But where from and where to? There are no lights, no cities, not even any houses.

Eventually we pass a village. At the entrance are huge portraits of Kim Il Sung and Kim Jong Il, the two smiling men both dimly lit by a spotlight. A light can be seen shining in some of the houses, before they disappear into the darkness. At a railway level-crossing I can see the contours of the level-crossing keeper against the dim moonlit sky. One oxcart after another appears suddenly in front of us, loaded with straw or sacks, or a sleeping, or at any rate exhausted, family. Ms Ok is also exhausted, and she repeatedly falls asleep. But each time she wakes to find herself resting her head on my shoulder, she sits bolt upright. And then she falls asleep again.

At a spot between Pyoksong and Haeju, in such absolute blackout that we hardly see we are passing it, we stop for a break. Myriad stars are like a thick porridge that engulfs us, as though we are swimming in the Milky Way, or are drowning in the total darkness. Ms Ok and I are standing a little aside, as we usually do. She informs me that the guide has told her to report to me that at this moment, the USA and South Korea are staging a military manoeuvre just south of the border. I already know, as well, that five officers from the Danish navy and the air force are located some few kilometres to the south of us and may, at this very moment, be involved in operational planning as a part of the huge, US-led manoeuvre known as Ulji Freedom Guardian.

Ms Ok asks me what I think about the Arab Spring. She herself has travelled in the Middle East, and lived in Syria for three years. I tell her about the Danish combat aircraft in Iraq. In the dark, I can faintly see her face, but her voice is not accusatory, simply curious, when she asks: 'How many countries does Denmark bomb?' The year after, in 2016, Denmark bombed Syria, Ok's second country.

In a country like North Korea, where it is difficult, if not impossible, to approach anyone at random on the street to communicate with the average citizen, one is prone to engage with those allotted by the state. In my case, those I could talk with easily were the cheerful Ms Ok and the heavy-drinking chauffeur, but not my guide, who was more like an ordinary bureaucrat, not dissimilar to those we know from the West,

It is important to realize that people in North Korea do not conform to our stereotypes of a uniform, grey, faceless mass of people marching in measured steps.

with qualifications in law and economy and acting as elites within the state bureaucracy.

As the weeks pass by, I discover that I can discuss absolutely anything with Ms Ok, from sexual issues to jealousy between siblings, or whatever seems otherwise awkward to touch upon in daily life. (In this respect she reminds me of my own daughter.) But it is not only her. It is important to realize that people in North Korea do not conform to our stereotypes of a uniform, grey, faceless mass of people marching in measured steps. On the contrary, they scold those who try to queue jump, regardless of their status. There are women who feel your leg muscles to see if you are fit enough to join them on a mountain hike. And in a newly harvested field in the remote countryside we see a group of farm workers – women and men in their working clothes – laughing and dancing together as we pass them by in our fast-moving car.

Such observations of everyday life in North Korea come as a surprise when I tell them to people back home in Denmark. It is as if North Korea is the only country on earth to have no sense of what is just, and what is not, no experience of joy or flirtation.

It is actually this misunderstanding that is the most remarkable thing of all. And also potentially the most dangerous, since it is the initial expression of the unconscious dehumanization of an entire population.

Ms Ok enjoyed a rather elite kind of lifestyle. When we visited the North Eastern provinces, the areas most affected by the famine in the 1990s and where most refugees to South Korea emanate from, I realized that here she felt just as alien as I did. She found nothing of interest here, yawned and asked if we could shorten the stay. This was not my intention, however. When we left the car, the local people looked as much at this woman with makeup and a fancy hairstyle, wearing a sports outfit with the word Adidas printed down the trousers and up the sleeves, as they did at me. Maybe they saw us both as foreigners.

Neither of us had anything in common with these women, who sat on the ground with their small pyramids of apples in front of them as contributions to the hastily growing private markets in the country. Nor, for that matter, did we share much in common with the inhabitants of the humble quarters of Pyongyang with their mud roads and shabby houses with tin-roofs and yards filled with heaps of foul-smelling coal-cinders and sewage.

My professional guide also had his positive traits. When we went for a walk in the parks, where mostly elderly women gathered around makeshift karaoke equipment to dance to, he often bought us beer. He was interested in discussing current American literature, and when we dropped by local bars, he was a pro at playing pool. When we accidentally ran into his daughter on a school outing, I felt a warmth in him that was not one gram cooler than that I have seen in many other parts of the world on such occasions or, for that matter, from what I know of myself.

Notwithstanding that, we 'know' that people in North Korea are cold and brainwashed, are likened to robots, and that their leader is an irrational psychopath. That very claim was voiced by the Danish National Broadcasting network on 6 January 2016, the day after North Korea had apparently tested a hydrogen bomb. One might ask whether it really takes the leader to be a psychopath to get hold of the worst kind of deterrents when his country is under heavy sanctions and surrounded by hostile powers without a peace agreement more than 60 years after an all-destructive war. One might also ask if the Danish National Broadcasting network would offer the President of the US a similar diagnosis?

A year before I left for North Korea, the same radio channel and most other major Danish media outlets announced some important information:

> The North Korean dictatorship is revealing still new characteristics. Now, all men in the country are obliged to cut their hair exactly as their leader does. This rule became obligatory for men living in the capital two weeks ago, and now, according to several media reports, all men in North Korea have to conform with this hairstyle. Before, men could choose from 10 different hairstyles, while women could choose from 18. ... No reports indicate how the men will be punished if they choose a different hairstyle.[1]

Could it perhaps be execution by shooting with anti-aircraft cannons? Or being cooked and used as dog food? Two stories about this scoundrel state that went viral. Even now, years later, people ask me after invited talks if the story about the obligatory hairstyle is true. I then tell them that I went into a hair salon in the capital and asked them to give me a haircut similar to the one Kim Jong Un is sporting. The three female hairdressers snorted, either because I have a bald patch, and

---

1. DR P1 (Danish Radio News), 26 March 2014 (editors translation).

how can that be a part of the marshal's hairstyle, or, because they were unaware of this order from the supreme leader.

It would have been exceedingly easy for the global media to have this information verified, or proved false, by contacting tourists, diplomats, businesspeople or others. But this did not happen and there were no retractions, which also, by the way, should apply to the information that there was a certain number of permitted hairstyles. Reportage on North Korea is not subjected to the journalistic criteria that we claim makes Western journalism superior. A similar story cannot be told about other countries, although also demonized, such as Iran, Venezuela and others before and after those two. North Korea is presumably the only place on earth where the people are not really human. When will that happen, that we will see them as human beings? When they introduce a stock exchange? When they flock to Instagram and Facebook? When they establish a welfare system and open up for immigration? Or, when they realize that, to be successful, one has to be wealthy?

The demonization of North Korea did not start with the Second World War and the establishment of the Kim Dynasty, replacing – or rather continuing – the old Confucian dynasties. We are all a part of history. It is said that in 1895, German Emperor Wilhelm the Second had a vision in which he saw a white woman laying desecrated on the ground, and above her floating the Buddha and a dragon. She was a metaphor for the guardian of the home whose virtue had been humiliated and broken by paganism and barbarity. It was an allegory for the demise of European Christian civilization in the face of the East Asian masses, *die Gelbe Gefahr*, the Yellow Peril.

Nowadays this is an expression few would use, but a hundred years ago it represented a widespread European view of its own civilization as superior, but with a fear of the oriental hordes threatening to flood the West. Apparently, the war in Korea, and Japan's victory over China, created this phantom in the German emperor's brain as Japan suddenly became an industrial and military power.

The Yellow Peril as a mass term removed any kind of individuality from the people it referred to and likened them to a swarm of locusts to be exterminated with DDT. The expression was akin to a dehumanizing powder sprayed over millions of human beings. During the Korean War, the phrase made it possible for the USA, after having used nuclear bombs over Hiroshima and Nagasaki in Japan, to openly threaten to use these dreadful weapons again in Korea. This did not lead to condemnation from Denmark, the small US ally, which supported the UN war in Korea with a hospital ship. The ship was placed under the Red Cross, but in this case the principle of neutrality was not upheld, meaning that not a single North Korean or Chinese person was treated on the ship, in contrast to South Korean soldiers, who often returned to the battlefield after treatment.

The Danish Ministry of Foreign Affairs described the efforts as a part of the nation's long and 'proud humanitarian tradition'. Official Danish foreign policy at the time was to work for détente and dialogue between East and West; Denmark took part in the UN peacekeeping actions, which after the war in Korea became non-aggressive. This changed when Denmark deployed combat troops in Yugoslavia in support of the NATO engagement in that civil war, a foreign policy change that was underscored in 2003, when Denmark supported the US attack on Iraq, without a mandate from the UN.

By that point, the incredible suffering that had been inflicted on the Korean people during the war was long forgotten in the West, while in North Korea, it still formed an important part of each new generation's upbringing and education. For Denmark, following the failed military interventions in Afghanistan and Libya, it would be wise to reconsider how close it chose to follow the USA in its next military adventure.

For the Korean people, this can have the most serious consequences, since next time around the Danish contribution is hardly likely to be a hospital ship.

No country other than North Korea has ever had a war waged against it by the UN, or been sided against by the Red Cross. But clearly, when the most distinguished and credible international organizations in the world are prepared to do this, it affects international opinion, meaning that the condemned must surely have placed themselves beyond the sphere of decent, civilized people.

The trinity of morally indisputable institutions also includes that of the Nobel Peace Prize. In 1906, Korean representatives went to the Second International Peace Conference in The Hague to protest Japan's decision to make Korea a Japanese protectorate. The delegation was not received at the conference. The peace treaty between Russia and Japan had secured the rights of Japan to protect its interests in Korea. This included the fact that Korea's foreign relations were to be taken care of by Japan, just as the Congo's foreign relations were taken care of by Belgium. The agreement was orchestrated by the US President Theodore Roosevelt, securing him the Nobel Peace Prize. In 2000, this prestigious prize came to Korea proper, when the South Korean President Kim Dae-jung was rewarded for his work for peace and reconciliation with North Korea, which culminated in a summit in Pyongyang. Were there not a counterpart present in that meeting? Anyhow, there was only one leader that received the prize.

The UN, the Red Cross and the Nobel Peace Prize are not seen by everyone as universal and absolute symbols elevated above bias and prejudice. In the places where they *are* seen as being beyond dispute, however, and where they have absolute authority, those who question integrity are seen as radically different and as outsiders who have placed themselves beyond the realms of the international community. As a result, blockades, sanctions, and in the last resort even war, are deemed to be the 'unfortunate' but unavoidable repercussions.

Denmark is a small country, but it is a member of NATO, a huge military alliance. The country used to be known as peaceful, though this is not the case any longer. And, remarkably enough, it is one of the countries where this shift has caused the least problems. The stationing of ground troops and the air force in remote 'Third World' countries has not led to heated public debates, as it has elsewhere. Even the fact that Denmark has a higher number of deceased and physically and psychologically injured soldiers per capita than any of the other warring countries has not provoked serious debate in its parliament or among its wider public. Nor have the people of Libya or of Afghanistan been collectively demonized, as the media in these instances has made the distinction between those who are warriors – and those who profit from the wars – versus the people at large. Not so with North Korea however, from where no stories of individuals are ever relayed, except those connected with defectors. Instead, regime and society are lumped together in descriptions of a country we know next to nothing about, when it comes to its history, religion, and culture. Rather than providing a reasonable and necessary critique of a family dictatorship, demonization emanates from a combination of ignorance and indifference. While no democratically minded and humanitarian-inclined person could defend the Kim Dynasty, which itself strongly demonizes 'the Other', is it nevertheless morally acceptable to include the whole population as the enemy in a 'humanitarian war of liberation'?

I was 30 years old when the Berlin Wall collapsed. Until it actually happened, I expected, as with most people, that this East–West division would remain in place throughout my life. The demonization of those on the opposite side was all-pervasive, had formed an integrated part of my childhood and schooling and was reflected in those media I encountered. What we were taught to expect from the East ranged from nuclear war, against which we had no real protection, to influencing agents and apologetically oriented fellow countrymen, whom we should be aware of and avoid.

I was, however, rather more curious than most other children and, in First grade, on the ferry to Bornholm, far out in the East Sea of Denmark, I threw a bottle into the water with a message posted inside. The following spring I received a postcard from a family in the GDR (the German Democratic Republic, or as we said, East Germany). Obviously, it was exciting to receive a message from the other side of the 'Iron Curtain'. I had not expected this, as I had believed it was illegal for them to send a postcard abroad. But it was also difficult to know how to handle this situation. My parents told me that it was my obligation to maintain the contact, as I had taken the initiative myself. So, the communication continued for a couple of years, but then ebbed away, possibly because the excitement disappeared when I found out that the family was just as ordinary as my own. I did learn, however, that dialogue obliges. And in my eyes the dialogue humanized those people, whose regime we had been taught to hate. It was not long after this that Denmark (together with the other Nordic countries) became among the very first Western countries to establish diplomatic relations with North Korea.

Now it is time to intensify the communication. It should probably make a soft – East Asian – start, taking its time and developing personal relations with counterparts. To succeed in this, it is important to show that one has knowledge of the Korea's history, and that one respects its suffering and its successes. This attitude was crucial for the outcome of my own visit to, and travel in, North Korea. If one fails to make a genuine effort – which now and then can be pretty difficult – to try to see the world through North Korean eyes, then dialogue is doomed. It is good to remind oneself about the democratic dictum that tolerance does not mean respect for the opinions of others, but to respect their right to maintain those opinions. Even in Northern Ireland, people succeeded over the years to reach an understanding between parties that had long seen each other as terrorists. If nothing else, both parties understood that the conflict could not be solved through violence. The same happened in the incredibly long civil war in Columbia, and soon in Syria as well: the impossible has to be made possible.

Maybe there was a hint of anxiety hidden in the question posed by Ms Ok under the starry sky in the darkest of North Korean nights. I do not know if I could have comforted her by sharing my own personal opinion: North Korea must not become just another country that Denmark is bombing to please our principal ally, or because of ignorance or fake news. Or, because the elimination of a people seen as nothing more than mere robots is considered little more than minor damage.

Kåre Bluitgen

A UK scholar-diplomat's personal account

HOARE'S PERSONAL ACCOUNT is that of a professional UK diplomat and scholar who has followed developments in East Asia longer than most of us. He takes us on a long journey from London to Seoul, Beijing and Pyongyang, where he was the first British diplomat to head the mission. Here, life and work for Western diplomats was a trial and error process, often with error as the most likely outcome. The author's posting to Seoul in particular, but also his earlier academic work on Japan, prepared him well as a representative to Pyongyang. Hoare shares his experiences with generosity: *Whatever the reality of life for ordinary people ... they did not behave as downtrodden slaves. They argued with police and other officials. They worried about their children just as parents did everywhere. They were cautious and careful among foreigners, but courteous and friendly when relaxed.* This is not the story of North Korea that the media chooses to paint. Instead, Hoare provides an insider's perspective based on UK and European foreign policies, offering first and foremost a solid view of the way in which North Korea engaged with the outside world. Hoare's critical pen does not spare any of the parties actively engaged on the conflict-ridden peninsula. His own position is clear: dialogue is possible and preferable.

About the Author: J.E. Hoare has a PhD in Japanese history from SOAS University of London, and is now a SOAS Research Associate and an Associate Fellow at Chatham House (Royal Institute of International Affairs). From 1969 to 2003, he was a Research Analyst on East Asia in the British Foreign and Commonwealth Office. He was posted to Seoul (1981–85) and Beijing (1988–91). From 2001 to 2002, he was the first British representative to the Democratic People's Republic of Korea. He writes and broadcasts, and has taught a course at SOAS on North Korea. He and his wife, Susan Pares, have produced several books about Korea, including *Conflict in Korea* (1994) and *North Korea in the 21st Century* (2005). A second edition of his *Historical Dictionary of the People's Democratic Republic of Korea* was published in 2019. A new edition of his *Historical Dictionary of the Republic of Korea* (2015) is in press.

CHAPTER THREE

Reflections on North Korea: Myths & Reality

Introduction

*I*n December 2000, Britain and the Democratic People's Republic of Korea (DPRK – North Korea) signed an agreement to establish diplomatic relations. It had been no easy journey. From the formal establishment of two states on the Korean Peninsula in 1948, Britain had been a firm supporter of the Republic of Korea (ROK – South Korea). This support had been maintained even when there were grave doubts about the policies of the Presidents Syngman Rhee and Park Chung Hee. The Scandinavian countries regarded the dissolution of the Korean War-era United Nations Commission for the Unification and Rehabilitation of Korea in 1973 as a removal of any legal barrier to recognizing the North, an interpretation shared by Britain's senior legal officers, but Britain continued to deny recognition to the North. There was some modification of this position after the two Koreas joined the United Nations in 1991, at which point Britain recognized the DPRK as a state. Nevertheless, ministers on both sides of the political spectrum declined to go any further and, even as late as July 2000, a proposal from officials for a change in policy was firmly turned down.

Yet the international relationship with North Korea was changing rapidly. Early in 2000, Italy had broken European Union ranks and established relations. South Korea, especially after the June 2000 North-South Summit, was keen that more countries should open relations with the North to end its isolation. The DPRK itself was reaching out. These factors all contributed to a change of position by ministers at the time of the Europe–Asia meeting in Seoul in September 2000.

The December signing (agreeing to establish diplomatic relations) led to the question of whether and how the relationship would be carried forward. Although it was decided that Britain would not open an embassy in Pyongyang, it was felt there should be at least one dedicated person to take relations forward. At that point, I was the only person at the right grade in the Foreign and Commonwealth Office (FCO) who had expressed a wish to go to North Korea if we ever established relations. Now I was taken at my word and I readily agreed.

Life before Pyongyang

In 1981 I was asked to go to the embassy in Seoul as head of chancery[1] and consul. We spent nearly four enjoyable years there. My wife, Susan Pares, taught English at the Ministry of Foreign Affairs training institute, then worked with the overseas service of the Korean Broadcasting System and wrote a regular column in a local newspaper. Our daughter, three when we arrived, started school and had a great time, even if she later said that she could not understand what we did. Eventually she concluded that since one of us had a striped jersey and we both went out regularly in the evenings, we must be burglars. Fortunately, she never revealed our secret.

These were the years of Chun Doo-hwan, the ROK's second military dictator. Politics was a dull affair but there was plenty to do, with visits, routine reporting and learning to know a new society. In 1982–83, we celebrated 100 years

---

1. The head of chancery performed several roles, as head of the political section, as co-ordinator of embassy work, and as advisor to the head of post. It no longer exists, being replaced by an American style deputy head of mission system from c. 1990 onwards.

of diplomatic relations, conveniently ignoring the break between 1905 and 1948 and the absence of any links with the North. It got me writing on Britain and Korea both for the press and for local academic journals. During the late 1970s, the then-ambassador had been an unambiguous supporter of the military dictatorship and would hear nothing against its policies, especially vis-à-vis the DPRK. This had changed by the time I arrived, but the North was still regarded as a threat. There was a nightly curfew, though it ended in 1982. Leaflets scattered by balloons regularly turned up in our garden; I still have a few. North Korean midget submarines were active and occasionally caught. The crews either committed suicide or were killed in fire fights. I knew several of those blown up in Rangoon in 1983. I made some 30 visits to Panmunjom, where the palpable tension added to the sense of menace.

We left in Spring 1985, just after Kim Dae-jung's return, but continued as commentators on Korea and produced our first joint book, somewhat unimaginatively titled *Korea: An Introduction*.

North Korea

In 1998, I finally made it to North Korea. Britain held the EU chair and I was the political adviser to an EU humanitarian team led by Britain's Department for International Development to assess DPRK requests for aid. After day trips in and around Pyongyang, we split into groups. Mine went first to flooded areas on the West Coast, and then across to the East Coast to see the consequences of economic decline. None of us had been to North Korea and I was the only one who had worked on the country, so there was a steep learning curve and occasional clashes with our guides. We had been assured in Pyongyang that we would be able to see markets but once on the road, we soon learnt that they would be seen only from a distance. In Wonsan, two of our number skipped a visit to the hospital to slip away to an obvious street market. As the rest of us emerged, they were being escorted back. There followed an argument between our senior guide – a cultivated man with a considerable knowledge of Shakespeare – and me over the bad behaviour of our group. We were told it was highly dangerous to go off alone since people might attack us. This would have been more convincing if 'the people,' including some who had seen the altercation in the market, had not stood on the other side of the road cheering us on. But all our pleading fell on stony ground. I fear that our final report, delivered in draft to the Korean side, was a disappointment. While we had seen flood damage, economic decline and clear evidence of food shortages in some areas, those who had been in other world disaster areas were not convinced that things were as bad as had been claimed.

That first introduction was what led me to say that if I was asked, I would go to Pyongyang again. In January 2001, I got my wish. A party of officials visited London that month to explore how we would implement our new relationship. The Koreans were happy that I was nominated as chargé d'affaires. Many of the people I had met in 1998 were still there, which proved most helpful. That winter was bitterly cold, revealing the lack of lighting and heating and poor maintenance of roads and vehicles. That was a short visit. I returned at the end of February to carry on the process of getting to know the North Koreans and to prepare for a planned visit in mid-March by the administrative head of the FCO, Sir John Kerr, the permanent undersecretary. The office had also agreed that Susan could visit, at public expense, to see what she might be letting herself in for.

Operating out of the Koryo Hotel and preparing a visit via unclassified fax and telephone was not easy, but it worked. My contacts at the MFA (Ministry of Foreign Affairs) were Kim Chun Guk and Thae Yong Ho, both of whom I had by then met several times, including during the 2000 negotiations in London. Sir John was known to them as he had signed the agreement on diplomatic relations, and they were pleased to have a senior British visitor. A good programme meant that Sir John was happy too. The Korean side smoothed out difficulties so that we saw sights normally off limits, including the Koguryo tombs just outside Pyongyang. And Kerr made a major decision: we would open a post in Pyongyang, which I would head. But, he warned me, times were changing and he thought that ministers were likely to take their tone from the new US administration of George W. Bush, whose hostility to North Korea was already clear.

I did not return to London until the end of March 2001. By then it seemed that enthusiasm for relations with North Korea had markedly diminished. There would be no fresh aid for the DPRK. But the post would remain open. I completed briefing, finished off medical visits and left for Pyongyang via Seoul and Beijing in late May. The Korean MFA was openly friendly, although it was soon clear that we would get no privileges because of that. Pyongyang was a very formal place, full of protocol. Conducting business was cumbersome for all; as in China until the early 1980s, the Diplomatic Note ruled. It was almost as if the telephone had not been invented.

We lived in the Koryo Hotel and worked at the German embassy, in the former East German embassy. As well as the Germans, who also had residential accommodation, the Swedish embassy had an office there, while the Italians maintained an aid office; there was no Italian embassy. We had half of the first floor. This had been earmarked for the US liaison office that was envisaged under the 1994 Agreed Framework, but the US was no longer interested. Until new office furniture arrived, we made do with old East German tables and chairs. Fortunately, there were plenty of these, since they showed an alarming tendency to disintegrate.

We had more serious problems. Our main task was to get the embassy established and running. One important component in that was communications, for which we were still completely dependent on an unclassified telephone and fax system, albeit now one we controlled, not the Koryo Hotel. The December 2000 agreement had clearly stated that we could secure the satellite-based communications that were being rolled out to all British diplomatic posts. When I raised the issue, I was told that it was impossible under DPRK law. The MFA denied that the agreement said anything different. Whatever we had thought, to them phone and fax were what was allowed. The message was regularly repeated from people from other ministries. We were also working on more permanent residential and office accommodation. The MFA had identified one property as serving both purposes. Our estates staff colleagues thought it might be able to become one or the other, but not both. If we could not have communications, there seemed little point in going ahead with hiring an office, so I stopped the survey work and told London we should not proceed. This was accepted, to the chagrin of the MFA who would have got the rent. The estates staff in the meantime decided that a semi-derelict accommodation block on the German compound was available and could be adapted for residential needs.

Then there were our diplomatic ID cards. We were told to apply for these but when we filled in the forms, we were told we had done so incorrectly. After this happened three times, I told the MFA at a meeting on another subject that we felt perfectly safe without ID cards. Since it seemed to be a problem, we had no wish to proceed. The cards duly arrived the next day, dated the day of our first application. And of course, we never had to show them. (We would later have a similar problem with driving licenses, which also turned out to be no problem. In any case, when I sat next to him at a reception, the head of the Pyongyang traffic police told me: 'Just drive. Nobody is going to stop you.')

This pattern repeated itself, no doubt to see whether we could be broken into their ways. A shipment of furniture was held all day at the docks over alleged 'South Korean writing' on the container but probably really to see if we would pay a bribe. We didn't and it was released. We had added an additional teacher to our programme of training for university English teachers, something the Koreans were very keen on. But we were told that there was no accommodation and she would have to live in a hotel separate from the other teachers. I said no accommodation, no teacher. An apartment was suddenly available. Books supplied for an exhibition, which were destined eventually for the Grand People's Study House, the national library, began to disappear during the exhibition. A frosty meeting with the official British friendship society got them all back. The same organization asked to be paid for arranging a dance performance at our British Week celebration even though nobody had asked them to do so.

Life was not all problems. The Koreans were always helpful over visitors even providing briefings for the journalists and academics who came as my guests. Family visitors were also entertained – the MFA clearly liked picnics. And about a year after the battle over communications had begun, we won. Having told them that I thought that, without secure communications, they ran the risk of us withdrawing, my old friend Kim Chun Guk called me over at a party and told me that we could have our communications, which was confirmed immediately in a Diplomatic Note. Not only had we succeeded where others such as the World Food Programme had failed, but we had won for everybody. I got fulsome thanks from colleagues. (Alas! Our budget for communications had already been spent, so the world-wide system could not be installed

immediately. As with the ambassador's residence, my successor benefitted.)

Being in North Korea was a most informative experience.
Whatever the reality of life for ordinary people – and these
were the years when much more information began to filter
out through defectors – they did not behave as downtrodden
slaves. They argued with police and other officials. They worried about their children just as parents did everywhere. They
were cautious and careful among foreigners, but courteous
and friendly when relaxed. While there were plaques everywhere commemorating visits by Kim Il Sung or Kim Jong Il,
the heavy political references that one used to find in China
were conspicuously absent. The outside world may have
been viewed with suspicion, but everyone from officials in
Pyongyang to farmers far off in the countryside would try to
drag you into the dancing and drinking sessions that seemed
to mark most weekends. Travelling around, one could see
why foreigners might be treated with suspicion – the handful of buildings that dated from before the Korean war were
mute testimony to the destructiveness of that conflict and the
country's helplessness in the face of Western firepower. It was
thought-provoking.

We left Pyongyang in October 2002 and I retired from the
Diplomatic Service soon after. Retiring did not break my links
with either Korea. I wrote, lectured and broadcast about both,
as well as taught. This included establishing and teaching a
course on North Korea for five years. Susan and I wrote *North
Korea in the 21st Century: An Interpretative Guide* soon after
we returned. We went back to North Korea together in 2004
and 2011, and I went on my own in 2018.

Mad, bad and dangerous to know?

Ever since leaving Seoul in 1985, I have pondered the myths and
assertions about North Korea. A word of caution: Kim Jong Il

told visiting South Korean journalists in 2000 that anybody who presented themselves as an expert on his country was a fool. I am inclined to agree. It is not that we know nothing about the country. The days when it was a deep mystery have long passed, if they ever really existed. Even when it was far more closed off than today, information did come out. But it was often seen through hostile lenses. This was especially true in South Korea, but happened elsewhere too. Since the 1980s, much has changed. More foreigners travel there and more North Koreans travel abroad. The diplomatic community in Pyongyang may still be small but they work together, and they are on the spot. Many embassies have several Korean speakers. International aid agencies have staff who get to remote parts of the country. New information and insights have come from defectors/refugees. Yet none of these really penetrate the inner workings of the system. One or two diplomats got close to Kim Jong Il; the Russian ambassador went hunting with him. Scholars from the former Communist countries often have a clear technical understanding of the system, but not necessarily how North Korea works in reality.

Indeed, just when it seems obvious how things work in the country, a new twist throws you off balance and certainties are swept aside. The number of disproved predictions about future policy or the chances of the country's survival is legion. North Korea is adept at allowing visitors to see only what it wants them to see. To attempt to get around this, you must keep your eyes and ears open and not take things at face value. Probe as much as you can, but be careful. Do not be rude and above all do not break the rules, however trivial they seem. What would cause no problems in most countries may not be treated with much tolerance in North Korea, especially if they are worried or – as some Americans have found to their cost in recent years – want to make a point.Demonizing North Korea is easy. For many commentators, it is the default mode. They do not analyse the country nor try to understand it. It is evil and its policies are wrong. The most famous exponents of this view were probably US President George W. Bush and his senior colleagues. They boasted that they did not negotiate with evil but destroyed it. For them, there was no question that any agreement negotiated with North Korea was a mistake and should be abandoned. So, the Agreed Framework, which had capped the most active and dangerous North Korean nuclear programme, was dumped. Unfortunately, the need to deal with the reality of a North Korean nuclear program proved stronger than the unwillingness to negotiate. But it was too late, and North Korea appears to be a nuclear weapons state. The Bush team were by no means alone. North Korea arouses strong emotions. The strength of those emotions can spill over into vitriolic exchanges on social media, in conventional media and even in academia. Nuance disappears, black and white prevails. If a negative interpretation can be found, let's go with it, seems to be the approach.[2]

The process begins early. Few use the country's official title – the Democratic People's Republic of Korea – or even the abbreviation DPRK. Some avoid the official usage because they do not want to give legitimacy to a state that, in their view, has no right to exist. To them, there should be no division on the Korean Peninsula. Korea was one for over 1,000 years. It was not divided, even under the Japanese colonial administration. For many people with little knowledge of history, the North is blamed for the division. The emergence of two separate states started in 1945, well before the Korean War when the United States and the Soviet Union agreed on the initial division, to take the Japanese surrender. The Cold War intervened, and

---

2. See a recent critique of the Washington-based Center for Strategic and International Studies: Daniel R. Depetris, "Reports of 'Secret' North Korean Missile Bases: Much Ado about Not Much", *38 North*, 28 Jan. 2019, at www.38north.org/2019/01/ddepetris012819/.

the two powers oversaw the development of separate states on the peninsula. The leaders of both states, each with a history of opposing Japanese colonialism, albeit in different ways, wanted unification. Each state denied the other's right to existence. (To some degree, they still do, summit meetings notwithstanding.) Belligerent noises and threats came from both.

The North struck first. Although the smaller in population, it had the means to do so thanks to the Soviet decision to give it an army. The US made a different decision. South Korea had a lightly armed super police force that proved no match for the North. Without outside intervention, the problem of Korean unification would have been solved in 1950. But intervention there was. The war settled nothing but left two even more hostile states facing each other across the division line; initial hostility had been made worse by the bitterness of war.

Relations between the two Koreas was not helped by the rest of the world. During the war, the United Nations had set up a Commission for the Unification and Rehabilitation of Korea (UNCURK) that pledged to bring about what the name denoted, unification. This followed on from its 1948 declaration that the South was the 'only legitimate government on the Korean peninsula.' Although the wording did not say that the South Korean government was the only government on the peninsula, it acted as though that was the meaning, as did Western countries. Only in the early 1970s, with the first substantive contacts between the two Koreas since the war and the winding-up of UNCURK, did the position change and Western countries began to open diplomatic links with the North.

From the war onwards, the default Western mode for referring to the two Koreas was 'Korea' for the South and 'North Korea' for the North. The implication, clearly, was that the South was the real Korea. (In the Soviet Union and other communist countries, it was the other way around, 'Korea' meant North Korea, and the South was always 'south Korea'. Something similar happened in the case of divided Germany and Vietnam.) The North was odd, an aberration. Of course, there were ways in which the North contributed to this image. It was a tough totalitarian regime that maintained a fierce independence. Few visited it. Even among the socialist states, it seemed a difficult partner, grasping and needy and going its own way.

The North was seen both as a threat and a strange, bizarre place. Both themes persist. Exaggerated claims about its military might abound. Its rhetoric is indeed ferocious. Yet it is in reality cautious, behaving like many small states surrounded by much bigger and more powerful ones. When not dealing with its alleged threat to world peace, press reports on the North are dominated by what is seen as its weird nature. In recent years, these themes have included the claim that the North believes in unicorns, or focused on the strangeness of the leader's hairstyle, while in July 2016, the British newspaper, the *Daily Mail*, reported that Kim Jong Un was devastated by international sanctions on luxury goods because of his love of Swiss cheese and watches. We have had giant rabbits, catfish and a regular diet of bizarre leaders doing odd things – all are jumbled together, whether true or not.[3] To many, it is the worst country in the world in a host of areas from human rights (yet look at some African or Middle Eastern countries) to architecture (most former Soviet cities could compete on that score).

A persistent theme is that the North is doomed to collapse any day now. Even the failure of this to happen so far does not stop the predictions. As with those who believe the end of the world is near, if it does not happen at the predicted time, it will certainly do so next time – or the time after that.

---

3. Many of these stories have been uncritically gathered together in Ruth Ann Monti, *North Korea in 100 Facts* (2019).

In 1949, the British Cabinet noted a report from the Seoul Legation that the North Korean army was disaffected, there was widespread starvation in the country, and that the regime was on the point of collapse. Forty years later, the British commentator Aidan Foster-Carter wrote, following the collapse of the Soviet Union, that North Korea would be next, if not in two years, certainly in five. When that did not happen, he twice more gave it five years, then stopped predicting.

This 'collapsist' view was always based on the mistaken belief that the North Korean regime was alien and imposed from outside. This was very much a stock theme in South Korean accounts until the mid-1980s. The North was a puppet state, run by the Soviet Union. It had rejected Korean traditions in favour of Soviet or Chinese ones. Its people were 'commies' or 'reds', not Koreans. (Again, the mirror image of the South in the North, was not dissimilar – South Koreans had sold out to American influence and were US puppets.)

Soviet forces had liberated the north of the peninsula in 1945. The Soviet Union may have enabled the Communist forces to dominate the area and undoubtedly played a major role in the establishment of North Korea. Dependence on Soviet guns to maintain its position was ended by 1949. It was China that saved it during the Korean War, not the Soviet Union. Unlike the states of Eastern Europe, from the 1950s onwards it moved to a more independent position, drawing as much on Korea's historical past and even on the practices of the Japanese colonial administration to give the state legitimacy. The collapse of the Soviet Union, which caused the collapse of Communism in Eastern Europe, worried the North, but it did not have the same effect here as it did on the European states. The fact is that the North has survived despite war, invasion, the longest sanctions' regime in the world, economic collapse, the end of its main trading relationships, famines, floods and drought.

Unification is still held out as a goal by both Koreas, but it is hard to see it happening. Despite all the talk over the years and the proposals put forward to end the division, most real effort has gone into building up separate states. Nearly 75 years of division have left only a few very elderly people with any experience of living in a united Korea. Even that Korea was dominated by Japan, so nobody now living knows an independent united Korea. The North still emphasizes unification, but on its terms. In the South, there is much indifference to the idea. People do not want to give up their current lifestyle to help the poverty-stricken North. Direct memories of the Korean War may have faded, but fear of the North regularly revives. The famine years of the 1990s showed that the North was no paradise. Most of its much-vaunted achievements were well in the past, indeed if they had ever existed outside the pages of glossy magazines. The costs of reunification in Germany proved far greater than anybody had expected. Even the mantra of 1990 – 'Unification but not till I have my second car' – has faded so that now it is only 'No Unification'.

The complication for North Korea is in some ways like that faced by the German Democratic Republic (East Germany) in 1989–90. Hungary or Poland could change government without fear of challenge, once the Soviet leader Mikhail Gorbachev made it clear that the Soviet Union would no longer support the Communist leadership. East Germany was different. Until 1945, it had been part of a unified Germany. Its people had been exposed to the German Federal Republic (West Germany) through radio, television and direct contact. Many wanted a return to a united Germany. There was opposition from other countries that had fought Germany in World War II and feared a united Germany would be too powerful. This was overcome, and the two German states merged into one. But an East–West divide persists. Although they had not fought each other, as the Koreas had, divisions had grown between the two Germanys that proved hard to overcome. East Germany had a smaller population than the West. Its economy, although widely regarded as the strongest in the former Soviet sphere of influence, lagged well behind. Its industries were old-fashioned compared to the West. In some areas, it is true, it was ahead. Social security and health provisions were more evenly distributed in the East, based on need rather than the ability to pay. There was one other problem in the relationship. Suspicions of the East in the now-dominant West led to many job losses amongst those who had worked for the East German regime. Some were tried and sentenced for having carried out state policies.

All this resonates with North Korea. The elite are aware of what happened in East Germany, in Libya and Iraq. Some know that there are voices in South Korea that call for revenge, not reconciliation. At best, the senior leadership sees unification as leading to loss of status and loss of jobs. At worst they see the prospect of prison or death. Avoiding such outcomes keeps them loyal to the system and its leader. The bottles of brandy, the watches or even the fast cars that Kim supposedly gives out from time to time may have some influence, but probably not much. Not many of us will voluntarily give up a privileged position for one of uncertainty. Even some high-ranking defectors, particularly those who took up residence in the South, have found it difficult to adjust to their changed status. Training and skills acquired in North Korea may not be of value in their new lives.

Even if the worst did not happen, the North Korea leaders have had many indications over the years that the South projects a quasi-colonial attitude towards their country. This became abundantly clear during the Lee Myung-bak and Park

Geun-hye presidencies (2008–13, 2013–17) South Korean companies and government see the North, if not quite virgin territory, as ready for exploitation. The South will help with developing existing resources and looks forward to exploiting a literate and obedient workforce. This does not bode well.

Unification thus seems unlikely in the foreseeable future. Perhaps one day, when all those who experienced the Korean War years have passed on and when the two sides get to know each other better, it may happen. But there is a long way to go. So, there is little choice but to deal with the North as it is, not as one might hope that it might be.

Here it would help if one got away from the overheated discussions on the threat from the North. Nobody would deny that the North has been an irritant to its neighbours, but beyond the South it is not a threat to their existence. Even in the case of South Korea, 2019 is not 1949. The balance of power has shifted to the South in most matters. The possession of nuclear weapons does not give a real advantage. The use of such weapons on the peninsula could have damaging effects on the North itself; radiation is no respecter of borders, and any use would probably ensure massive retaliation and the end of North Korea.

A real threat to the US or, even more unlikely, to Europe, seems far-fetched. A potential threat is, of course, useful in justifying US military spending and forward bases. In the past, US officials did not deny that North Korea was often used when the real worry was China. Today, they are less circumspect. The North is an irritant but cannot threaten the existence of the US, whatever its wilder claims. Former US Secretary of Defence William Perry pointed out the huge discrepancy between the North and the US. If North Korea were to use any of its small nuclear arsenal against the US, it would face a counterattack that would certainly mean the end of the regime and possibly the complete destruction of the country. (This would be President Donald Trump's fire and fury with a vengeance.) And while the North has shown that it will practice brinkmanship, it has not shown itself suicidal.

Kim Jong Un has made threats and paraded warlike scenes. The armistice agreement has been denounced. Declarations of war are regularly flung about. But nothing happens. The North still respects the armistice. There have been so many DPRK assertions that this or that development is an act of war that it is hard to take them seriously. Kim in the control room would look more authentic if the computers were plugged in and the telephones were connected. Or even if the map on the wall did not look suspiciously like a blown-up airline route map rather than the rocket trajectories against the US that it claimed to be. While it helps if this makes foreigners think twice about risking an attack on the North, what is often forgotten is that such pictures are primarily for internal consumption, showing a leader in control and standing up to the North's enemies.

That North Korea does not stick to its treaties and agreements is by now another well-established mantra. The DPRK is certainly a tough negotiator. Like other East Asian countries, it is usually more attached to the general spirit of a document than to the precise text. If, however, it is to its advantage to be more precise, it will be. What its negotiators do expect is that there will be equal and mutual advantage. If there is backtracking or a lack of reciprocity, to the North that excuses it from meeting its side of the bargain. Essentially that is what happened over the 1994 Agreed Framework. The North believed that it had stuck to the agreement since it had capped and halted its plutonium-based nuclear program. That was all that was covered in the agreement. When the US did not seem to be pursuing its side of the agreement – by 2002, it was estimated that the project to supply light-water reactors was eight years behind schedule and the Bush administration was showing signs of hostility – the North began pursuing an alternative route towards its original goal. The US could have raised its concerns quietly under the terms of the Agreed Framework, as happened in the Clinton administration. But, 'to confront evil', it chose a different path. This choice was not wise; it opened the way to the situation we have today. Yet the lesson was not learned, and agreements continue to founder because of a wish to add new conditions or to change the terms. For most of the period since 1945, North Korea was seen as an awkward nuisance at best or as a potential source of trouble at worst. Rather than engage with it in the hope of effecting change, it was isolated. It is hard to argue that such a policy was successful, given what happened during the short period (1998–2002) when South Korea and the US followed a different approach. Yes, it cost money, but there were real achievements. A nuclear program was capped. The South began to build a new relationship with its neighbour, as did the US and many other countries. For some in the US, the hunt for the missing in action (MIA) during the Korean War allowed them a degree of closure, but it was also an important confidence-building measure between two military organizations that were on the worst possible terms. Even Japan began to benefit. Nobody got all they wanted from the improved relationship, but it was the start of a process.

If the momentum of the Clinton years had been kept up, who knows where it might have led? President George W. Bush, however, returned to the demonization of the past, typified by John Bolton's boast in his 2007 autobiography, *Surrender Is Not an Option*, that he had driven a stake through the heart of the Agreed Framework. A fine boast, but it did not kill the DPRK nuclear programme, but hastened it, with the first nuclear test in 2006. Frantic efforts under the second Bush administration failed to halt it, while the Obama administration gave up trying. Then came Donald Trump. He had sent mixed signals while campaigning, offering to meet Kim Jong Un. In office, he became increasingly hostile, mocking Kim Jong Un as 'Little Rocket Man' and threatening North Korea with annihilation. The response was a flurry of DPRK threats. Yet while the rhetoric became strident, the North was, as usual, pulling back. Threats were not matched by actions. As early as July 2017, while the insults and threats flew, Kim Jong Un indicated that, as the DPRK was now a nuclear power with the means of delivery, further testing was not necessary – although it might be resumed if need be. This was repeated in Kim's 2018 New Year's message, with an offer to attend the Winter Olympics to be held in South Korea.

Although dismissed by many as 'North Korea up to its old tricks', this was to lead to what appeared to be a major break-through. Kim Jong Un did not attend the Olympics but sent his sister, who was ostentatiously boycotted by US Vice-President Mike Pence who defended his action on the grounds that the United States does not stand with 'murderous dictatorships'. South Korea's President Moon Jie-in received an invitation to visit North Korea. In the following months, Kim also met the Chinese leader for the first time, as well as meeting Moon several times and signing a number of significant agreements. And whatever Mr Pence's view, President Trump eagerly seized upon an invitation to meet Kim.

That meeting, in June 2018 in Singapore, appeared to go well. Trump, who clearly heard what he wanted to hear, claimed that there would be complete North Korean denu-clearization and announced that he was cancelling a number of joint US–South Korean military exercises. The North made gestures towards dismantling parts of its nuclear and missile-related system but was clearly hoping for some relaxation of the sanctions regime, which had been steadily tightened dur-ing 2017. By the end of 2018, both the US and North Korea were bemoaning the lack of real progress. Yet talks behind the scene led to another US–North Korea summit in Hanoi in February 2019. Both sides seemed optimistic, indicating a pre-meeting agreement. Yet on the morning of the second day, the talks abruptly ended without an agreement, lunch or a communique. Trump and his entourage, which included John Bolton, then-national security adviser, returned home, while Kim Jong Un carried out a planned state visit to Vietnam.

The recriminations began almost immediately. The North Koreans said that the United States had made unacceptable new demands on the pace of denuclearization and other issues. The Americans claimed that the North Koreans had demanded the full lifting of US sanctions. Each rejected the other's claims. There was a brief moment in June when Trump met Kim at Panmunjom – with a rather-neglected President Moon taking part in a photo shoot – but the Hanoi summit seemed the effective end of the process that had begun in January 2018.

To the United States administration, the fault lay entirely with the North Koreans. Bolton argued that it showed that the DPRK could not be trusted. Others were not so sure. The president seemed to believe that his relationship with Kim Jong Un was still strong. Although formally still committed to the UN sanctions regime, Russia and China turned an increasingly blind eye to evasions by their nationals. The standoff continues (March 2020). While North Korea has said that its self-imposed moratoria on long-range missile and nuclear testing is over, it has not in fact done either.

What is to be done?

Clearly there remains a glimmer of hope that all is not lost, but it requires some more imaginative thinking than we are used to. The first need is to accept that the DPRK is here to stay and to act accordingly. It is not East Germany, Eastern Europe or even the former Soviet Union. Unification offers little for the elite. At best they would lose their status, at worst their lives. Isolation and sanctions have not and are not likely to make North Korea more co-operative. The effort devoted to them would more profitably be expended on providing training and exposure to the outside world. Show the elite that there are other ways of doing things than those currently used in their country.

Patience is required. Do not expect overnight change. Get to know the North Koreans. The US should make a real effort to establish a presence in the country, to improve knowledge and to impart it. This was done in Moscow and Beijing; there seems no reason why it should not be done in Pyongyang. Do not expect the nuclear issue to be solved quickly. Work in stages. A cap is better than a continued development programme. The end of the latter should remain the long-term goal, but that does not reduce the benefit of progress on intermediate stages. Stress the positive.

James Hoare

The consequences of demonization

AS A SEASONED OBSERVER OF THE KOREAS from the perspective of political culture, the author sees the demonization of North Korea by the West as more keenly based on the Western inability – or unwillingness – to understand East Asian political culture than the fact that North Korea is seen as a 'communist threat'. Pointing at several common and similar features in the two different polities of North and South Korea, due to their shared traditional political cultures, it appears that the seed of a solution to the conflict might be hidden in what both systems, and the Korean people writ large, recognize as both acceptable and 'theirs'. This makes the international dimension of the conflict yet more disturbing and problematic, as it can be assumed that a positive development in the relations between the two Koreas – a gradual reduction of the animosities and eventually a solution to the division of the country – would come more easily without US interference. In addition to this, and with potentially grave consequences, come the international aspects of the inter-Korean conflict where China and the USA comprise the main conflicting actors. For the USA, a 'military solution' forms part of the diplomatic menu. For Beijing, that is a totally unacceptable anti-solution and is perceived as a threat directed against China.

About the Author: Geir Helgesen has a PhD in cultural sociology and has focused on Korean affairs since the early 1980s, with a special emphasis on the political cultures of the two systems on the Korean Peninsula. His main works are *Democracy and Authority in Korea: The Cultural Dimension in Korean Politics*; *Politics, Culture and Self: East Asian and North European Attitudes*, co-edited with S.R. Thomsen; and *Dialogue with North Korea? Preconditions for Talking Human Rights with a Hermit Kingdom* with Hatla Thelle. He has drafted reports for Nordic Foreign Ministries on the situation in North Korea; co-organized training courses on doing business in South Korea for the Confederation of Danish Industries; and organized Track-2 events with North Korean counterparts sponsored by three Nordic ministries of foreign affairs. He is a regular commentator on Korean affairs in the Nordic media.

CHAPTER FOUR

A Case of Successful Demonization and Its Consequences

*T*he first time that I visited North Korea was in 1984. I still clearly remember that on several occasions during this visit, I found myself wondering whether this was where George Orwell's novel 1984 had actually been set. Many visitors to North Korea, both pre- and post-1984, have shared the same experience and the same considerations, almost certainly breathing a sigh of relief once they had left and were on their way back home to a completely different and freer society. But as a young researcher in cultural sociology, with a great curiosity and a certain degree of courage, I returned to Korea several times after 1984. At first I visited only the North, but later also the South. Korea became my destiny and I write this piece following 35 years of 'active service' as a researcher, lecturer and so-called 'expert' (a term used by the media that is not chosen for oneself but rather awarded by others, deservedly or otherwise). This chapter is based primarily on my own experiences, though it of course draws on knowledge generated by my predecessors and my peers.

Opening considerations

A very large majority of people in the West (Europe and the USA) undoubtedly regard North Korea as an enemy state. Aggressive by definition and a threat to peace in the region, as well as to the wider world, its leader is perceived to be a demon of the very worst kind. As a result, North Korea is not only seen and portrayed in a demonizing way but is indeed viewed as a *de facto* enemy and a *de facto* demon. What, then, is the difference between these two positions?

When discussing enemy images and demonization, we should be open to the possibility, or rather the probability, that these images omit some elements of the overall story. We know that blending truth with myth can produce images different from 'realities'. But these images do not provide the full picture and tend to be clearly black and white, without any intermediate shades of grey. This should be implicitly acknowledged in any discussion of images of the enemy; but it is not. The Democratic People's Republic of Korea (DPRK) and its leader, the third in the Kim family line, are not, therefore, examples of an enemy image and a demonized leader respectively, but rather they are instances of an enemy state and a dictator, respectively: both of which are demons. The image has become a fact; it cannot be nuanced or modified. Trying to do so means to side with the demon, the monster.

A view of the country, and a corrective

The starting point of this chapter is that the North Korea we know of in the West is, to a large extent, a construct based on fragmented information about the country's current situation, especially via terrifying or abnormal images and statements taken out of context and, in particular, taken out of their cultural context. Things are seen, presented and commented on, *as if* they were taking place in the West. As a result, the people's exaltation of their leader becomes a point of ridicule, despite the fact that this phenomenon is found, to a greater or lesser extent, as a central feature of political culture throughout the East Asian region. In cases where Asian leaders are seen to reflect the West's own cultural and political values, the uncritical veneration of their leaders is instead thought to be admirable and highly worthy of respect, such as, for example, the case of Thailand's devotion to late King Rama IX, a hero of pro-US Cold War relations. In another instance of ridiculing what is different from the Western norm, when a North Korean female television presenter reads the news in a traditional, high-pitched voice, she is reported as being utterly ridiculous, because that would have been the case had she performed in that way in the Western news media. But is she ridiculous in the local context of North Korea? Hardly so! Some of the 'reality' of the demonized North Korea that we have constructed in the West can therefore be shown to have emerged from a lack of willingness, ability, knowledge, effort or time to try to understand foreign Others in their *own* social environment, and in their *own* cultural context.

In addition to this, it is also problematic to focus on the North Korean nation in isolation from its history, geography and geo-political conditions. When all that we see of North Korea is the regime's ('ridiculous') perception of itself and its selective, negative stories of a hostile external world, then it is

> A crucial prerequisite for ... rebalancing the currently dominant view of North Korea is to deal with the country and the regime in a larger regional and international context.

these fragmentary images alone that we base our assessments on. And this can only lead to serious problems.

A crucial prerequisite for, at the very least, rebalancing the currently dominant view of North Korea is to deal with the country and the regime in a larger regional and international context. As a result of this reorientation, it becomes clear that any conflicting relationship involves several different parties. This reality is rarely raised, however, as doing so would complicate and undermine the veracity of the 'persistent enemy' image North Korea is condemned to uphold.

Despite the recent (2019) somewhat positive development in the relationship between the two Koreas and between the

North Korean leader and US president, it was only a matter of months earlier that war was regularly mentioned as a possibility. There was talk of the imminent danger of war, and it is a historical fact that the worse the image of the enemy is, the greater the fighting spirit of the home forces becomes, while at the same time assuring one's own population of the necessity to deploy armed force in a conflict situation. To prevent war, it is therefore imperative to make an effort to balance the existing negative view of this country and its regime. It does not, however, follow from this that to problematize the creation of an enemy image equates with an act of whitewashing.

A relevant comparative perspective

In an effort to see North Korea as a part of the world, although different from 'ours', what would then be an appropriate basis for comparison? The closest example of a country with a basically similar political culture, and with a similarly troubled past, is South Korea. During the series of military dictatorships in place over a 45-year period, from 1948 to 1993, the country's active opposition, which included hundreds of thousands of industrial workers and students, was very badly treated. The main reason why South Korea avoided being labelled by the West as a dictatorship, and why its image remained largely untarnished, despite serious human rights abuses, was that this country by definition belonged, via its relationship to the United States, to the 'free world' - that is to say, the West. The repressive actions of the military regime were presented as a necessity due to tense relations with the North, and due to threats emanating from the North which were, by extension, threats from a wider Communist bloc. The military and the riot police in Seoul and in other major cities reacted with perhaps unnecessary harshness, yet their reaction was deemed a required response to a smouldering, mortally dangerous threat.

In short, demonization and the production of enemy images are, to a large extent, coloured by relationships and alliances. Regimes belonging to 'our' camp receive gentler treatment, even when guilty of violent acts meted out on their own citizens. When we turn to look at the record of physical abuses and the repressive system in place in North Korea, we do not find the same degree of international indulgence. Neither threats from the South nor from the United States have been sufficient to explain away prisons or prison camps. It is evident that a large number is placed under lock and key in such facilities, a number corresponding in percentage to that of those detained in the United States. In both countries, this figure stands at around two per cent of the population, which is clearly too high a proportion, in both locations. Nevertheless, we hear far more about the prison population of North Korea, despite the fact that the actual number of inmates is far higher in the United States.

An important observation is that enemy images become cemented over time. A particular belief and image takes root (as in the way that the Western media portrays North Korea). This enemy image then constitutes a filter, which colours what we see and what we hear. This filter is formed and solidified by repetition. Very few people have any actual experience of North Korea, yet almost everyone has read, heard and seen the most spine-chilling report of things this country has to offer. This then become the basis of people's experience which, over time, is stored as *what we know*, or rather think we know. It is interesting for a seasoned North Korea observer such as myself to note that even one's own family and friends express skepticism when the media-shaped image of this dictatorship in East Asia is questioned. Even when people make the effort to get off the couch and venture out on a cold winter night to pay good money to hear a different version of events, such as the ones I might offer at a public lecture, they are nevertheless difficult to convince. Their usual response is: *well, but all newspapers and radio and TV tell us something else!* And so they do, with the most unfortunate consequences.

Some years ago, I joined an EU delegation to North Korea. Travelling with delegations of officials and political representatives is a good experience in that it provides ample opportunity to discuss what you observe and encounter with people who are decision-makers and advisors. Particularly interesting, on this occasion, was that both civil servants and politicians from the EU system agreed that it would be positive, from a humanitarian standpoint and in terms of necessary change, if the European Union committed itself more fully to engaging with North Korea. The EU representatives on this mission stressed, however, that such a task is difficult to fulfil when European voters see the country as a virtual hell on earth. When the 'researcher-observer' then asked if it was rather not worthwhile to nuance this picture a little, when we actually saw that not everything was pure misery, so came the following reply: *yes, you may be right, but that is a pretty difficult task.* In other words, the effects of demonization have made themselves fully felt and are self-reinforcing, even among people who have seen, with their own eyes, evidence to the contrary.

One further and important factor is that East Asia, including the Korean peninsula that is centrally located in this region, does not lie in Europe's backyard, but rather in the backyard of the United States. The relationship between the United States and North Korea has, until recently, been poised 'on the brink of war'. The bloodbath that ended with a ceasefire in 1953 was never replaced by a peace agreement. *Formally, the weapons only rest, say the North Koreans, so technically we are still at war with the USA.* At the top of North Korea's wish list when they meet with the United States is a peace agreement – something rarely referred to in the Western media, probably because it does not fit with the image they themselves have created over the years.

A temporary but honorary member of the 'Axis of Evil'

The Axis of Evil is a designation of recent times, dating more specifically from the immediate aftermath of 9/11, when then-US President, George W. Bush, in response to this violent attack on central and emblematic institutions of the United States, took on the role of godfather of the war against terrorism.

'Well-informed sources' – as one says when actual names should not be mentioned – claim that the reason why North Korea found itself in a collection of 'evil countries' was that they were all otherwise Muslim. Advisors to the US president warned against creating a group of solely Muslim enemies, which could easily grow and which could make it appear as though the United States was launching a religious war, by blowing into the embers of an already smoldering fire. A bright spark (so it is said) among the president's staff, therefore, proposed the inclusion of North Korea in this group, to provide the justification that this was *not* a confrontation driven by religious difference. And since North Korea undoubtedly fitted the definition of 'evil power', the proposal was resoundingly approved. The North Korean government was in fact among the many around the world that had sent a letter of condolence to the United States after the 9/11 attacks, but this was regarded as mere hypocrisy and as 'playing to the gallery'. As so often before, the object of the demonization process was not amenable to sympathy, not to mention support. North Korea had become so closely aligned with its enemy image that dialogue was virtually impossible.

One interesting observation in this regard is that, by including North Korea in the group referred to as the 'Axis of Evil', the United States provoked widespread shock in South

Korea. Apart from that country's most steadfast antagonists, most believed that this dehumanization of the North Koreans was far from permissible, and that it revealed more about the US government than it did the North Koreans – who are, after all, their native brothers and sisters.

In an interview study he conducted in South Korea in the late 1990s, a colleague of mine, Fred Alford, examined the perceptions of and attitudes that (South) Koreans held towards the question of evil. He was surprised, he said, to find it was almost impossible for one Korean to describe another Korean as evil. While they recognized that people were capable of committing evil acts, it broke with their perception of their fellow men as actors in one or more in-groups to actually *be* evil. Their actions were thus seen as situational and greatly influenced by their position in the group and by the group's own situation and relationships.

The US rejection of North Korea's expression of sympathy and North Korea's corresponding skepticism toward the US exemplifies the normal relationship that existed between the two countries until Kim Jong Un and incumbent US president Donald Trump met, to the surprise of most people, in Singapore on 12 June 2018. This makes it clear, therefore, that something extraordinary was needed, something which broke the mold and disrupted the long-standing, institutionalized pattern of enemy relations, in order for hopes of peace and reconciliation to be expressed.

If you see, as I do, how the press in large parts of the world handles the question of North Korea on a daily basis, it would seem that we are still a far cry from releasing the country from its straitjacket of demonization. There may be a single, or even two news items devoid of a clearly negative angle, but the rest remains a mixture of description, assumption and conjecture, all of which underline what we already 'know' in advance, namely that North Korea continues to oppress, militarize, cheat and deceive. In short, North Korea is not to be trusted. When stories in the news media are more than plain juicy, they are often copied by others and brought to light across most of the globe as news from 'the court of hell'. An obvious example is the murder of the leader's uncle, who was allegedly thrown to wild dogs, who attacked and killed the poor uncle in a bestial way, as hungry predators do. It was subsequently revealed that the story had been invented by a Chinese blogger who wanted to see if it was possible to get Western media and their readers to bite. Although this fictitious story was published worldwide, the media made no room for subsequent corrections.

Something beyond ideological differences appears, however, to support the image of North Korea as a country where the inhabitants live as if in a large and heavily monitored prison, and under a government that is demonic. That something is, as I see it, the culture of a country that is *foreign* to us. A broadly similar culture is also to be found in China, South Korea and Japan, as well as in Singapore, Thailand and Vietnam. However, the latter places are also influenced by the West, most notably in the cases of Singapore, Thailand, South Korea and Japan, as a result of which their mores become merely and acceptably 'exotic'. By contrast, North Korea is least affected by the West, as the country's isolation from the outside world almost from 'time immemorial' was a strategy to avoid foreigners, be they Japanese pirates or colonizers, Western trade delegations, or military and religious missions. The country was referred to as 'the Hermit Kingdom in the East' and its centuries-long isolation explains much of their values and norms, ideas, rituals and behaviours that are difficult for Westerners to understand.

The West against the rest, as the tectonic plates of history shift

The West has maintained global dominance for the past 500 years. For the last century, we have experienced a political-ideological division in our own world, and this division has existed between countries and systems, in the form of free and democratic vis-à-vis communist systems. Moreover, this contradiction has also emerged within individual countries, between opposing political groups, especially until the collapse of the European Communist systems around 1989.

The communist collapse was celebrated in many places and, in that same year, the American political scientist Francis Fukuyama wrote an article that proclaimed nothing less than the end of history. It was not just the collapse of an ideological, political, economic system, but the end of an era in human history. It was now clear that the capitalist market economy and the political form of liberal democracy, represented the endpoint of history itself. It was now just a question of waiting for the rest to reach this magic stage and to become part of 'the civilized world'. This was the end point of human socio-cultural evolution, a theme developed by Fukuyama in 'The End of History and the Last Man' (1992).

What this American social scientist expresses is a widespread perception in the Western world: *we* are more highly developed than 'the rest', *we* have reached a further civilizational stage, and therefore *we* also have a tradition for helping the others (unless they harbour enmity towards us). Our assistance is termed development 'aid' and it includes the promotion of democracy and human rights, as well as, not least, the market economy. 'Peacemaking' is also a part of this recent tradition, although the West can still adopt the opposite position when our great allies feel it necessary. In short, we have been expecting to govern and regulate the world, as far as possible, and we have not found it important to familiarize ourselves with the basic beliefs and ideas of Others, since they are approaching their expiration date. That assumption has proved, however, to be incorrect. So what now, little white world?

What we see now, on an almost daily basis, is that Fukuyama was categorically wrong. The Western world now finds itself in great trouble. Not only has the crushingly effective capitalist economy closed its eyes to the consequences of its 'efficiency', which now pose enormous challenges both in terms of the cohesiveness of societies and the destructions of climate change, but the civilized world is scarcely civilized any more. Wealth exists in abundance, but the distribution of that wealth is being shared ever more unequally. If globalization on Western terms was the goal of the economic and political elites, the belief that this goal can be achieved and sustained has lost momentum. In leading Western countries, strong forces are turning their backs on the 'system', for they no longer believe that this system exists for them, but rather for itself and, simultaneously, for the upper echelons of society.

In East Asia we have seen economic miracles, among which the major ones were Japan, subsequently South Korea, and currently China. Other countries may be in the starting pits. Asia, where more than half of the world's population resides, is on the rise. The century of Asia is a phenomenon that the West has not dealt with easily. Are we witnessing tectonic

The West is tormented by the demonic image of China: that there are so many Chinese people, that they are growing more and more wealthy, that they are tourists with money in their pockets, plaguing our cities and our countries all year round.

changes with global consequences, or will Asian miracles also lose their momentum? We are already seeing a change of attitude in the West. A growing skepticism is being expressed in regard to non-democratic regimes in Asia. A disappointment perhaps, after we had almost celebrated the end of history and the ultimate victory of the West. A growing hostility towards China's leadership may be a sign that uncertainty and fear also promote processes of demonization. The West is tormented by the demonic image of China: that there are so many Chinese people, that they are growing more and more wealthy, that they are tourists with money in their pockets, plaguing our cities and our countries all year round. Their companies, whether public or private, or a mixture of the two, buy out 'our' influence where they can. Can we trust China? What does it want from us? Will it take over the role of the United States as the next superpower? If so, should we give in? Or should we retaliate?

One thing is certain: our general perception of the outside world as black or white, true or false, right or wrong, simply does not hold. This binary good-and-bad dichotomy is far too narrow to help us grasp and understand the world outside our own cultural circles. North Korea has been made into a demonic place where there are no positive spots, no rays of hope. By focusing on North Korea only, and almost consistently failing to see the conflict as a piece in a much larger regional and international relational dynamic, a caricature of reality is created. The demonization of North Korea has resulted in a very clear outcome: it has held the country in a state of fear of the outside world and thus placed it in a highly defensive position; this defense has often taken the form of aggressive expressions that then has added reasons to maintain the external pressure towards the regime and the country. A vicious circle. One obvious consequence has been that this has so far blocked the path toward change and development in North Korea.

Reasons for this situation to prevail could be that North Korea is seen as a convenient enemy. It was useful to include the North into the Axis of Evil, and it might be useful from a military strategic point of view to maintain the North in its enemy position, especially if one sees China as an enemy in the making. This perspective is not as bizarre as it seems, and it was brought to the table by several observers as a reason for the USA to deploy THAAD to South Korea. THAAD is the US Army's Terminal High-Altitude Area Defense system, the most advanced interceptor in the world, designed to shoot down ballistic missiles in the terminal phase of their approach to a target. Beijing, however, maintains that the system's radar can penetrate its territory and thus undermine the whole regional security balance.

Viewed from this perspective, the demonization of North Korea can be deemed successful: it has served a greater purpose in the global military-strategic perspective of the USA. At the same time, however, it has added fuel to the flames on the Korean peninsula. Some would likely say that the goal sanctifies the agent, and that has also been the excuse for maintaining constant military tension. It should then be remembered, however, that this strategy has been extremely costly for Korea, considering the great harm it has inflicted upon the people on both sides of the demarcation line. Life in the shadows of an extended threat of war cannot but undermine people's quality of life; it leaves scars on the soul.

Geir Helgesen

Sources of particular relevance

Alford, C. Fred (1999) *Think No Evil. Korean Values in the Age of Globalization*. Ithaca and London: Cornell University Press.

Almond, Gabriel (2000), 'The Study of Political Culture' in L. Crothers and C. Lockhart (eds) *Culture and Politics*. New York: St. Martin's Press.

Almond, Gabriel and Sidney Verba, (1963) *The Civic Culture: Political Attitudes and Democracy in Five Nations*, Princeton: Princeton University Press.

Diamond, Larry, (1994) *Political Culture and Democracy in Developing Countries*. Boulder and London: Lynne Rienner Publishers.

Eckstein, Harry, (1996) 'Culture as a Foundation Concept for the Social Sciences', *Journal of Theoretical Politics*, 8(4): 471–498.

Fukuyama, Francis, (1993) *Historiens Afslutning og det Sidste Menneske* [The end of history and the last man]. København: Gyldendal.

Fu Ying, (2017) 'The Korean Nuclear Issue: Past, Present, and Future: A Chinese Perspective'. John L. Thornton China Center at Brookings, May 2017. https://www.brookings.edu/wp-content/uploads/2017/04/north-korean-nuclear-issue-fu-ying.pdf

Hahm Pyong Choon, (1986) *Korean Jurisprudence, Politics and Culture*. Seoul: Yonsei University Press.

Harrison, Lawrence and Samuel P. Huntington (eds) (2000) *Culture Matters. How Values Shape Human Progress*. New York: Basic Books.

Helgesen, Geir and Søren Risbjerg Thomsen (eds) (2006) *Politics, Culture and Self: East Asian and North European Attitudes*. Copenhagen: NIAS Press.

Helgesen, Geir and Hatla Thelle (2013) *Dialogue with North Korea? Preconditions for Talking Human Rights With a Hermit Kingdom*. Copenhagen: NIAS Press.

Huntington, Samuel P., (1996) *The Clash of Civilizations and the Remaking of World Order*. New York: Simon & Shuster.

Inglehart, Ronald and Marita Carballo (2000) 'Does Latin America Exist? (And Is There a Confucian Culture?): A Global Analysis of Cross-Cultural Differences', In Crothers and Lockhart (eds) *Culture and Politics*. New York: St. Martin's Press.

Moon Chung-in and David I. Steinberg, eds. (1999) *Kim Dae-jung Government and Sunshine Policy*. Seoul: Yonsei University Press.

Nielsen, Ras Tind and Geir Helgesen (eds) (2012) *Ideas, Society and Politics in Northeast Asia and Northern Europe: Worlds Apart, Learning from Each Other*. Copenhagen: NIAS Press.

Osgood, Cornelius, (1951) *THE KOREANS and Their Culture*. New York: The Ronald Press Company.

Pye, Lucian W. (1985) *Asian Power and Politics. The Cultural Dimension of Authority.* Cambridge, Massachusetts: The Belknap Press of Harvard University Press.

Getting North Korea right

IN THIS SHORT CONTRIBUTION, Han S. Park emphasizes what may seem obvious but which most scholarly and news media reports alike neglect: to understand the present situation and what made North Korea the way it is, one must avoid seeing it as an isolated entity. While the North, as well as the South, are strongly affected by a common traditional political culture, their post-division trajectories have led them to appear today as opposites. There is no reason to search for which is the most important influence of the two, tradition or modernity, since they coexist; in the development process, two different entities – apparently opposites – have been shaped albeit sharing a strong underlying basis. That this may provide a firmer positive foundation for the normalization and eventual reunification of the two Koreas is a given in Park's argument; while recognizing this and taking the wider geopolitical interests into consideration as well, he shows us that there are good reasons to take North Korea seriously.

About the Author: Dr Han S. Park is University Professor Emeritus of International Affairs and Founding Director of the Center for the Study of Global Issues (GLOBIS) at the University of Georgia. Among all the excellent contributors to this volume, he has been active the longest, as a scholar and as a communicator with a particular focus on Korea and Korean affairs. Born in China (Manchuria) to immigrant Korean parents, he received his education in China, Korea and the United States, with advanced degrees in Political Science from Seoul National University (BA), the American University (MA) and the University of Minnesota (PhD). Throughout his life, Han Park has endeavoured to find new ways to use his talents and abilities to serve the global community. He has been fortunate to have had the opportunity to do so in several capacities: as an educator, a publishing scholar, an opinion leader, a humanitarian and a peacemaker.

CHAPTER FIVE

The De-Demonization of North Korea

*D*emonization is a concept that has been used to characterize terrorist culture in which some human beings are regarded as useless and their rightful fate is no better than death itself. Such a concept is most commonly depicted in the Christian system of values, in which some souls are believed to be evil and demonic. In Cold War culture, the US-led free world customarily demonized the Communist world to justify the destruction and killing of people of Communist persuasion. For a prolonged period of time, the Soviet Union was demonized, as were all other states in the Communist bloc. But none was demonized more acutely than the DPRK (North Korea). In the West, led by the United States, North Korea has been characterized as a barbaric system where people are capriciously slaughtered by the ruling elite. It is a living hell where mass starvation is pervasive and human rights are completely undermined. Such a derogative perception of North Korea is common in the US-led 'free world.'

As long as North Korea feels that it is demonized and isolated from much of the world, including US-backed South Korea, the system will be defensive and arrested by this siege mentality. A person or group driven by such a mentality is bound to believe that the world is hostile and that no one is trustworthy; and that if you do not protect yourself, you will be destroyed. If such a person is demonized, then the siege mentality is intensified and the desire for self-protection is heightened.

Juche as the product of a siege mentality

The ideology of *Juche* is the founding doctrine of the republic established by Kim Il Sung. *Juche* adheres to the principle of self-reliance: no one else but oneself may be trusted and relied upon. The doctrine of *Juche* was first developed in the early years of the Kim regime, even before the promulgation of the political system in 1948. An extremely inhumane and exploitive, imperialist Japan governed Korea from 1905 to the end of World War II in 1945. Following the Japanese surrender, the two primary victors of the World War, the United States and the Soviet Union, occupied the Korean peninsula, each taking half and both using the peninsula to further their hegemonic struggle to rule the world. After three years (1950–53) of intensive military conflict resulting in millions of human casualties, the United States dominated the southern half of the peninsula. This domination has been complete and extensive. Throughout this time, the United States never ceased to demonize North Korea.

Sources of demonization of North Korea in South Korea and beyond

Inter-Korea demonization from the Korean War. The inter-Korea hostility during the brutal Korean War, and afterwards during the ensuing decades of Cold War politics, made the two Korean regimes mutual devils in which they single-mindedly accumulated weapons and strengthened military capability: one became completely dependent on the United States and the other ultimately achieved coveted nuclear power status. Due to the ideological confrontation of the Cold War by the superpowers, the two Korean systems soon engaged in a 'legitimacy war': both systems cannot be legitimate, and the Other must therefore be demonized.

Missionaries and demonization. After the division in 1948 and especially after the Korean War that rolled into a prolonged period of truce in 1953, American missionary activities exploded and missionaries from the West (mostly from the United States) penetrated all segments of South Korean society. They are largely responsible for orienting Koreans to believe that North Korean communists are so evil that their only rightful fate is death.

Ignorance from misinformation and disinformation. Peoples in both the north and the south have been subjected to heavy indoctrination to believe that the other side is wrong and unjustified. The indoctrination begins early on in educational institutions and continues through mass media and government programs. In South Korea, the most popular source of information is from defectors from North Korea whose views are unsurprisingly biased against the system which they defected from. Often information is manufactured by the South Korean conservative establishment.

Prejudice and bias: the power of indoctrination. The politics of the Cold War was itself one of indoctrination and mutual demonization, and the two Korean regimes were little more than mouthpieces for the superpowers. All Koreans in the north and the south have been subjected to intense political education and ideological indoctrination. In South Korea, the predominant sources of information about the north have been selectively chosen or approved by the intelligence community of the government with the possible exception of the current Moon Jae-in government that came as a result of the Candlelight Democratic Revolution.

The challenge of de-demonization: The DPRK is a normal state

Logically, de-demonization requires neutralizing or reversing each of the sources of demonization itself. I have no ambition, however, to denounce and reverse the above sources of demonization of North Korea. Instead, I intend to advance the argument that North Korea is a normal and healthy political system. With an understanding of North Korea as a normal system, one may be able to see past the four sources of demonization.

The Democratic People's Republic of Korea is a normal state with a normal leadership. It is a developing socialist system with unique characteristics that stems from North Korean culture and its historical legacy. From the inception of the government in 1948, the Kim Il Sung regime has pursued for generations a set of policy goals that are universal to all political systems of the world, especially developing systems. These policy goals are regime legitimization, security and prosperity.

Legitimacy

Legitimization provides the political system with a reason to exist and it is usually achieved through a political ideology that is a system of values and norms. An ideology is a legitimizing tool for a regime, and no regime can justify its existence without the help of an ideology. When a government is formed, a governing authority must be created. 'Authority' connotes not just physical power, but also 'legitimate' power accompanied by ideological justification. All ideologies, liberal and illiberal, have been used by a variety of regimes to generate authorities out of mere physical (military) forces. North Korea's Kim Il Sung did exactly that. The creation of *Juche* ideology and its meticulously guided evolution is designed to generate a legitimacy that is superior to the ideology practiced in South Korea. Kim, as a legendary nationalist leader under Japanese colonial rule, embraced nationalism as the core of his political views. National sovereignty and independence became the driving forces behind the ideology. Its evolution through the decades, especially under Founder Kim's leadership through the 1960s and 1970s, made the ideology an integrated system of world views, normative values and policy programs. Several ideas that developed in the evolution of *Juche* are worth pointing out as they contributed to integrating people's belief systems and effectively generated loyalty and patriotism among the entire population:

Man-centeredness (humanism), not materialism. Socialism is basically atheism plus materialism, but North Korean socialism deviates from this norm. There is a saying that everyone in that society feels, 'if we are spiritually motivated, there is nothing we cannot accomplish!' which suggests that history is crafted not by material or economic determinism but by human and cultural determinism. This phenomenon may be further instigated by Confucian 'spiritual determinism.'

Juche theory. According to *Juche* theory, there are two different lives that everyone lives: a *biological life* and a *political-social life*. Biological life is the life everyone is born with before socialization; the other is the one that has advanced to a mature person through education and socialization. Education and proper socialization contribute to the development of a set of human attributes that a mature person can achieve: (1) social *consciousness*; (2) *independence*; and (3) *creativity*. These human attributes are directly reflected in government policies, both domestic and foreign. The process of attitude formation begins during the early stages of children's education and continues throughout their lives. This process is remarkably effective in converting natural biological beings into political/social beings.

The inter-Korea 'legitimacy war'. North Korea as a state has been decisively affected by the existence of South Korea. With the progressive development of the South Korean economy in the 1970s onward, especially in the downturn of the Communist bloc centered around the Soviet Union, the North Korean economy has continuously lagged behind South Korea even after the emergence of a new leadership under Kim Jong Un. The youthful leader found that there was much to be done in order to catch up with the South. But Kim Jong Un, following in his father's footsteps, has refused to 'learn' from the south. Anyone who suggests the South Korean model as a desirable pattern of development is purged, or even executed.

Socialism with Korean characteristics. North Korea is basically a Confucian society, and it has developed a peculiar version of Confucianism that is meshed into North Korean socialism, creating what is referred to as Paternalist Socialism. In this, the entire country is regarded as an indivisible extended family. Kim Il Sung is believed to be the 'father' of the entire people. As in Confucianism itself, loyalty to the head of the family is regarded as more significant than to the head of government. Kim Il Sung elevated himself as the *father* of the nation, thereby designating himself the ultimate authority and power. In revering the father, *Juche* made Kim the brain of the body politic (*suryongnim*).

Security

Once legitimacy is reasonably established, national and regime security become the universal goals of the political system. Laws and legal institutions are designed to achieve domestic stability. North Korea, with its central authority system centered around the Korea Labor Party, is one of the most secure and stable systems in the world. There is absolutely no possibility of mass uprisings or military coups against the regime. However, security from outside forces – including South Korea – is a different matter. The US military presence in the south, which has been a constant since the Korean War began in 1950, continues to be a tremendous source of insecurity to North Korea.

After the passing of Kim Il Sung in 1994, his successor Kim Jong Il waged an all-out campaign to meet the challenge of keeping the country secure from external threat under the banner of Military First Politics (MFP). MFP is designed for both the militarization of the people and the civilianization of the military, so that the military and general public become indivisible and, together, ensure maximum national security. With the US–South Korea security alliance, the two affluent powers conduct joint military drills on a regular basis, causing an intense sense of insecurity and threat to North Korea's survival. With a sagging economy, North Korea is not capable of meeting the security challenge by stockpiling conventional weapons, whereas the south is capable of purchasing large quantities of sophisticated conventional weapons from the United States. This situation, combined with the fact that the political systems of Libya and Iraq were uprooted overnight by the US-led Western forces, decisively drove Kim Jong Il into a corner, and led him to conclude that nuclearization is the only rational response to be made.

> ... a sagging economy ... combined with the fact that the political systems of Libya and Iraq were uprooted overnight by the US-led Western forces ... drove Kim Jong Il into a corner, and led him to conclude that nuclearization is the only rational response to be made.

In fact, North Korea's nuclear ambition traces back to the time of Kim Il Sung. When Kim witnessed the massive power of the atomic weapons deployed in Hiroshima and Nagasaki in 1945 that instantly brought the emperor of Japan to his knees, Kim was overwhelmingly impressed by the weapon and was convinced that this weapon was all he needed for the defense of his country. However, the United States was far ahead with nuclear weaponry and American tactical nuclear weapons were believed to have been distributed to South Korea. The realization of the US-led nuclear preparedness in South Korea persuaded Kim to declare the denuclearization of the entire peninsula, not just of South Korea. Kim Jong Il succeeded with this policy, although he wanted to continue to build on the nuclear program.

At the time of Kim Jong Il's unexpectedly death in December 2011, North Korea had not completed the goal of achieving nuclear status in the world community. But his son, Kim Jong Un, was quick to declare that the country had achieved the goal of nuclearization after the sixth test in September 2017. Kim Jong Un was confident that his nuclear state would not be attacked by any external nuclear state, including the United States. His declaration of being a nuclear state has been effectively confirmed by the US's inability or unwillingness to put North Korea to the test.

Prosperity

I offered the view that Kim Il Sung and Kim Jong Il had achieved their respective goals of the state. If Kim Il Sung was effective as a leader in establishing regime legitimacy through the creation and development of *Juche* ideology, Kim Jong Il perfected the Military First Politics to bring about national security with the development and possession of nuclear weapons. The current leader Kim Jong Un was likely then inaugurated for the purpose of creating prosperity through economic development. While perfecting the unfinished job of nuclearization by Kim Jong Il, the young leader, who was exposed to and experienced with the environment of Western life in Switzerland, proclaimed that his role is to provide for the people's basic needs and especially food security, so that 'the people do not have to suffer from a tightly tightened belt.'

Historically, North Korea's most reliable food source is China. The vast stretches of arable land in Northeast China's Jilin, Liaoning and Heilongjiang provinces produce great quantities of rice, the majority of which has been exported to North Korea, often free of charge, from the inception of Maoist China. This practice continues today. For food, no country is as important to North Korea as China. Coupled with security alliances and culturally and politically intimate relations, North Korea is expected to value China over the United States or South Korea as a trustworthy source of food.

Current Security Map

Beyond the case of food, however, the United States and South Korea are noteworthy as sources of economic development. Yet, as long as the US–South Korea security alliance remains intact, problems in both countries' economic relationship with North Korea will continue to mount. South Korea needs the north to remain the primary enemy in order to justify its military alliance with the United States who, in turn, markets weapons to South Korea. In this regard, Washington's not-so-secret objective is to deter China more than North Korea. Pyongyang, on the other hand, has a security alliance with China, who is a reliable source of assistance both economically and in relation to security.

Japan also remains an important player in the region. Among the systems there, Japan – like South Korea – is a strong security ally of the United States, with a large number of US ground troops stationed on its soil and with a shared interest in deterring China. Thus, East Asia has become a complex and confusing area in which diverse political systems are to find a new security structure surrounding the Korean peninsula.

North Korea's willingness to accept demands for denuclearization from foreign countries is due to it already having achieved the status of a nuclear state. The DPRK is not expected to relinquish its nuclear ambitions. As North Korea cannot run into conflict with the United States, Pyongyang wishes to secure a guarantee of non-aggression from the United States, for which Kim Jong Un demands a peace treaty as a precondition for accepting the CVID (Complete, Verifiable, Irreversible, Dismantlement) demands. The CVID measures are not operationally definable, let alone implementable. Regardless of practical feasibilities, both Kim and Trump seem to share an enthusiasm for pursuing denuclearization on the peninsula.

For Kim Jong Un, it is motivated by national prosperity or economic development; for Donald Trump, it is driven by the potential political payoff from a diplomatic breakthrough with North Korea.

Final Words

Ever since the Korean War, North Korea has been continuously subjected to demonization. This was later facilitated by the Cold War decades, in which both Koreas were swept up by the Security Paradigm. For peace and eventual reunification, the Security Paradigm is harmful. To achieve the de-demonization of North Korea, one must revisit the sources of demonization such as the paucity of information on North Korea, and the prejudices and biases against the people, the ideology and the political system of the north. At the same time, it is vital to interpret and understand North Korea as a normal or ordinary state, so as to neutralize the demonization process through formal education and mass socialization in South Korea and her allies, such as the United States and Japan.

Han S. Park

Juche, the North Korean Ideology

It is tempting to translate *Juche* directly, which would then be *Self Reliance.* This would not convey the full meaning of the concept, however, but rather how *Juche* is perceived within a Western cultural context. Han S. Park has penetrated the very essence of *Juche.* While he notes that 'Scholars and observers of North Korea have found striking similarities between today's North Korea and what was depicted in George Orwell's famous novel *1984*' (p.1), he convincingly explains that *Juche* is the locus of the country's political culture, and central to understanding its political behavior.

'[T]he *mindset* of North Koreans [...] dictates the policy-making process and its output. In this process, it is imperative to examine the nature and ramifications of *Juche* ideology. This ideology is pervasive. It is more than a political system of values; it is a way of life.' (p.3)

'I contend that one should understand and react to the perceptions of reality of the North Koreans themselves. I further contend that no perception is inexplicable if one is willing and able to put oneself in the shoes of the perceiver. Only with such empathy can one begin to find rationality in seemingly irrational and random patterns of behavior.' (p.9)

'Citizens of North Korea have been effectively shielded from the uncontrolled environment of the external world. They are not only physically confined but also mentally isolated within their own surroundings.' (p.61)

'Without interruption in the progression of socialization for several decades, *Juche* has been able to deeply penetrate and assimilate itself into the mass belief systems. The degree of rigidity and saliency of beliefs may have reached a point at which external disturbances may not easily cause psychological dissonance.' (p.63)

~ Han S. Park, *North Korea: The Politics of Unconventional Wisdom.* Lynne Rienner Publishers, 2002.

Sovereignty matters

HAZEL SMITH REMINDS THE READER that the aim of this edited volume is to provide a reality check on 'received wisdom' in respect of North Korea. Smith shows how over-simplification occludes analysis and shuts off debate about interesting and consequential matters for inter-Korean relations. Smith unpacks one of these tropes, which is that North Korea claims to be the sole legitimate government of Korea. Smith investigates the complex issue of where sovereignty resides on the Korean peninsula and with what political entity. Smith evaluates North Korean and South Korean policy on sovereignty, showing that while North Korean policy is of recognition of legal division; South Korean policy suffers from some difficult contradictory impulses. On the one hand, President Moon Jae-In explicitly rejects the policy of 'absorption' of the North and *de facto* government policy is to negotiate with the DPRK as a sovereign equal. South Korea's *de jure* state structures, however, deny DPRK sovereignty. These contradictions raise doubts as to the sustainability of ROK policy past the electoral cycle in which Moon remains President.

About the Author: Hazel Smith is a Fellow of the Woodrow Wilson International Center for Scholars, Washington DC, Professorial Research Associate at SOAS University of London and Professor Emerita in International Security at Cranfield University, UK. She received her PhD in International Relations from the London School of Economics and has held competitive fellowships at the Woodrow Wilson International Center for Scholars, the East–West Center, Honolulu, Kyushu University, the United States Institute of Peace and Stanford University. Professor Smith has researched, written, published, consulted and broadcast internationally on East Asian security and North Korea politics, economics, society and international relations for nearly 30 years. She lived in the DPRK for two years while working for United Nations humanitarian organisations, earning a (still valid) North Korean driving licence.

CHAPTER SIX

Sovereignty Matters: North Korean Pragmatism and South Korean Contradictions

T he 2020 pandemic sweeping the world pushed major conflict off global news feeds and policy agendas but it was not long before, in 2017, that inter-Korean relations were at such a low point that serious commentators were talking about the potential of another global disaster in the shape of a nuclear war, a catastrophe that could not have been confined to the Korean peninsula. These conflicts remain unresolved. At the same time, the 'demonization' agenda that saturates the international negotiating environment with over-simplistic generalisations, hyperbole, skewed data and highly opinionated assertions, often masquerading as factual analysis about North Korea, paralyses serious action as policy-makers fear being accused of being 'soft' on North Korea should they step outside ubiquitous 'received wisdom' parameters. This is not a question of holding a view about the very real failures of the North Korean government. It is that to mis-use and skew the data prevents careful evaluation of complicated social realities and the development of real-world policies designed to deal with those complexities. What I have called the 'securitisation' of DPRK analysis prepares international actors for war; the logic is that if North Korean government and society are so far outside the bounds of any normal society, then the extreme solution of war can be justified to enforce change.

The broad aim of this edited volume is to provide a reality check on much of the 'received knowledge' about North Korea. This chapter unpacks one of these tropes, which in one form or another repeats the common assertion that North Korea claims to be the sole legitimate government of Korea. According to Nicholas Eberstadt, for example, writing in the respected *New York Times* (25 April 2018) 'the existential objective of its [North Korea's] ruling family, the Kims, has been to wipe the state of South Korea off the face of the earth.' It is a fairly simple matter to show that this assertion does not have much of a factual base. The substantive point of this chapter, however, is to show how such over-simplifications occlude analysis and debate about more interesting, complicated and consequential matters for inter-Korean relations. These emphatic declarations rule out by fiat (because the question has already been decided) an investigation as to where sovereignty resides and with what political entity, and how this may have changed over time.

This chapter compares the sovereignty claims of North Korea (formally the Democratic People's Republic of Korea or the DPRK) to those of South Korea (formally the Republic of Korea or the ROK) and finds that, while the DPRK explicitly limits sovereignty claims to the northern part of the peninsula, the ROK makes assertive constitutional claims to sovereignty over the entire Korean peninsula. South Korea is by far the more powerful actor in inter-Korean politics; its policies and activities are crucial in shaping the possibilities and frameworks for success in inter-Korean negotiations. Yet South Korean policy towards the North suffers from some very difficult contradictory impulses. On the one hand, President Moon Jae-In explicitly rejects the policy of 'absorption' of the North and pursues an activist conciliation policy with the DPRK. On the other hand, the ROK's Constitution and legislation do not recognise DPRK sovereignty. The contradictions between the existence of *de jure* state structures based on the denial of DPRK sovereignty and government policy of negotiating with the DPRK as a *de facto* sovereign equal, raise some doubts as to the sustainability of ROK policy past the electoral cycle in which Moon remains President.

Sovereignty: what is it good for?

Sovereignty is an intangible but nevertheless powerful idea that provides the organizing concept of the international system in which we all live. Sovereign states are political and territorial entities that are recognised by other sovereign states as possessing supreme authority within their territory. Sovereign states are equal to and independent of other sovereign states. Sovereignty has provided the core foundational principle of international law and the constitutive principle of the international system for several hundred years. The entire planet is divided territorially and politically into jurisdictions demarcated as sovereign states. Today the United Nations, the nearest we have to a global, universalist organisation, recognises 193 sovereign states as members. Sovereignty, albeit an abstract concept, is a highly prized political commodity because it provides international legitimacy and because it is inviolable, irrespective of the quality or type of government ruling over the state.

Sovereignty endows important privileges. It is sovereign states, not governments, that are the constituent members of international organisations (like the United Nations). It is sovereign states that sign the treaties that govern almost every aspect of modern social, economic and political life, from the environment to human rights to tariffs to poverty. Treaties are signed between sovereign states that vary in size and capacity but which, in international law, enter into international agreements on the basis of legal equality. Non-sovereign political entities cannot authoritatively deal with states as equals in international law and cannot easily act for their populations in any sphere of activity that involves international transactions.

Sovereignty provides a powerful regulator of international norms and behaviour. The principle of non-interference in the affairs of other states, for example, is a corollary of the embeddedness of the foundational idea of sovereignty. It is illegal under international law, as codified in the United Nations Charter, to extinguish the sovereignty of another sovereign state by force. The 1990–91 United States-led intervention in Iraq was thus legally justified because Saddam Hussain invaded and attempted to annex the sovereign state of Kuwait.

Sovereignty does not of course mean the same thing, in theory or in practice, as power. States are clearly unequal in terms of power – whether understood as capacity (resources), relational (the ability of A to get B to do something they wouldn't otherwise do) or agenda setting (the ability to control narratives and by doing so to exclude debate on alternatives). Nevertheless, powerful states have historically shown a perhaps surprising reluctance to challenge sovereignty norms and often seek to justify military interventions abroad as upholding sovereignty claims. In 2014, when Russia expropriated the Crimea from Ukraine, it was careful to try to justify annexation on the grounds of historical claims to sovereignty and principles of self-determination; it argued that a referendum proved that the population supported the transfer of sovereignty from Ukraine to Russia. The majority of the world, as expressed through United Nations resolutions, thought differently. For them, Russian annexation was an illegal abrogation of Ukraine's sovereignty. Neither party sought to argue that sovereignty did not matter; on the contrary, both referred to the doctrine of state sovereignty to justify and support their actions.

In the post-Cold War era, the fragmentation of the former Soviet Union and Yugoslavia did not result in a call for a new type of international system; instead political and territorial entities fought (in the case of Yugoslavia) and negotiated (in the case of the former Soviet Union) to achieve sovereign statehood. In 1990, the Federal Republic of Germany (FRG) succeeded in absorbing East Germany after a series of negotiations based on the consent of the politicians and the population of East Germany (albeit begrudgingly in some parts of the former Communist state). In 1990, South Yemen and North Yemen also achieved a merged sovereign state through negotiations. More common, however, is the propensity of sovereignty disputes to end in war – as in the Vietnam War, in Korea itself in the 1950s and, more recently, in the brutal conflict that ended with recognition of East Timorese sovereignty in 2002.

The idea of sovereignty has shown enormous resiliency and potency. The principle of sovereignty coincides with the inclination of powerful states to exclude 'outsiders' from intervening in their domestic affairs. Powerful states may attempt to undermine the legitimacy of foreign governments through political, economic or propaganda means, but do not commonly call into question the sovereignty of the state. The more common argument is that governmental incumbents in the target state are illegitimate and should be replaced by alternative governments. Small states also value the condition of sovereignty; for them, it provides protection against unilateral intervention by more powerful states.

International lawyers, diplomats and scholars have argued that, as weak as it is, international law based on the notion of sovereignty is valuable as a preventive of the war of all against all, which would likely be a corollary of living in a world that was only run by brute power. It is not just scholars, however, that value sovereignty; bloody, brutal and prolonged wars are fought for sovereign status. Attempts to force the derogation of sovereignty from one state to another, do not have a record of easy success. Today's most well-known sovereignty dispute is that between the People's Republic of China (PRC) and Taiwan; but even the PRC, a superpower in today's global system, cannot exert its will on Taiwan through the use of brute power.

Sovereignty: the fight for legitimacy on the Korean peninsula

In 1945 the United States and the Soviet Union, then wartime allies, divided a Korean peninsula-wide political entity that had been united for at least 600 years (and more if every pre-modern polity is taken into account), giving each of the allies a sphere of influence in Korea. Between 1950 and 1953, the Democratic People's Republic of Korea and the Republic of Korea fought a very bloody, brutal, internationalised civil war for sovereignty over the entire Korean peninsula, which left millions dead, mostly Koreans, on both sides. The 1953 Korean War concluded with a military armistice that acknowledged a *de facto* existence of two sovereign states on the Korean peninsula. Initially, neither of the two Koreas anticipated that the political and ideological division of the Korean peninsula would last and both continued to hope for unification on terms that would have meant capitulation of one side to the other. The first political negotiations between the two Koreas did not start until two decades after the Korean War, when Korean division was beginning to appear to both to be more permanent, the problem of reunification more intractable and the support of superpower allies less reliable. Superpower détente of the 1970s, between China and the United States and the Soviet Union and the United States, resulted in both Koreas fearing the loss of military support from their respective superpower allies.

The North–South Korea talks were not based upon a fundamental change of attitude to each other's political legitimacy, but the signing of the 4 July 1972 North–South Joint

Communiqué by the two Koreas confirmed *de facto* mutual recognition of each other's sovereignty. By 1973, however, the agreement had unravelled, and deadly skirmishes involving North Korean, South Korean and United States soldiers in the oxymoronic Demilitarized Zone continued. Neither Korean state engaged again in an all-out attempt to unite the Korean peninsula militarily, but continued hostility over unresolved legitimacy claims provided the context for now-well-known incidents involving the murder of civilians. These included the assassination of South Korean President Park Chung-Hee's wife in 1974 (in a failed attempt to kill the President) by a North Korean sympathiser and the 1983 atrocity when North Korea bombed and killed a South Korean political delegation in Yangon, Myanmar. Twenty-six Korean and Burmese politicians and civilians were killed, including ROK Foreign Minister Lee Beom-Seok, and 46 were injured.

It was not until the end of the Cold War in Europe that a more definitive (compared to the 1972 Agreement), mutual recognition of *de facto* sovereignty occurred, after both Koreas joined the United Nations as sovereign states in August 1991. The *de jure* position, however, remains complicated, especially on the part of South Korea, which explicitly claims sovereignty over the entire Korean peninsula. The current South Korean Constitution, established in 1987, states that the 'territory of the Republic of Korea shall consist of the Korean peninsula and its adjacent islands.'

North Korea: getting the facts right

Sovereignty for the DPRK is a well-understood concept and is congruent with the theory and practice of international understandings of sovereignty. The key components of sovereignty as *equality with* and *independence of* other states are exactly synonymous with the DPRK state ideology of *Juche*, or self-reliance doctrine.

Sovereignty is an important concept for the DPRK but is not conflated with a claim to hold sovereignty over the entire Korean peninsula. The 2016 Constitution contains broad-brush aims to 'reunify the country [i.e. the Korean peninsula] on the principle of independence, peaceful reunification and great national unity' but it explicitly confines sovereign jurisdiction to the 'northern' half of the peninsula. Secondary legislation mirrors these rather circumscribed claims. Alongside persons born in the DPRK, the Nationality Law recognises as nationals every person 'who possesses Chosun [the name given to pre-1945 united Korea] nationality before the establishment of the republic, and their children' but adds the qualifying phrase 'and who has not renounced the nationality.' South Koreans and Koreans living anywhere in the rest of the world, including United States citizens, can thus claim DPRK nationality if they wish to do so, on the grounds that one of their ancestors lived in the Korean peninsula between 1392 and 1945, but there is not a general expectation that they would do so. The nationality law explicitly gives preferential jurisdiction to other states in which Koreans reside in terms of nationality status. Article 16 asserts that 'in the case when the DPRK nationality law and the nationality related treaty established with other countries are inconsistent, the treaty with other countries shall be applied instead.' There would, in other words, be nothing to prevent the DPRK entering into an agreement with South Korea to formalise mutual recognition of the sovereignty of the two states in respect of nationality and citizenship.

North Korea's position may be explained by pragmatism or cynicism. By the 1980s, North Korea was already the less-powerful party of the two Koreas. Since 1971, North Korean reunification proposals have been based on 'two systems in one country', which envisages North Korea and South Korea operating two different political systems, while uniting in a single independent, confederated Korean state. Kim Il Sung had hoped that such a confederation would allow 'Leftist' elements in South Korea to take over the South Korean government and generate unification by absorption of the south into the north. In these more realistic times, with Kim Jong Un admitting to South Korean President Moon that North Korea is not anywhere near as economically attractive as the South, it is hard to find evidence that North Korean unification plans continue to be based upon similar assumptions to those of the 1970s. Today South Korea's military and economic capacity is far superior to that of North Korea. South Korea's annual spending on its military is bigger than North Korea's entire GDP. Despite the possession of a nuclear capacity, the DPRK could not win a war against South Korea and its allies and cannot reunify the peninsula by force on its own terms. The DPRK can only move towards the economic development it seeks through a negotiated settlement.

> South Korea's annual spending on its military is bigger than North Korea's entire GDP. Despite the possession of a nuclear capacity, the DPRK could not win a war against South Korea and its allies and cannot reunify the peninsula by force on its own terms.

Negotiating with South Korea on a state-to-state basis is not presented in the state media or in government emissions in an ideological context or as providing any existential threat. The DPRK is not a democracy; any expressed support for South Korea has been brutally suppressed in the past and would still be today. Nevertheless, the government has hitherto sought to justify key initiatives to the public via state media, for example the nuclear programme. Inside North Korea, however, well-publicised meetings with the South Korean presidency are today presented to the population as a recognition of the DPRK as a sovereign equal with what the entire population of the DPRK knows is a much more prosperous and successful state than their own.

North Korea's position on state sovereignty does not constitute much of a research puzzle, theoretically or practically. Theoretically, as far as analysis of the DPRK approach is concerned, it is simply a question of getting the facts straight. Practically, as long as the leadership can keep North Korea's ruling elite united, the issue of where sovereignty resides on the Korean peninsula does not provide an obstacle to inter-Korean negotiations.

South Korea: democratic divisions and institutional contradictions

South Korea, unlike the DPRK, is a democracy and must secure domestic support for domestic and international programmes and activities. The administration of President Moon Jae-In was elected in 2017 on the basis of a political programme that included initiating negotiations with the DPRK. In contrast to the previous engagement-oriented South Korean administrations of Kim Dae-jung and Roh Moo-hyun, President Moon has this time round been supported by the United States. South Korean diplomacy has worked pro-actively with the United States, China and others to ensure that key international actors are in step with each other in the process of inter-Korean conciliation. This is partly to assuage United States and Japanese fears that South Korea might go it alone with the DPRK and consequently weaken the tripartite alliance, but also because the South Korean judgement is that without the United States actively involved, the process has no chance of long-term success.

President Moon's policy is of negotiations between *de facto* sovereign equals and the rejection of reunification by absorption of North Korea into a South Korean-dominated polity. Nevertheless, as one would expect in a vibrant democracy in which opposing views are articulated and debated, there is a significant section of domestic opinion that does not support engagement with the DPRK, unless it is on terms of DPRK abasement. More problematic for President Moon's policy is the continued existence of a Constitution, legislation and political institutions that assert and advocate South Korean sovereignty over the entire Korean peninsula. The well-known National Security Law imposes punitive sanctions, including lengthy jail sentences, on those who are deemed to have expressed support for the North. The less well-known National Unification Advisory Council (NUAC), a state institution established by the South Korean constitution, provides another challenge for President Moon's policy towards North Korea, in that one of its functions is to organize and appoint a government-in-waiting for the DPRK.

The NUAC started life in 1980 as the Advisory Council on Peaceful Unification Policy, when South Korea was still governed by military leaders. The 2009 National Unification Advisory Council Law gave the organization a new lease of life and it was instrumentalized by former Presidents Lee Myung-bak and Park Geun-hye (both now imprisoned after corruption scandals) as an activist organization at home and abroad. In 2018 the National Unification Advisory Council had 18,000 government-appointed members, including, according to its website, 'overseas council members stationed in 122 countries around the world'. The NUAC's stated remit abroad, among other items listed, is to:

- push for active peaceful public diplomacy
- strengthen unification ability and public diplomacy
- strengthen its role as hub of the overseas unification network
- continuously remind the global community of the North Korean nuclear problem through relations with influential foreign politicians, civic groups and media

The UK chapter of the National Unification Advisory Council, for example, regularly convenes meetings to which it invites former North Koreans domiciled in the UK, South Koreans and high-profile UK persons interested in Korea.

The challenge to the government policy of negotiating a peaceful settlement with the DPRK arises from the institutional and legal foundations of the NUAC, which by statute deny the sovereignty of the DPRK. By law, the National Unification Advisory Council is comprised of South Korean citizens appointed by the South Korean government as putative governors to North Korean provinces. The National Unification Advisory Council also has the legal responsibility to convene provincial assemblies for North Korea. President Moon is ex-officio president of the National Unification Advisory Council. On the one hand, therefore, as head of government, President Moon forswears any intention of regime change aims or unification through absorption. On the other hand, President Moon heads a well-funded institution that was designed to undermine the legitimacy of the DPRK.

South Korea's nationality law reflects similar contradictory impulses towards DPRK sovereignty. The Constitutional assertion of peninsula-wide sovereignty might logically be taken to imply that DPRK citizens are automatically considered South Korean nationals. Yet ROK law does *not* grant North Korean citizens an automatic right to ROK citizenship. Instead, the South Korean Nationality Law states that those wishing to 'reinstate' their nationality (i.e. DPRK citizens) may *apply* [my emphasis] to do so but they will *not* be granted South Korean citizenship if they are a person:

- who has inflicted harm on the State or society;
- whose conduct is disorderly; or
- for whom the Minister of Justice regards the reinstatement of his/her nationality as inappropriate, for the purposes of national security, sustainment of order or public welfare.

To become South Korean citizens, North Koreans must first be screened by the Ministry of Justice, which in practice means the South Korean intelligence agencies. Because South

Korean citizenship is conditional on the intelligence services determining that the person is not inflicting harm upon society, every North Korean choosing to apply for South Korean citizenship must agree to submit to intrusive investigation during the application process. They must also accept permanent surveillance after the granting of citizenship, to ensure that nationality conditions are not breached. Apart from the intelligence agencies, the organisation charged with oversight of former North Koreans, is the National Unification Advisory Council, whose remit includes 'supporting the successful settlement of North Korean defectors [in South Korea].'

Explaining the contradiction in South Korean policies

The ambiguity in respect of South Korean approaches to DPRK sovereignty is not accidental or inexplicable but reflects significant tension and division in South Korean domestic politics and institutions over how to deal with North Korea and inter-Korean conciliation. This is not a division in respect of an ethical assessment of the DPRK government; there would be only a small minority in South Korea today that would claim that the DPRK is a state to be admired. This is rather a dispute as to whether the DPRK should be treated as an equal sovereign state with which a deal can be negotiated.

Post-Cold War ROK administrations reflected these different perspectives, careering between the non-belligerent but non-engagement of the President Kim Young-Sam (1993–1998), to what were understood at the time as revolutionary engagement policies of Presidents Kim Dae-Jung and Roh Moo-Hun (1998–2008), to the vigorous non-engagement policy of Presidents Lee Myung-bak and Park Geun-hye (2008–2017). President Moon Jae-In's approach is to assume a relationship of sovereign equality and to negotiate for conciliation and nuclear disarmament.

The Constitutional commitment to ROK sovereignty over the entire Korean peninsula reflects a still strongly held view that the North Korean government is ethically illegitimate and with which South Korea should not negotiate as a matter of principle. Given the continuity of authoritarian politics in the DPRK, it is not very surprising that many find abhorrent the idea of offering any concessions to North Korea. This is, after all, a state which as recently as 2017 was implicated in the assassination of the half-brother of the current leader in an international airport using nerve gas.

In a democracy, minority views cannot be ignored and in South Korea such views are not held not by a small minority, but throughout large swathes of the society. For President Moon, then, the issue is one of pragmatism. The president needs to recognise the practical fact of DPRK state sovereignty for negotiating purposes. At the same time, as a democratic leader seeking continued office for his party and political programme, the president needs to respect and be sensitive to the continued strength of anti-North Korea feeling in South Korean society. To engage in attempts to change the Constitution of the Republic of Korea in order to limit sovereignty claims to the southern half of the peninsula or to alter the institutional structure of the NUAC, would be to generate a wave of vocal opposition from those who still see engaging with the DPRK as supping with the devil. It would necessarily involve the dissipation of political attention away from the core government goal of achieving substantive progress in inter-Korean conciliation and denuclearizaton of the Korean peninsula. For these reasons, it is a logical policy to adopt a political fudge of continued embedded denial of *de jure* sovereignty combined with *de facto* acceptance of DPRK sovereignty.

Sovereignty matters

We should be wary of common knowledge claims about North Korea – irrespective of where they are published, be it on online encyclopaedias, 'quality' journalism, 'academic' articles or policy analysis. The example in this article is of the oft-repeated assertion that North Korea claims sovereignty over the entire Korean peninsula. A simple fact check shows that North Korean legislation and policy confines its jurisdictional claim to the north of the peninsula. This does not mean that the DPRK leadership argues for the political legitimacy of the South Korean leadership, but it does allow for a reconsideration of what DPRK, and ROK, sovereignty claims actually entail in the context of the urgent and complex problems of inter-Korean conciliation processes. This then is the job of scholars and analysts; to focus on using the analytical and disciplinary tools available to us to investigate the complications, contradictions and messiness of real-life international relations.

Most studies of international relations converge around the idea that conflict resolution through diplomacy is intrinsically about reaching agreements between adversaries who do not share common values, not about coming to an agreement between allies. Being ethically unpleasant is not a barrier to sovereign recognition for the purposes of entering into negotiations or agreements in the international system. If it were, the international system would cease to function. The reason adversaries engage in diplomacy is because they cannot achieve their separate aims through other means, and because the status quo is too costly and too risky. The North Korean government and the South Korean government are in precisely this position; neither can achieve their goal through the use of power and both are left with the option of continuing with a risky status quo or of engaging in diplomatic negotiations to achieve a compromise deal both can accept.

The Democratic People's Republic of Korea is not a minor player in the inter-Korean conciliation processes. From the perspective of the North, the nuclear programme gives it a negotiating edge. For much of the world that nuclear programme provides urgency to the pursuit of a political solution to the security conflicts on the Korean peninsula. Nevertheless, North Korea is negotiating for survival, not to expand its sovereignty throughout the peninsula. This does not mean that the DPRK government will voluntarily cede sovereignty to South Korea, as East Germany effectively did to West Germany in 1990. Nor is it all clear that the North Korean population looks to South Korea as an appropriate model for their future. The limited data that is available indicates more of an affinity with prosperous if non-democratic China, whose political and social system is more familiar to North Koreans than full-on capitalist South Korea.

President Moon Jae-In has achieved enormous and unprecedented success in taking forward a brave and transformative process of conciliation with South Korea's old adversary. South Korean manifestations of 'unification by absorption', however, complicate negotiations between the two Koreas. DPRK negotiators may not take seriously the appointment of alternative government officials for North Korea by a South Korean state institution, but what must be visible is the continuing constitutional, legal and institutional embeddedness of, at best, ambivalence towards negotiating with the DPRK, and, at worst, regime change norms. The continued existence of a structural disinclination to treat the DPRK as a sovereign partner implies that, should there be a change of government in South Korea, inter-Korean agreements would be easily reversible by an incoming South Korean administration disinclined to push a conciliation policy based on the sovereign equality of the two states. In the end, change to institutions at home may be just as important for the success of President Moon's policy as change abroad.

Hazel Smith

Sources of particular relevance

For those interested in any of the issues raised above, a short list of primary sources is appended below. I also list two publications in which, among other things, I evaluate why conventional and basic rules of analysis including fact checking, avoiding over-generalisation, careful periodisation and avoiding speculation, are so often flouted in writing about North Korea. For those wishing to pursue further research, please feel free to contact me, and I will be happy to provide further references.

Constitution of the Democratic People's Republic of Korea, http://www.naenara.com.kp/en/politics/?rule, accessed 6 December 2016.

Constitution of the Republic of Korea, http://korea.assembly.go.kr/res/low_01_read.jsp?boardid=1000000035, accessed 6 December 2018.

Nationality Law of the Democratic People's Republic of Korea (DPRK), https://www.ecoi.net/en/file/local/1396555/1930_149 0686222_58d3c5f24.pdf, accessed 6 December 2018.

Nationality Law of the Republic of Korea, http://elaw.klri.re.kr/eng_mobile/viewer.do?hseq=18840&type=part&key=7, accessed 6 December 2018

Smith, Hazel (2015) *North Korea: Markets and Military Rule.* Cambridge: Cambridge University Press.

——— (2000) 'Bad, mad, sad or rational actor: Why the "securitisation" paradigm makes for poor policy analysis of North Korea', *International Affairs*, Vol. 76, No. 3 (July 2000) pp. 593–617.

Making sense of North Korea

THIS CHAPTER FOCUSES ON THE IMPORTANCE of taking North Korea seriously. Most people who have followed how the country has been reported on in the media will know that it is seldom, if ever, taken seriously, and that demonization and ridicule are instead the norm. This in turn has created an abnormal picture of North Korea, which is the goal of the demonization process. Spezza admits that his initial interest in North Korea was due to a negative fascination, something he probably shares with a majority of Korea watchers. Most people's knowledge or assumed knowledge of North Korea is media-created, and professional observers and scholars can hardly avoid being tainted by this. This is particularly important because, after the Cold War ended, the Korean conflict went from being a local to a global conflict. The author offers excellent examples where media coverage of actual as well as fake occurrences made global headlines and contributed to shaping people's views worldwide. Two sources of news on North Korea are highlighted; the *rumour mill* and the *refugees* ('*defectors*'). It is enlightening to read from where a big part of 'news and views' on the Korea conflict originate, how this information is spread and repeated, and why studies that take the country seriously, including its government and official material, are much needed.

About the Author: Gianluca Spezza earned his PhD in 2017 from the University of Central Lancashire under the supervision of Professor Hazel Smith, on the strength of research on the cooperation between UNICEF and the DPRK in education and childcare. Dr Spezza is an assistant professor of international relations and a senior researcher at the DPRK Strategy Center at KIMEP University in Almaty, Kazakhstan; he is writing a monograph on education, international cooperation, and human capital in North Korea (Palgrave 2021). His work on the DPRK, articles or interviews, can be found, among others, on the websites of the BBC, The Guardian, The Diplomat, IRIN News, NK News, DR.dk, Newsweek Korea, and El Confidential.

CHAPTER SEVEN

The Unwillingness to Take North Korea Seriously: Media Stereotypes, Problematic Sources and the Rhetoric surrounding the DPRK

Introduction: The Evil Twin?

*M*y first encounter with North Korea goes back to 2001; I had just moved to Seoul, unaware of what lay north of the DMZ. One day, on my way home from work, I noticed small leaflets placed inside the subway. The leaflets displayed a 'smiley' cartoon slightly peeled off, under which they revealed another one – looking malignant, stained with blood. There was a caption accompanying the image. My Korean was quite poor at the time, so I noted down the caption, and asked a colleague to translate it for me the next day. She explained that it was a political message, something along the lines of 'They look like us, they are among us, but they are not like us. Be vigilant.' 'They' were the North Koreans, and the poster was part of a countrywide government effort to maintain alertness among the population in order to help authorities locate North Korean spies.

The episode sparked my interest in North Korea and inter-Korean relations, and it was marked by a 'negative fascination' of sorts. I became intrigued with the idea that the country I was living in faced an 'evil doppelgänger' just 50km north of

115

Seoul. In hindsight, I realize that despite my curiosity, *I wasn't taking North Korea seriously.* The poster – and the explanation I received about it – shaped my first impression of North Korea: a country that would seek to infiltrate the South, as a consequence of which South Koreans had to remain alert. I didn't have too many questions about *what made the North hostile to the South.* In my partial defence, had I attempted to look further, I might not have found much material in Seoul due to legal restrictions placed on North Korean materials, but more on this later.

Time has passed and my view of inter-Korean relations has evolved. I learned that just as Pyongyang periodically sent spies to the South, so did Seoul to the North, and that there is much more to inter-Korean relations than espionage. I realized that understanding what the DPRK *really is* requires due consideration of the interests and identity of *the North Korean state,* that is, taking the polity seriously without either taking its propaganda at face value or dismissing the entire country as a freak show.

The following pages centre on this idea: *explaining the importance of taking North Korea seriously, just like we would any other country.* This is a reflection on the suspension of common sense and a general lack of evidence-based analysis that characterizes mainstream western media reporting on the DPRK. There is a constant contradiction in international reports on North Korea: it is portrayed as the ultimate 'irrational' place, yet everyone tries to *predict* its behaviour; at the same time, there seems to be no agreement on the underlying motives of its domestic and foreign policy.

If we consider how much the media can influence policymakers, the common habit of caricaturing or demonizing North Korea appears like a risky exercise in international relations, even riskier since North Korea's major antagonist – the US – embarked on a dubious course of foreign policy under President Trump.

I want to clarify one thing before moving on. When I propose 'an understanding' of the interests of the North Korean government, I mean understanding *why* things with the DPRK are the way they are. This is vital information, if we wish to know *how* the present state of affairs can be improved or changed and *at what cost*. In no way do I want to hint at justifications for the evident shortcomings of the North Korean government or the hardships endured by most of its citizens. In fact, it is precisely because there can be no doubt that ordinary people suffer enormously in the DPRK and that the DPRK government *is the cause of its own problems*, that North Korea should be rationally investigated, rather than mocked and oversimplified.

I begin with an overview of the *status quo*. Then I explain the misinformation that clouds mainstream reporting on North Korea, providing examples of how common sense is often suspended; finally, I summarize the main issue: *the North Korean question is one of national survival*, which has been overlooked for far too long.

At the roots of rivalry: Two Korean states and a zero-sum game.

Why do two rival Korean states, so different from one another, coexist on a peninsula inhabited by the very same people?

The conventional terms of 'North Korea' and 'South Korea' refer to two separate governments that have led two separate states on the Korean peninsula since September 1948, when North Korea proclaimed itself an independent state in response to South Korea doing the same thing one month earlier.

Since 1948 and until the late 1990s, the DPRK and the ROK made use of the education system, the media and any other means at their disposal to foster a set of values that shaped their national discourse and 'the other Korea' in polarized terms: *all the good on one side, all the bad on the other*. No middle ground.

International media and academia have generally paid one-sided attention to this phenomenon, focusing on aspects of North Korean propaganda such as magazines, posters or children's books. These publications contain falsifications of historical facts; among others, the Korean War is described as a war of aggression by the US, with the complicity of the UN and the 'puppet regime' in Seoul. School texts espouse hatred of US troops and American missionaries. Until recently, these books depicted South Korea as a 'US colony', where destitute Korean children are forced to work and women to prostitute themselves to American G.I.s, but where the population longs to reunite with their northern brethren under the red star banner.

The other side of the coin is less known: up to the late 1980s, in South Korean school books, North Korea was quite literally *the devil*. Those who went to school in South Korea before the democratization of the 1990s remember that school texts depicted North Koreans as red-coloured, demonic figures with horns on their head, constantly plotting evil schemes. This practice disappeared with the end of military rule in Seoul. Today Seoul endorses 'Unification Education', which presents North Korea as a separate state – where the government is still capable of bringing trouble to the South – but one where people share common roots with the South and are genuinely in need of help.

The two states remain at odds. On the one hand, South Korea maintains a strict national security law forbidding all pro-North activities, the diffusion of DPRK media and publications, and contacts, remittances or migration to the north. The Moon Jae-in administration has shown a softer stance on these issues, but the law remains in place. On the other hand, Pyongyang has until recently referred to the government in Seoul as a 'puppet regime', rarely lowering its tone. Before the Moon government and the recent improvement of inter-

Korean relations in 2018, South Korean presidents were routinely addressed as 'traitors'. Years ago, the state news agency – KCNA – referred to former US president Barack Obama as a 'wicked black monkey' and to former South Korean president Park Geun-hye as an 'impudent bitch'. The DPRK government has often delivered public threats to Seoul; though mostly rhetorical, these were occasionally followed by actions as with the Yeonpyeong Island shelling in 2010. Seventy years after their birth, the two Koreas offer a tense terrain to researchers and journalists.

Where we are today. The spillover of Korean tensions, from local to global

The problems between the ROK and the DPRK became an issue of international concern after North Korea announced its humanitarian emergency to the UN in 1995. Since then, North Korean rulers and the people alike have been depicted in bizarre ways by most western media. Why is this? Indifference towards and trivialization of the DPRK could be considered a spillover from the practice of the 'vilification of the enemy' that was a normal aspect of the confrontation between two rival states since the start of the Cold War. As two part-nation states,[1] North and South Korea competed for the same territorial and ethnic entity through to the ideological demolition of the Other. Rationally speaking, they had no other choice because their legitimacy was predicated on the illegitimacy of their opponent. The question is: why has the rest of the world come to demonize North Korea?

It was not always the case that North Korea was seen as the last bastion of dictatorship. Until the late 1980s, troubles on the peninsula were largely considered an affair between two authoritarian regimes. Even when North Korea occasionally surged in the news – as with the Pueblo Incident in 1968

---

1. I borrow the definition from Barry Buzan (1983).

or the KAL858 flight bombing in 1987 – each episode was framed within the scenario of the Cold War. The presence of a military dictatorship in Seoul, with its negative record on human rights, somehow balanced things out with the DPRK, as this was conventionally understood as a state akin to those within the Eastern Bloc.

Noteworthy, during the Cold War, North Korea enjoyed much better consideration from international institutions and media than it does today. The United Nations Development Programme (UNDP) opened its office in Pyongyang in 1980. UNESCO reported positively for years on many aspects of socioeconomic life in North Korea – particularly education – while UNICEF compared DPRK social indicators favourably to those of South Korea as late as 1987.[2]

Everything changed with the end of the Cold War. Between 1990 and 1995, the North Korea issue left the peninsula to become a *world problem*. First, there was the simultaneous admission of both Korean states to the UN in 1991. A newly democratized South Korea re-established diplomatic ties with Russia (1990) and China (1992), the historical patrons of North Korea, casting doubts on the economic survival of the DPRK. Then there was a crisis between the US and the DPRK due to the withdrawal of North Korea from the Non-Proliferation Treaty (NPT), followed by temporary detente

---

2. UNICEF (1987), Draft Board Submission, UNICEF-ROK Programme of Cooperation (1988–1992) Seoul. While many UNESCO and UNDP publications had reported near-universal enrollment and lit-eracy rates at all school levels for both genders during the 1980s, this UNICEF report stated that only 1.7 percent of children in the ROK attended kindergarten until 1970; this figure rose to 57 per cent in 1986, yet still lower than DPRK figures for the same period. Similarly, breastfeeding, infant and maternal mortality, and immunization rates for the ROK were worse than those of the DPRK, even though South Korea was projected to join the group of advanced countries in the 1990s, and no longer be a development aid recipient.

with the 1994 Agreed Framework. Finally, North Korea saw the outbreak of a humanitarian emergency, with the intervention of UN agencies and international NGOs in the country by late 1995. The ensuing famine catapulted the DPRK onto the world stage under the worst possible conditions. International reports showcased North Korea to worldwide audiences for the first time since the Korean War, with very graphic images.

The emergency lasted officially from 1995 to 2005, a decade in which new mass media drastically altered the fruition of information. With images and video readily available to a non-specialized public, North Korea quickly went from zero to total exposure. The production of analytic work, statistics and archival material – all necessary to gather a deeper understanding of complex issues – simply could not keep up with the pace of online opinion-makers or sensationalist accounts.

Suddenly the Soviet Union and the Eastern Bloc were gone, and – open to the public – there was an 'obscure country' coming out of the Cold War, stricken by famine, subject to authoritarian rule and a cult of personality that demanded loyalty in the midst of starvation. Under the spotlight, North Korea was a country about which very little specialized knowledge seemed to be available *and consequently* a country about which almost anything could be said, and it would somehow still sound plausible.

> The diffusion of social media and the possibility of visiting the DPRK ... does not seem to have changed things: in the absence of solid evidence, opinions are often dressed up as facts.

The diffusion of social media and the possibility of visiting the DPRK – albeit under a strict set of rules, and only with guided tours – does not seem to have changed things: in the absence of solid evidence, opinions are often dressed up as facts. One example: often referred to as 'communist' or 'Stalinist' by mainstream media, North Korea has long deleted any reference to communism from its constitution, and purged every single piece of literature or media of any reference to the Soviet Union for decades. North Korea's official discourse has a distinct focus on ethnonationalism. The government stresses the cultural and ethnic homogeneity of its people on every occasion, be it through propaganda or in its dialogue with international institutions. The actions of the DPRK government (with, until very recently, priority given to military strength over economic improvement) are in contrast to the basic tenets of Marxism-Leninism; and yet the label lingers on.

Another example: the DPRK is routinely represented as 'mysterious', 'irrational', and 'isolated'. The history of its foreign relations and participation in the UN system show that these definitions are inaccurate. In fact, the documentation produced by the North Korean government in over three decades of cooperation with international agencies constitutes a goldmine for researchers. From just one set of documents – the reports on the CRC (Convention on the Rights of the Child), one can learn, for example, that North Korea admitted to instances of corporal punishment, episodes of domestic violence, the presence of street children, the rehabilitation of teenagers caught smuggling pornographic materials.[3] These problems are somewhat downplayed, but not hidden. At the same time, the UN–DPRK documentation demonstrates that through a learning curve, North Korea has absorbed – if selectively – international norms. Whenever possible, the government likes to stress its own achievements, like universal literacy and free healthcare; it also seeks to distance itself - morally - from countries that tolerate 'prejudicial practices' such as forced marriages or female genital mutilation.[4]

---

3. UN-CRC (2003). Written replies by the DPRK government to issues on the second periodic report, Geneva: UNICEF; UN-CRC (2003), DPRK Second periodic reports of States parties due in 1997, Geneva: UNICEF.

4. Ibid.

Finally, the DPRK has shown remarkable adaptability to an international system that has sustained the country with humanitarian aid since 1995 (and it does so in spite of the evident human rights abuses) while seeking to correct its course of nuclear proliferation with sanctions that North Korea manages to evade to a considerable degree. Far from proving the DPRK's irrationality, these contradictions rather highlight the inconsistencies within the UN system.

North Korea and the suspension of common sense

Misinformation about the DPRK should not come as a surprise. North Korea was considered a non-subject in South Korean academia and a niche topic in US universities until the early 1990s. As for the media, after two decades of gradual access to the country and to a growing number of data, the majority of news reports on the DPRK still relies on two major sources: one is known as the *North Korea rumour mill*; the other is the community of former North Korean citizens – or *defectors* – living in South Korea.

The North Korea rumour mill fabricates stories so absurd that they should be easy to dismiss, were it not for the fact that they have influenced nearly all mainstream media reports for over 20 years.[5] Let's consider this episode: in a piece of news that made world headlines in the summer of 2013 – after circulating on the South Korean press – Kim Jong Un's ex-girlfriend, singer Hyon Song-wol, was allegedly arrested for violating North Korea's pornography laws, then rounded up with 11 other performers and machine-gunned to death in front of her family. Gruesome enough, and perfectly believable in the case of North Korea, *except that it never happened.*

---

5. On the rumour mill, see: https://www.nknews.org/2014/01/inside-the-north-korean-rumor-mill/; https://www.38north.org/2016/09/aabrahamian090216/; https://www.nknews.org/2012/12/the-top-ten-most-bizarre-rumours-to-spread-about-north-korea/.

Months later, she resurfaced on national TV, perfectly alive and well. As if that wasn't enough, in early 2018 she was chosen as North Korea's first Olympic representative and scouted South Korea for appropriate locations to host DPRK athletes and cheerleaders. Her journey to Seoul was treated on par with visits from international pop stars: she was surrounded by crowds and foreign correspondents in Seoul covered her every move with enthusiasm. The fact that the tales of her gruesome death were at this point blatantly false was rarely mentioned. South Korean newspaper *Chosun Ilbo*, one of the main sources for Hyon's alleged death news in 2013, still reported her dead by execution during – and after – her visit to Seoul in 2018. Nobody ever bothered to correct the blunder, and it is unlikely at this point that someone will.

The North Korea rumour mill, however, is not just the fault of the press. Seasoned DPRK watchers have explained how ROK embassies and the ROK intelligence service established over time a network dedicated to leaking tampered intelligence on the North Korean leadership.[6] This has been standard operating procedure for as long as North Korea has existed. The explosion of digital, real-time information, however, has acted as a catalyst for an even less verifiable stream of gossip that replaces actual journalism. The main issue is that South Korean officials have long been allowed to give information to the media without being identified or otherwise held accountable. The aggravating factor in the age of social media is that too often it doesn't matter that the rumour hasn't been confirmed, or that no one actually has the chance to verify any of the sources, if and when these are detailed – and most times they are not: they are just referred to as 'a source' in Beijing, Seoul, or Tokyo.

---

6. Aidan Foster-Carter offers insightful analysis on these issues, see: https://www.38north.org/2020/04/afostercarter042820/.

The rumour mill begins to roll, and some journalists fuel it rather than checking facts. Nevertheless, rumours can only spread if there is a persistent unwillingness to take the North Korean state seriously, and at the same time, if there is an inclination to take the crudest – or most ridiculous – accounts at face value.

Among a few examples are: the Kims have god-like attributes; the population is in a uniform state of robotic numbness; Kim Jong-un's uncle was devoured by a pack of 120 hungry dogs … the list goes on. If statements made about the DPRK are questionable, then the questions seem to be even worse. When North Korea was consolidating its nuclear arsenal in the early 2000s, international media speculated with diligence on how many bottles of expensive Cognac or how many golden Rolex watches the Kim family imported, and how many mistresses would sleep with its supreme leader.

A reminder that such myths on North Korea are hard to dispel is that it took two trips to Pyongyang in 2000, from the highest levels of US and South Korean politics, to validate the notion that Kim Jong-Il *wasn't crazy* – or at least was 'not that crazy'. For years, books and documentaries were happy to report whatever the rumour mill fabricated about the former DPRK leader, including allegations of raging alcoholism, mental retardation and sexual depravity.

The testimony of former North Korean citizens is a more complex issue. North Korean *refugees* can provide essential insights on many aspects of daily life in North Korea, even though they are often asked mono-directional questions, sometimes with morbid curiosity, about their personal tragedies, the famine that plagued the country and the torture of political dissenters.

A different issue is whether they can be considered a viable source of information *on the ideas and interests of the North Korean government* – and if so, under what conditions. In general – while respecting individual stories of people who certainly suffered in their journey to freedom – this is unlikely, for two reasons. First, due to the highly regimented and hierarchical nature of North Korean society, and the non-transparency of institutions towards the average population, the number of North Koreans who can provide accurate information on policy-making processes is very low: a handful of individuals – a recent example being the former DPRK ambassador to the UK, Tae Yong Ho. Average North Korean citizens are excluded from institutional and political life in the DPRK.

Second, the characteristics of the defector population itself make them a non-viable source on the nature of the North Korean state, and what it seeks to achieve. According to the South Korean government, the number of defectors passed the 33,000 mark as of 2019, but their composition is rather imbalanced: 74 per cent of them are women in an age cohort of 25–50 years. Around 76 per cent of the total number of defectors, male and female, originates from only two of the country's nine provinces: North Hamgyong and Ryanggang, both in the northeastern corner of the peninsula. This part of the DPRK has historically been disadvantaged in socio-economic terms. The harsh climate and unfavourable terrain make agriculture nearly unsustainable, and the regime has periodically transferred to this region any individuals or groups deemed disloyal, diminishing *de facto* their opportunities to survive. This has given rise, from the early 1990s, to the predominantly economic character of North Korean migration, a fact acknowledged in publications that derive most of their arguments from defector testimony; furthermore, the South Korean government estimates that before they left North Korea, 45 percent of them were unemployed.[7]

---

7. Data on North Korean defectors from https://http://kosis.kr/bukhan/ and https://www.unikorea.go.kr/unikorea.

The total population of the DPRK stood at 25.3 million in June 2020, but the North Koreans living in the South amount to just 0.13 per cent of this number; even this tiny proportion overstates the range of information provided by refugees. Only a few thousand have participated in surveys, and those whose stories have been presented in the West numbers less than a hundred.

Even fewer than this – totalling around a dozen prominent names – are those who have achieved a relative degree of popularity in South Korean, US and European media, or have managed to become authors themselves. Notable examples include Kang Chol-hwan, Shin Dong-hyuk, and Park Yeonmi. The latter two in particular have gained fame, but discrepancies in their stories have emerged over time, giving rise to speculations that their accounts may not be fully transparent or genuine.

Once again, this is not to dismiss the plight of North Korean defectors as a whole. Rather, it is to point out that if we want to understand *what the North Korean government wants* – then we ought to consider that anecdotes and personal accounts from a statistically skewed portion of the population cannot be our only source.

The myth of the 'information black hole': What do we know about North Korea, and how do we look at it?

Where do we turn for information about, or from, the DPRK? Of all the different layers in the general misunderstandings about North Korea, the most consequential is the myth of the DPRK as a *tabula rasa*, a unique black hole of history and information. There is truth in saying that the DPRK is institutionally opaque at best. Field research is not possible, nor is free tourism or unfiltered interaction with the general population. But while it is true that what is seen by journalists and tourists outside-in is strictly controlled, this does not necessarily make North Korea a black hole in the age of digital information.

As of early 2020, a Google search for 'North Korea' returns on average 1.38 billion results. These include statistics reports produced by international organizations at work in the DPRK for 25 years, government documents, academic articles, imagery from the country – taken by tourists and international workers alike – videos, satellite pictures and news. We can add to this the numerous specialized sources available in Korean language, but yet not digitalized: North Korean materials (which can be used – with *caveats* on their biases – as they offer unique insight) and studies by the South Korean government. North Korean websites are also available, and they have increased manifold over the last two decades. Today they number around 60, and provide a unique window on culture, some government activity, foreign relations and society. Through a number of them, the government monitors international affairs, never missing a chance to join international criticisms of President Trump, for example.[8] Then, there are 'mirror statistics': data gathered by the DPRK's commercial partners, particularly useful for economic studies as they show at least one side of the trade equation. The lack of materials doesn't seem to be an issue. What about our curiosity for the DPRK?

In 2017 – at the height of its latest nuclear crisis – 'North Korea' was the fourth most popular search topic on Google for all news worldwide. However, the scope of that interest appears to be narrow. The most popular online queries related to 'North Korea' in 2017 and 2018 were: 'Donald Trump', 'war', 'missile', 'nuclear', 'news', 'Dennis Rodman' and 'Kim Jong Un'. Other queries – tracked by Google since 2004 – include 'hu-

---

8. Other than the Party organ, *Rodong Sinmun*, and the state news agency, KCNA, the best sites to examine North Korean media discourse are: Naenara, Arirang-Meari, and Uriminzokkiri.

man rights', 'torture', 'famine' and 'war'. This is mostly what North Korea is known for. Why?

The short answer is: *we tend to pay attention to North Korea only when it behaves badly.* The rest of the time, as far general interest goes, we don't really care. Online queries for 'North Korea' since 2004 are infrequent, but there are periodical spikes in this otherwise stable trend. These peaks of interest correspond exactly to (i) the dates when North Korea announced or conducted ballistic or nuclear tests; (ii) the times when the UN imposed sanctions on the DPRK; and (iii) times when tensions between Pyongyang, Seoul and Washington rose dramatically.

In sum, conventional reporting perpetuates the notion of *an unknowable country*, when evidence suggests that it is rather stereotyped and poorly analyzed. This notion favours speculation to the detriment of common sense: if the assumption is that *nothing can be really known about the DPRK,* then a caricature is as good as an analytic report.

Back to square one: What is North Korea and what does it want?

Can we make sense of North Korea (the state, the government, the institutions)? We can, and we should, but we rarely do. Within the realm of international relations, the DPRK is still *an intractable problem.*[9] Stereotypes and vilification eschew analysis so that what we read on North Korea ends up being rather binary.

North Korea is either devoid of agency (hence the monikers of 'hermit kingdom', the 'failed state', the passive recipient

---

9. I borrow this definition from the title of a conference organized in 2014 by my former doctoral supervisor, Professor Hazel Smith. The term has stuck with me ever since. Of the many shades of meaning associated with the word *intractable,* the elements of being *obdurate* and *unmanageable* seem to encapsulate the salient traits of North Korea as a subject of many media reports, and the tone of many debates on North Korea.

of international aid) or a strategic liability (a 'garrison state' ready to fire at the US, if threatened). These descriptions assume the country to be uniquely *reactive*, as if the DPRK did not have any governance nor a vision for its future. In other words, according to this view, *everything North Korea does is a response to external stimuli.* This framework is problematic, because it perpetuates the status quo – of either endless charity or confrontation.

A series of events throughout 2018 gave rise to some cautious optimism. The demonization of North Korea *tout court* has temporarily given way to the opposite phenomenon: a curiosity for the more human – and humane – aspects of the Kim family, more rosy depictions of Kim Jong-un as 'a rational leader' during several inter-Korean summits, and even a few speculations of a possible Nobel peace prize nor only for Kim, but for President Trump as well, after their first meeting in June 2018.

I believe too much optimism is as bad as too little, and the fact that these early enthusiasms gradually vanished throughout 2019 and the first half of 2020 seems to confirm this. So, here's a counter-proposal: rather than speculating on North Korea or dismissing Kim Jong-un as a mere caricature, we should *take the North Korean state, the government and the leaders at their word,* considering that the DPRK has defined its own identity and interests quite clearly, since 1948. What we should be asking is: 'What kind of state is North Korea?', 'What is the ultimate goal of its government?' and 'What are they prepared to do to achieve their goals?'

We can learn much about what ordinary North Koreans endure by reading defectors' accounts; however, in order to understand *what the government wants,* it could suffice to read North Korean documentation – both that published in the constraining awareness that the outside world will read it (the constitution, government documentation, the party organs and national news), and that intended to remain secret (diplomatic notes from the Cold War era, archival material and internal propaganda smuggled by refugees).

This material points clearly to one conclusion: the DPRK has developed a specific national identity, mutually constitutive of its interests, whereby sovereignty, independence and a certain ethnic pride are considered inalienable. Economic success, on the other hand, appears as a variable that doesn't affect the durability of the government.

Let's consider this: in 1997, in the midst of the humanitarian crisis, the International Monetary Fund (IMF) visited the country to discuss financial aid and economic reforms. North Korean authorities were adamant in their response: financial aid was welcome, but political and economic reforms were not. This attitude was not different from what the government espoused during the 1970s and the 1980s, while seeking technical assistance from UN agencies and international loans. The same attitude was displayed in 2005, when the DPRK unilaterally declared that it no longer wanted to receive humanitarian aid, and wished to switch to development assistance instead. Things did not go that way and in 2006 the DPRK began its nuclear and ballistic tests, aiming to be recognized as a *de facto* nuclear state.

If we take the North Korean state at its word, it seems clear that it pursues national interests with ruthlessness and rationality; these interests ultimately entail a withdrawal of US troops from the peninsula, and the pursuit of a confederate project with Seoul that would see both Korean states addressing reunification without external interference. Whether the rest of the world finds this course of action more or less suitable has never been much of a concern for the DPRK government, but it is worth reminding ourselves that Seoul has now agreed to this confederate scheme three times: in 2000, 2007, and 2018.

In conclusion, rather than simply 'obscure', the DPRK can be understood as a country that has lost the competition to a more successful rival state, after falling off its initial developmental path. It is a country where the government has employed a wide array of measures – often draconian ones – to ensure its own survival. These measures include the development of nuclear weapons, a strict limitation on individual freedoms, and a totalitarian ideology. These, however, are not uncommon features and are shared by a number of other countries. They certainly do not make the DPRK an unknowable entity, refractory to the inquiry of the social sciences. Perhaps, understanding how North Korea envisions its own survival could be the key to future – more successful – negotiations.

Gianluca Spezza

Sources of particular relevance

Alford, C. (1998) *Think No Evil: Korean Values in the Age of Globalization.* Cornell University Press.

Buzan, B. (1983) *People, States and Fear: The National Security Problem in International Relations.* Brighton: Wheatsheaf Books.

Frank, R. (ed.) (2012) *Exploring North Korean Arts.* Vienna: University of Vienna Press.

Ho, Y.Y. (1993) 'The question of Nations and national sovereignty', in K. Hirano (ed.), *The State and Cultural Transformation: Perspectives from East Asia.* Tokyo: United Nations University Press.

Eberstadt, N. (2007) The *North Korean Economy.* London: Transaction.

Kim, B. Y. (2017) *Unveiling the North Korean Economy: Collapse and Transition.* Cambridge, UK: CUP.

Kwon, H., Chung, B.H. (2012) *North Korea: Beyond Charismatic Politics*. Lanham: Rowman & Littlefield.

McEachern, P. (2010) *Inside the Red Box: North Korea's Post-totalitarian Politics*. New York: Columbia University Press

Myers, B. R. (2010) T*he Cleanest Race: How North Koreans See Themselves and Why it Matters*. New York: Melville House.

—————— (2011) North Korea's State-Loyalty Advantage, *Journal of International Affairs* 65(1): 115–129.

—————— (2015) *North Korea's Juche Myth*. Busan: Sthele Press.

Park, Han S. (2005) *North Korea: The Politics of Unconventional Wisdom*. London: Lynne Rienner.

Smith, H. (2005a) *Hungry for Peace. International Security, Humanitarian Assistance and Social Change in North Korea*. Washington DC: USIP.

—————— (2005b) 'Disintegration and reconstitution in the Democratic People's Republic of Korea', in S. Chesterman, M. Ignatieff and R.C. Thakur (eds), *Making States Work: State Failure and the Crisis of Governance*. Tokyo: United Nations University Press.

—————— (2015) *North Korea: Markets and Military Rule*. Cambridge: Cambridge University Press.

Red complex in South Korea

SPORTS DIPLOMACY HAS PROVED TO BE an effective, well-known and oft-practiced method of breaking the ice between people and countries where relations are disturbed by political and ideological differences. Gyuseog Han looks into a recent case of exactly this: South Korea's hosting of the 2018 Winter Olympics. In this chapter, Han reviews the history of demonization in the South, and how it has affected people's view of the North, as well as how this activity colours the entire political scene in South Korea. Based on personal experiences, and with a background in psychology, Han shows us how demonizing has worked on the individual as well as on the societal level, and why it still makes up a strong force in his country. The author has not been able to survey the demonization of South Korea as practiced in the North (where his brother lived for 57 years until his death in 2017), but this practice is obviously carried out in both halves of the Korean peninsula. What becomes clear, however, is that demonization is a negative and clearly destructive force with dire consequences at to both individuals and societies. Particularly important but seldom considered is that the overall negative consequences of demonizing the Other create an almost impossible environment for dialogue; this is why the practice affects both the demonized and those who demonize.

About the Author: Gyuseog Han holds a PhD in social psychology and is now an emeritus professor of the Chonnam National University in South Korea after serving there for 32 years. His academic interest broadly covers the socio-cultural psychology of Korean people. Realizing the limits of Western-centric modern psychology, he is working towards a new theory of moral development based on the Korean worldview in collaboration with other scholars. He has investigated the psychology of social hierarchy, which he understands to be affected by honorific language, relational stress in social relationships and indigenous constructions of mind. His publications include social values, the history of psychology in Korea, and theoretical issues in psychology. His social interests concern multiculturalism, unification, environmental issue, and animal rights.

CHAPTER EIGHT

The Red Complex in South Korea: The 50-Year Legacy of Demonizing North Korea

Introduction

Every Korean, including myself, cheered for the Korean women's ice hockey team in a game against the Swiss in the 2018 Winter Olympics. The team included athletes from both North and South Korea and the idea of building a joint team came when the North Korean leader Kim Jung-un made a New Year's address to the people of North Korea, just a month before the start of the Olympic Games. The announcement of his intention for North Korea to participate in this world sports festival was a surprise to everyone. It came after a six-month standoff between North Korea and the USA that was marked by serious nuclear threats and demonstrations. US President Donald Trump appeared ready to take military action against North Korea when he threatened Fire and Fury instead of seeking diplomatic solutions. The newly elected government of South Korea, which replaced a conservative regime with a progressive one, immediately seized the opportunity for joint South–North action. The former government, together with other conservatives, voiced their opposition and suspicion. They regarded joint participation, holding the flag of the blue silhouette of the Korean peninsula on a white background, as a strategic manoeuvre by North Korea.

Amidst all the worries, fears and threats, the fact that a unified team could march under one flag during the opening ceremony of the Olympics is a beacon of hope, for most people in this land, for the future reunification of the peninsula.

In this chapter, I illustrate with examples from my own personal experience the consequences of demonizing North Korea. By reviewing interactions between the South and the North, I reveal how the act of demonization has taken place both intentionally and unintentionally. The effect of demonization is profound, but the long history of one nationhood of the two sides renders it far from straightforward. The so-called 'red complex', which I discuss below, is the lasting legacy of demonization that continues to exert a powerful influence on politics in South Korea.

Demonizing North Korea and the Red Complex

I vividly recall a personal episode from 1981. I had just arrived in the US and was crossing a university campus in San Francisco, when I spotted a group of people a hundred feet away. They wore the traditional dress of common people of Korea – white jackets and black skirts for ladies and a black work uniform for men – a style that to me seemed quite outdated. From their appearance I immediately gathered that they were from North Korea. I was then very surprised by my next thought: 'They are humans!'; but I did not dare to approach them and speak. It is true: I expected people from North Korea to be something other than *normal* human beings. But in fact, they appeared to be *only* human.

That North Koreans are abnormal is the sort of image most South Koreans had. It is an image that was imbued in the people of South Korea through the consistent demonization of the North. The deliberate manipulation of information and constant censorship instilled an evil image of North Korea and communism in the minds of the people in the South over the generations, and especially among those born after the Korean War, like myself. My reaction was therefore likely an inevitable consequence of living through a long period of the demonization of North Korea.

Demonization proceeded over the four decades following the Korean War, which lasted for three years and came to an end with an armistice treaty in 1953 between the USA (representing the UN) and North Korea. The war entirely destroyed the Korean peninsula, with 2.5 million deaths and 10 million family members separated. Numerous hostile activities have taken place since that time, including espionage, propaganda, infiltration of territories, incidents of murder and even small-scale bombing of the other's territory. The two states have remained arch enemies. All communication between them is banned and any breach may be taken as an act of violation of the national security law. For example, a South Korean student who participated in the 1989 International Students Conference held in Pyongyang, North Korea without government permis-

> That North Koreans are abnormal is the sort of image most South Koreans had. It is an image that was imbued in the people of South Korea through the consistent demonization of the North.

sion was sentenced to a five-year jail term when she returned. For three decades, the military regimes in the South exploited this stalemate and the law of national security to suppress people's yearning for democracy. They took every opportunity to portray North Korea as an evil state that was trying to do anything it could to undermine and destroy the system of the South to achieve the unification it had pursued in 1950 through brutal force.

The demonization of North Korea by the South succeeded in imprinting in the minds of people in the South the notion that North Korea was a state ruled by merciless dictators who instil fear and hostility through the brutal execution of prisoners, a massive military build-up including nuclear bombs, the suppression of human rights, and the killing of innocent South Koreans. For ordinary South Korean citizens, this harsh rhetoric has had the effect of their perceiving North Korea as a thoroughly evil country.

Official lines of communication between the South and North only opened up sporadically, for humanitarian reasons. As a consequence of the work of the Red Cross on both sides of the border, a few members of separated families were allowed to meet each other briefly for the first time in 1985. While these types of meetings continue to take place, they have often been halted for political reasons. There remain many people who have never met their family members, including me. My eldest brother was drafted when the Korean War broke out in 1950. My parents were informed that he was killed in a battle, yet fifty years later, we were informed that someone in North Korea was searching for the names of my family members. It was my brother, who had not been killed after all, but captured on the battlefield and taken to North Korea. After confirming his presence in the North, we were able to establish an informal communication channel through an intermediary relative in Canada, as direct communication of any sort, including letters and emails, were and still are not permitted.

To watch television or listen to radio broadcasts from the other side is still completely forbidden. For half a century, any activities associated with communism have been barred in South Korea, including simply reading the classic works by Marx or possessing materials positive towards North Korea, let alone writing anything in favour of the North or of communism. To do so is considered a criminal act and is heavily penalized. To this day, no political party in the South is allowed to claim that they adopt any kind of Marxist doctrine. The strict censorship of news about North Korea is taken for granted. The few portrayals of North Korea that are covered on the TV evening news are limited to items such as military parades, other mass gatherings where all people as one applaud the national leader, party statements, and demonstrations of weaponry including ICBM and nuclear missiles. Such portrayals often feature the miserable faces of starving people and the dismal record of human rights violations. The demonic image of North Korea and its leaders has had its consequences. While overt demonization stopped in South Korea two decades ago, in reality, beneath the surface, the psychological effects of 50 years of demonization can still be keenly observed among the population of the South.

This fear of being associated with communism is what I refer to here as the 'red complex'. The red complex and another term, *Jongbuk Jwapal*, which literally means 'a person complying with North Korea and the left is communist', is the legacy of demonization. Being labelled as communist in South Korea is like a death sentence. Anybody who associates themselves with North Korea or with communism is considered a criminal exposing a threat to national security and must be placed behind bars. Many innocent students and workers have been accused of being associated with North Korea and spent many years in prison. Under torture they made false confessions and testimonies. In the 1950s and 1960s, many thousands of people were killed as a consequence of being labelled as *Jongbuk Jwapal*. Between 1970 and 1990, executions were rare, but many of those accused served prison terms for dubious reasons.

People were accused of being partisan if they engaged in any activities related to being pro-North Korea, pro-labour unions, anti-USA, or opposed to the conservative regime. Naming any person or party as *Jongbuk* (supporting the North) or *Palgaengi* (red people, meaning partisans) brought with it the fear of threat to national security and the surrender of the South Korean nation to the North. This fear played a critical role in salvaging the conservative party of the previous regime (2008-2013). Even when millions of candle-holding people protested on the street in 2016, demanding the impeachment of President Park Geun-hye for her corrupt and inept ruling of the country, a group of counter-protesters assembled on another street. This latter group always held the Korean national *Taeguk-gi* flag and US stars and stripes to symbolize their 'loyalty' and their pre-occupation with national security. They blamed North Korea for masterminding the candlelight rally, attended by millions of people. Despite overwhelming support for the newly installed regime, the conservative party has survived by appealing to the red complex. The fifty-year-long campaign of demonizing North Korea and communism has proved very effective in the politics of South Korea and remains so even today.

Limited interactions between the South and the North: Why the red complex remains

The relationship between South and North Korea has been like a rollercoaster, depending on the regime in power in the south. Official communications were filled with hatred until the progressive party took power for the first time in 1998. Until then, only a few members of separated families were allowed to visit the other side of the peninsula where, under close supervision, they could meet their relatives for a few hours. In 1998, changes were made to allow ordinary South Korea citizens to visit the *Kumkangsan* (a mountain famed for its beauty) tourist area in the North for a couple of days, though they were not given the freedom to interact with the people around them. This policy remained until 2008, when a South Korean tourist who disregarded signs about where not to go and failed to hear North Korean armed guards calling her back. She was shot dead. After that, South Korea stopped allowing their citizens to visit the North.

The long standoff between South and North faced a new challenge in 2000, when the leaders of both countries held their first-ever summit meeting. After the summit, South Korean President Kim Dae-jung announced his tension-reducing Sunshine Policy. This policy lasted for two consecutive governments and, in 2004, led to the founding of the *Gaesung* IIndustrial Complex in North Korea. The South provided technology, capital and supervision, and the North contributed the labour force. Close to 1,000 supervisors from South Korea used transit buses for work on weekdays. These supervisors were the only South Koreans who could freely interact with workers from the North during working hours. The complex was suddenly shut down by a South Korean presidential order following a nuclear test by the North in 2016.

In 2017 there were more than 30,000 escapees from North Korea living in the South. The numbers of escapees increased sharply in the early 21st century and there are now over one thousand new arrivals each year. Most of them reach South Korea via a circuitous route that begins at North Korea's northern border with China. When they arrive, they receive five years of various forms of government support, including housing, healthcare, education and employment. In addition, hundreds of people working for non-governmental organizations interact with and seek to support the refugees. Despite these assimilation efforts, however, many refugees experience difficulties living in South Korea. Insufficient job training and a scarcity of good jobs for people with little education pushes them into the low-wage bracket. Many seek every opportunity to make easy money, and some become criminals. A 2015 survey revealed that 20% of these refugees had considered committing suicide for various reasons. These people have the potential to provide truthful facts about North Korea, but that seldom happens.

The small number of South Korean staff who worked at the *Gaesung* complex and NGO workers who help settle North

Korean dissidents are the only South Koreans to have had direct contact with people from the North. Most other South Koreans have had no contact or have received information only through the media. One popular TV talk show in the South is *Moranbong club*, named after a hill in Pyongyang (the capital city of North). In this show, a couple of hosts invite North Korean refugees from a variety of backgrounds to chat about life in their home society. All of the topics relate to things like misery, human rights violations, famine and forbidden activities such as watching South Korean dramas. The hosts never fail to highlight such stories. Spectators are left with sympathy for the 'victims' but also with a disdainful feeling both for the people and for the regime in North.

I often worry about the images that the South Korean audience might take away from watching such shows. While these programs may not constitute demonizing as such, they nevertheless fuel the derision of the entire population of North Korea on an unconscious level. The people are portrayed as stupid puppets without guts and brains, unconditionally obeying the supreme leader, who is a merciless tyrant. People show no signs of resistance or revolutionary intent except for some surreptitious activities on a personal level. This framing leads the audience to believe that such people deserve to suffer as they do. Nobody likes to be friends with such kinds of people. This image of stupidity and of being a lesser kind of human being only serves to put more hardship on the lives of the refugees from the North.

Demonizing North Korea can have a strong effect in South Korean society because factual information about the North is hard to obtain when people are exposed only to the negative aspects of the North. However, unlike Afghanistan or Iraq, which are very remote, North Korea is our neighbouring state; South Koreans feel a sense of brotherhood, and a longing for reunification. This aspect of cultural history certainly goes against the simplistic treatment of the demonization effect in South Korea.

A shared cultural history counteracts the uniform effect of demonization

The division of the Korean peninsula is a modern history. For over a thousand years, Korea maintained a singular nation state of one ethnic group that shared the same language. Despite numerous invasions by foreign powers such as China, Japan, and Mongols, Korea maintained its sovereignty for most of this time. And it is because of this long history that, although currently divided, reunification is taken as being for granted. In fact, according to the constitution of South Korea, North Korea is not a separate nation state. Rather, it is a territory to be reclaimed, which is the very reason why all refugees arriving in the South are provided with citizenship and governmental support. For this reason, contrary to the effect of demonizing another state thousands of kilometres away, there are different dynamics to consider in the demonization of North Korea by the South. There are two aspects I would like to highlight here: political orientation, and generational shifts among people in South.

In every society, two political orientations can be observed. The conservative party in South Korea espouses national security, tradition and state control, while the progressive party espouses individual freedom, human rights, and welfare. It is well known that conservative people uphold paternalistic views and progressive people have multiple criteria for their moral and political judgements. At the core of the conservative orientation lies national security and a demonic view of North Korea; no attempt to endanger this view can be tolerated. It is ridiculous *not* to think of North Korea as a demonic country. The conservative's perception of the opposing party and its members is much affected by the demonic frame and its associated stereotypes and prejudices. For such people, demonizing North Korea ignites the fear of the red complex and the contingent threat to national security. When, for example, an IOC member from North Korea suggested that his country should participate in the Winter Olympics in the middle of the fiery exchange of nuclear threat in 2017, the conservative party objected, warning of North Korea's hidden motives. But the incumbent progressive party hailed their participation and quickly proceeded with a plan for putting together a joint team and inviting hundreds of cheerleaders and an orchestra from the North. In fact, until recently, many members of the progressive party were victims of decades-long demonization.

Is the longing for unification equally strong for everybody in South Korea? Recent surveys show that reunification is almost a moral mandate for the older generations, but it is more of a practical matter for the younger ones. Young people fear the economic burden that the South will bear as unification cost. They tend to have a somewhat reserved attitude about helping and cooperating with North. Empathic concern toward the North operates strongly among old people, even though they easily fall victim to the language of demonization. Since young people have not been as much exposed to the demonic rhetoric of the North, they are not much swayed by demonizing rhetoric against North Korea.

Concluding thoughts

A demonized version of any group or any person is far from the truth of that group or person. It does not reflect the actual reality of the target of demonization but rather reveals how one wants to see and treat that target. The human system of cognition is nonetheless vulnerable to such treatment. In any society, some people will fall victim to the rhetoric of demonization. A demonic view coupled with harsh rhetoric will, almost always be reciprocated by the target, which serves to escalate conflicts. We can reignite our hope for a better future only when the demonic view of the other party is checked and abandoned. The psychology of the red complex must be played down through proper education and factually accurate information that reflects reality.

Gyuseog Han

Sports, media and demonization

It is already clear that the media plays a significant role in demonization. Traditionally, mass media are the main channel for public information – and, as we shall see, also for disinformation. M.K. Kang has a research background in the field of media and communication and in this chapter, he comments upon what happened during the 2018 Winter Olympics, when the two Koreas decided to join forces and create unified sports teams for this major international event. While sports events can function positively as 'sports diplomacy', as mentioned in the previous chapter, such an event can also be used to highlight and demonize imagined hidden agendas of the enemy Other. Kang focuses on how speculations and media hype became a prominent aspect of mainstream media coverage of North–South cooperation during this event. He clearly demonstrates that a free press can be one-sided and politicizing, as if the guidelines on reporting came directly from the political authorities.

In this particular case the media counteracted and undermined efforts by the incumbent government, which sought to create an environment of reconciliation. When expectations formed by two generations of demonizing the North Korean system meet reality, and reality fails to meet expectations, then mainstream South Korean media reporting tends to cling to expectations. The normal becomes abnormal, as the effects of prolonged demonization overrule the current reality.

About the Author: Myungkoo Kang is Emeritus Professor of Media and Cultural studies at Seoul National University, where he had been director of the Asia Center and dean of the College of Liberal Studies. He convened a series of international conferences on hate speech in Asia and Europe in cooperation with the University of Detroit, Paris 7 and Ritzumeikan University, leading to the publication of an edited volume by Routledge. He has also published a book on the public sphere in East Asia, entitled 'Humin (訓民) and Enlightenment (啓蒙): A Historical Formation of Public Sphere in Korea.'

How a Gaze Becomes Violence: Representations of the North Korean sports team at the PyeongChang Olympic Games

Introduction

*T*his chapter addresses how the mainstream media in South Korea views North Korea from within the framework of 'a gaze of violence'. One can look at the Other in different ways: from the completely positive angle with eyes of love and consideration; or from a fundamentally negative angle through a lens of exclusion and disgust. In this chapter, I demonstrate that mainstream media in South Korea views North Korea through a lens of *exclusion* and *disgust*. This way of seeing the Other may be considered a double collective punishment, because it generalizes the North Koreans as a negative Other at the same time that it mobilizes the South Korean people to accept this view; alternatively, it enforces silence.

The way one sees things reveals the desires of the individual as well as those constructed by society. When the two overlap, this produces a strong position that is difficult to challenge. This chapter reviews journalistic reports about the North Korean sports team, the delegation of representatives and the cheer squad during their visit to South Korea at the

PyeongChang Winter Olympics where they participated with South Korea as a unified Korean team. This analysis shows how mainstream South Korean media produces and reproduces hatred of North Korea, that is, how it demonizes the Northern half of the peninsula.

The Anticipation of War: the Anxiety of a Fabricated Future

The possibility of a North Korean nuclear attack (be it on the US or on South Korea), a pre-emptive strike by the US, or a land war on the Korean peninsula continues to produce an unrelenting, faint anxiety in many South Koreans. A sense of anticipation does not correspond to real events, yet endlessly repetitions of the possibility certainly can stimulate anxiety. Among those living on the Korean peninsula today, the anticipation of war provokes different reactions, from 'there really is no way it will actually happen' or 'this is just a passing phase' all the way to 'war may break out tomorrow!' In addition to traditional forms of media (TV and newspapers), social media platforms such as Twitter and Facebook also warn of the dangers of war, sometimes proclaiming it to be imminent, almost as if the breakout of war is desired.

Is this anticipation of war a fantasy, or is it real? We can say it is a fantasy because it does not exist in reality, but rather only in words spread by the media. And yet it is real, because the expectation of a possible war creates internal fear, which extends its reach beyond the state of mind of individuals to the psychology of people in group settings. The negative portrayal of North Korea's team of athletes at the PyeongChang Olympics by the mainstream South Korean media, made possible by appealing to the fantasy of an anticipated war, demonstrated an undeniably real effect.

The continued state of division and coexistence of North and South Korea is shaped by post-war antagonism. The area around the 38th parallel, the demarcation line or 'de-militarized zone', is actually the most heavily militarized place on earth; now more than ever, the possibility of military clashes has increased because of North Korea's nuclear missile testing.

Every time North Korea tests a nuclear device or a delivery system, it is common to hear claims that an American pre-emptive strike is imminent, or that it is necessary. These claims are developed under the rationale that *the responsibility lies with North Korea's belligerent behaviour; the South has continually pointed this out and has sent warnings.*

THAAD (Terminal High Altitude Area Defense), an anti-ballistic missile defense system, was deployed by the Americans in South Korea to protect against a North Korean attack. It has received continuous coverage on TV news and in mainstream newspaper articles that warn of the imminent threat of war. After the Pyeongchang Olympics commenced, this type of reporting became more frequent and widespread.

In its 1 February 2018 broadcast of 'News Focus', Yonhap News TV, an affiliate of the government-controlled Yonhap News Agency, reported on North Korea's military parade and claimed the possibility of war. All of the expert panelists quoted below were current or former employees of defence organizations.

Statements on 'pre-emptive strikes against North Korea'

Panelist Kim Jeong-bong:
- When we claim one as an enemy, we may want that person dead. However, when America considers one an enemy, it is a target that must be beaten, broken and destroyed. So it is very frightening when the US determines one to be an enemy.
- There is no other way to see this than as US efforts to find reasons to justify an attack on North Korea.
- It has become highly likely that the US will make decisions unilaterally, be they military or diplomatic, regardless of the intentions of the South Korean government.
- I think we should hold the view that war could happen at any time, regardless of the intentions of our government.

Panelist Shin In-kyun:
- Doesn't it really feel like the US will attack North Korea right now?
- The US is at the phase of strategically gathering justification for an attack on North Korea at any time.
- There is an increasing potential for the realization of the US military option.
- The US Airforce has removed the reflectors off of F-22s so that they will not show up on the radar. This suggests this is a real battle.

Panel Host Park Sang-ryul:
- Is it possible to suggest that preparations are being made for the next step with the real intention of immediate action if necessary?
- We can interpret that, if really necessary, the possibility of a pre-emptive strike is not a falsehood.

Panel Host Park Ga-young:
- They have prepared as many military options as we expected, and perhaps more.

Source: Citizens' Coalition for Democratic Media Weekly Monitoring Report, February 2018

Kim Jeong-bong, former Department Head of the National Intelligence Service, and Director Shin In-kyun of the Korea Defense Network are both permanent participants at News Focus, a live TV broadcast aired by Yonhap News TV. Kim Jeong-bong repeatedly made unsubstantiated claims, such as 'there is anticipation that North Korea's military parade will display weaponry that will aggravate the US and the international community' and 'Who can win a war against the US? North Korea also knows that it would face annihilation.'

Live broadcasts that focus on 'news' about a possible or even likely forthcoming war serve the purpose of maintaining widespread fear among people, and this fear is furthered by stories in the written news media, as exemplified in the following quotation from *Dong-A Ilbo*, a major conservative newspaper in South Korea.

> If we transition to a 'peace regime' as they (North Korea) desire, it is unknown how much longer the North Korean people will have to suffer through a hell of human rights abuses. If the US–ROK alliance is broken and a North Korea-led unification occurs, just like Kim Jong Un seems to want given his 12-time use of the word 'unification' during his New Year's Address, *our daughters may face the same fate and sacrifice as the majority of North Korean defector women who experienced trafficking and prostitution in China.* (emphasis added by author)
>
> Yet in this country, the leftist camp that cries out for human rights generally remain silent when it comes to North Korean human rights. It is a waste of breath to state that this is hypocrisy.
>
> – Column by Kim Soon-deok, 12 February 2018

The warning and danger of an event that has not occurred is referred to as 'premediation'. Richard Grusin (2010) has previously conceptualized it as *premediated terrorism* that is witnessed in person as well as in news that reports on the warning and dangers of terrorism.[1] In a way, this kind of warning has become habitual in South Korean society, and the average person living on the Korean peninsula has become accustomed to threats of war. Normally, 'events' that do not occur go unreported in the media. But war is understood as something that could immediately be actualized on the Korean peninsula. The possibility of war breaking out has been a constant repetition in news reporting since the Korean War. Reporting on North Korean nuclear developments is based on a hypothetical North Korean launch of a nuclear attack on the

---

1. In the book *Premediation: Affect and Mediality After 9/11* (Palgrave 2010), Richard Grusin uses the concept of 'premediation' to critically explain how predictions and warnings about terror or dangers lead to actual situations, and how viewers become accustomed to these predictions, resulting in an international phenomenon of helplessness and lethargy.

Photo still from YouTube video

President Moon Jae-in meets with Kim Yo Jong at the Blue House in Seoul. The meeting came after Kim Jong Un's sister and other North Korean delegates attended the opening ceremony of the Winter Olympics on February 10th.

US mainland (very similar to the assumption that convicted Saddam Hussein's regime – without evidence – of possessing Weapons of Mass Destruction before the War). As a result of this premise, action plans, countermeasures, and strategies are constantly discussed. It is noteworthy that a situation that has not been realized (although anything is possible at any time) has had the effect of creating warnings and anxieties that are now firmly rooted in the minds of the Korean people. It is upon this rooted anxiety and fear that the demonizing of North Korea exerts its influence.

The North Korean Olympic team that 'directed a Pyongyang Olympics': belittling and careless treatment

Daily statements and reports by the New Korea Party, Chosun Ilbo, and multiple news channels mocked the PyeongChang Olympics as *the Pyongyang Olympics*. A selection of these mockeries are examined here to review the various ways of seeing, and how they instigate hatred by objectifying and degrading women.

'Freckles and Moles Visible on Skin' and 'All-Black Fashion and Colour Makeup' were descriptions used to portray North Korean delegates. Additionally, a video clip of Vice Department Director Kim Yo Jong (sister of the North Korean leader) shaking hands with Hyun Song Wol (leader of the North Korean Olympic delegation) was played repeatedly and Kim's clothing and body became the subject of detailed critical discussion. One reporter stated:

> Many experts have noticed that Kim's stomach is slightly enlarged, as seen under her coat. The Korean National Intelligence Service has previously revealed that Kim Yo Jong gave birth in 2015, and she wore a similar coat during that time. Judging by her posture of leaning with her back out and waist in, it appears that she is five months pregnant. An obstetrics specialist has confirmed this. However, the specialist could not be certain without a direct examination.[2]

Others faced similar treatment:

> Hyun Song Wol, head of the [North Korean] Moranbong Band, enters the meeting location with a light smile on her lips. She wore a two-piece business attire in navy blue with black high heels. It is a different look from the military uniform she wore when she cancelled the performance in Beijing.
>
> She dressed up her hair with a flower pin.
>
> Despite rumours that had circulated about romantic involvement with Kim Jong Un, today she wore a ring on her left ring finger. The green leather purse seen when she took out her notebook is a product of the famed European luxury brand 'H', and is estimated at 20 million Korean Won, if original.
>
> Today's meeting, a 'working-level contact of art troupes', took place as the North's counterpart to our 'senior working-level talks'.
>
> – TV Chosun, 15 January 2018. 'Hyun Song Wol
> Appears with Luxury Bag and Wedding Ring'

2. At the time of the reporting, Kim Yo Jong's pregnancy had not been confirmed. It was clearly beyond rational reporting guidelines to report on such a private issue such as the pregnancy of the North Korean special envoy when she herself had not mentioned anything of it.

As seen in the quotes above, the focus on the rumour of Hyun Song Wol's romantic relationship with Kim Jong Un, ring on her left hand, hair pin, and luxury alligator bag put Hyun Song Wol in the sole context of being a woman instead of as a delegate of the art troupe working-level meetings. The statements belittled her, and reporting on the ring seemed to express a certain disappointment about the falsity of the rumour linking her to Kim Jong Un.

Captured Bodies of the North Korean Cheer Squad

Every broadcaster began their report with a picture of the legs of the North Korean cheer squad. This view clearly objectifies women's bodies. They were first commodified by North Korea, which selected only beautiful women as objects to be exhibited in the South; they were commodified a second time in the South, by the South Korean media.

What must be questioned is why it was possible for news broadcasters to report so carelessly on the North Korean delegation, *despite ongoing governmental efforts to decrease war threats via the PyeongChang Olympics.* Criticisms can be made and blame placed on corporate journalism, or on the objectification of women, but it is difficult to accept these as sufficient explanations for such journalistic practices. There remains an important need to interrogate the ways in which the mainstream media persists in viewing and representing issues and events.

Constructing Normality and Abnormality

As evidenced in the above examples, the physical appearance of the members of the North Korean delegation, and especially that of women leaders, were objectified in a particular way. Sophisticated fashion, beauty and smiling faces are the norm, and the media in general tends to hold views that objectify women and put them on display. However, the way the South

Korean media cameras looked at the North Korean delegation this time surpassed the usual level of objectification, and did not conceal its expression of confusion or the inability to accept what was being seen. Firstly, Kim Yo Jong and Hyun Song Wol's manners, facial expressions and fashion appeared rather normal relative to the expectations of the South Korean media. The media searched for deviations and anomalies in their smiling faces, sophisticated and calm movements, and speaking patterns, but found them not to be extraordinary in any way.

According to popular expectations, Kim Yo Jong and Hyun Song Wol's behaviour and speech should have typified the abusive nature of the North Korean regime, symbolized by missiles and military assemblies, where participants acted like robots, ready to shout 'Great Leader' at any time. Instead, they gave normal handshakes and greetings, laughing and conversing as they did so. When those who are expected to be abnormal act normally, one must look even closer to find abnormalities. This is the reason for the mainstream media's focus on Kim Yo Jong's pregnancy and her freckles, the rumours of Hyun Song Wol's romance, and her luxury bag and scarf, among other things.

> **When something goes against expectations, one tends to rationalize it by pushing it into the realm of the abnormal.**

In fact, Yonhap News even aired a recording of cheer squad members waiting in line inside the women's restroom.[3] When something goes against expectations, one tends to rationalize it by pushing it into the realm of the abnormal. A sense of abnormality is produced here by juxtaposing luxury goods and sophisticated fashion with freckles and a pregnant female

---

3. The reporter's action of following the cheer squad into the women's restroom with a hidden camera to take pictures is what is strange and abnormal. What sort of abnormality was it that the camera hoped to capture?

body not as a productive body but rather as a body that has conceived a dangerous child. This parenthetical goal itself becomes the justification for producing an irrational report.

The normal behaviour and manners of the North Korean delegation, the Blue House (the official residence of the President of *South Korea)* and the ruling party treating them as normal diplomatic partners, and the image of South Korean citizens welcoming the delegation all appeared 'abnormal' in the context of the South and North Korea's symbiotic antagonism – so leading to instability. For South Korea's conservative powers, this can only be seen as a threat, as their existence is one of the results of this antagonistic relationship. Symbiotic antagonism is maintained, not only through military and political power, but also via the mentality of a divided system.

The Voyeuristic Gaze: Subjects Thrown into Defenceless Circumstances

The North Korean cheer squad was comprised of women selected by the regime specifically for display purposes. The women knew they would become objects to be watched in the South, and it is assumed that they were always aware of this fact. They were now under not only the gaze of the North Korean regime, but also the constant gaze of South Korean cameras, whose images and matching stories would be transmitted within South Korea and around the world. Actions and words cannot be very natural or free when one is conscious of being under someone else's gaze. It is impossible to laugh freely, or to choose not to laugh. It is difficult to speak, yet one must speak. The media maintained its relelentless, voyeuristic gaze on this defenseless group.

Why should the North Korean cheer squad watching South Korean TV in their hotel rooms be seen as something strange and newsworthy? *TV Chosun* narrated the following while broadcasting this point.

> At night, they watch our TV shows. This act doesn't seem to be secretive, as two people sit side by side watching TV.' '(When those people turn the TV on, they see our channels, right?) When I checked the rooms the day before yesterday, all the [South Korean] channels worked. They work fine, but who knows what happened.

The report states the strangeness of North Koreans watching South Korean TV when it should (according to our expectations) have been prohibited. The report itself reveals that the photo was caught by zooming-in and peeping through an open window using a telephoto lens. This raises the question of the significance of the voyeuristic gaze.

Methods of looking at a counterpart who is difficult to face directly include sneaking peeks and taking glances. The most representative is the gaze of misogyny. As misogynists, men select physically weaker women as the target of their hate and disgust in order to disguise and hide their own vulnerabilities, weaknesses and deficiencies. These men generally cannot face women as equal agents. Consideration of others and helping others is not possible for them. It is unimaginable to help and be considerate of others when the self is empty and vulnerable. They hide their vulnerabilities and ignore those of others. And, because they must hide their deficiencies and position, they sneak peeks at others, believing the objects of their view to be abnormal and impure.

The North Korean delegation and cheer squad were subject to this kind of voyeuristic gaze, and though the cheer squad knew they would be exposed to South Korean cameras, they were nevertheless defenceless. They had no other option but to be exposed in front of the camera as captured bodies that had to laugh (though not mindlessly!) that could not get caught watching TV, that should have made sure not to have in their possession a luxury bag. To prepare their bodies as objects, they of course had to wear makeup, freedom af choice played no role in their actions. In this sense, the gaze of the South Korean mainstream media on the North Korean delegation and cheer squad can be seen as both abusive and violent. As an act of demonization.

Concluding remarks

As examined above, the violence of the gaze derives from the viewer's anxiety and feelings of danger posed to one's own conditions of existence. It is therefore necessary to change the current antagonistic coexistence of North and South Korea to one of peace and togetherness, for only then will a safe and secure life be guaranteed for those living on the Korean peninsula. North Korea's nuclear threat has provided a favourable condition for the vested interests of North Korea's governing system and the conservative powers of South Korea that have depended on antagonistic coexistence to maintain their power. The Abe administration in Japan also safely overcame political crises thanks to North Korea's missile launches.

The joint North-South entrance into the PyeongChang Olympics under the Korean Unification Flag (a silhouette in light blue of an undivided Korean peninsula on a white background), a unified ice hockey team, and the cheer squad had to dwell in the sphere of abnormality and illegality because the delegates were seen as representing North Korea's propaganda strategy. Their natural actions and behaviours, casual laughter and conversations were a difficult 'normal' for the mainstream media to accept. It had even in its unsuccessful search for their abnormal, deviant, awkward or strange actions.

A country and a people united by a common history and culture, but divided by ideology and military power, that for years was enforced by a mutually antagonistic political education, needs first and foremost to re-establish and build normal relations. To bury animosities internalized in childhood and later maintained via schooling and a variety of publication channels can only be successful if the urge for change is widespread and strong on both sides of the demarcation line. Paradoxically it seems that the free media in a democracy has great difficulties in contributing to such a development. This bodes ill for peace on the Korean peninsula.

Myungkoo Kang

Directed and Executed Attacks?

ONE SERIOUS PROBLEM OF A CLOSED COUNTRY is lack of transparency and hence the difficulty for the outside world to reach judgements based on facts. But perhaps it also includes the risk of exaggerating the negative aspects and wrongdoings of the given regime? In this chapter, Park-Kang challenges conventional wisdom by posing unconventional questions about the disappearance of a South Korean civilian airliner over the Indian Ocean in November 1987. The number of victims was 115, and North Korea was seen as being behind this massacre. The author asks controversial questions, though not claiming that he knows the truth of the incident. What is important in this contribution is that it reveals how the case was used in what was still a Cold War on the Korean peninsula; and that institutions specialize in dealing with such cases, of which there are several in post-war Korean history. Investigative journalism and research still have a long way to go and much remains to be achieved. A general satisfaction with the present state of affairs seems to be widespread; there are two Koreas, the really bad one, and the generally good one, which has a reasonably well functioning democracy and a strong economy. Nevertheless, the reality is more complex, and Park-Kang reminds us of that.

About the Author: Sungju Park-Kang is Adjunct Professor at the Centre for East Asian Studies, University of Turku, Finland. His research interests include international relations, inter-Korean relations, narrative, memory, gender and methodology. Park-Kang was formerly Assistant Professor of International Relations and Korean Studies at Leiden University, the Netherlands and the University of Central Lancashire, UK. His work has appeared in the *Review of International Studies* and *Millennium: Journal of International Studies*, among others, and he is the author of *Fictional International Relations: Gender, Pain and Truth* (Routledge).

CHAPTER TEN

North Korea over the Rainbow: A Mysterious Demon?

'Sister, I am sorry', whispered a woman almost in tears and leaning on a female interrogator from the South Korean intelligence agency. It was winter 1987. She had been arrested following a failed attempt to commit suicide in Bahrain and had been brought to Seoul for interrogation. With only one day to go before the presidential election, her arrival captured all the attention of the South Korean media and its readers. As a North Korean secret agent, according to the authorities, she had bombed a South Korean plane, under instructions from the North Korean leadership to disrupt the Seoul Olympic Games, killing 115 people. According to the official account, this was the truth of the case of Korean Air (KAL) Flight 858. It was not just the families and relatives who had lost their loved ones who were grieving and in shock, but also the entire people of South Korea. The bomber made her public confession at a national press conference. In contrast to the conventional image of terrorists, she looked beautiful, innocent and pained. Soon after the press conference, the US government referred to this case as it designated North Korea a state sponsor of terrorism. With great concern, the United Nations (UN) Security Council held an emergency meeting. The alleged bomber was sentenced to death, but was immediately granted a special pardon by the South Korean president.

Nevertheless, troubling questions about the truth began to arise: there were no dead bodies and the black box was never recovered. No proper wreckage of the plane was recovered, either. Furthermore, the bomber's statements had substantial contradictions that later resulted in reinvestigation campaigns by family members of the passengers. Subsequently, the government twice reopened the case. It was also revealed that the bomber's first confessional words during the investigation – 'Sister, I am sorry' – were made up by the South Korean spying agency as part of the government's propaganda strategy. Meanwhile, in a film based on the official findings, she was described as a *virgin terrorist*. Since then, she has been a hidden time bomb ticking at the centre of the controversies and sensitivities of the Korean peninsula.

Background

Based on the above story of the virgin terrorist, this chapter explores how North Korea is demonized in international politics and inter-Korean relations. It acknowledges that North Korea, as with any other country, deserves criticism for its wrongdoings. But more importantly, the chapter attempts to show that North Korea is very often subjected to demonization with confirmed and unconfirmed accusations. To become familiar with the case itself and the political climate of that time, it is useful to start with a brief account of the 1980s on the Korean peninsula.

From the South Korean side, the 1980s began with a mass killing in Kwangju, a city in the south-western area. People in Kwangju protested against nationwide martial law imposed by Chun Doo-hwan, a military general, and hundreds of them were killed by a Chun-led government force in May 1980. Soon after this crackdown, Chun became president of South Korea. Throughout his illegitimate military regime, democratization movements were organized. Subsequently many people were arrested, tortured and sometimes died in suspicious circumstances. The year of 1987 was a crucial moment in contemporary South Korean history. In January 1987, a college student was tortured by police and died. The government authorities attempted to cover up the case, but failed. This manipulation attempt triggered a widespread protest against the military regime, which was intensified with another student's tragic fate in police hands in June, which eventually led to the so-called June Democratic Uprising. In response, the military regime agreed to take various democratic policy measures, including the direct presidential election on 16 December. The case of KAL 858 happened right before this highly significant election.

From the North Korean side, the 1980s began with a transition programme in the top leadership. The North Korean Workers' Party held a congress, where it officially acknowledged Kim Jong-il as the successor to Kim Il-sung, the country's founding leader. In October 1983, North Korea was accused of killing South Korean government officials in a bomb explosion in Rangoon, Burma. These officials were waiting for President Chun Doo-hwan, who was on a state visit to Burma and managed to escape the explosion. The accusation was rejected by North Korea, but widely-circulated official findings were hard for that government to explain away. The Rangoon case subsequently caused the already conflict-ridden relations between North and South Korea to deteriorate even further. It is important to note that North Korea was slowly beginning to implement various opening-up policies, particularly in terms of its economy. For example, the North tried to attract foreign investment by introducing related legislation in 1984. And the year of 1987 was a starting point for another economic review policy in North Korea, with continuing gradual commitments to opening up further. Meanwhile, as the 1988 Seoul Olympic Games were approaching, North Korea was in negotiations with South Korea to stage some of the events in the North.

Then the Korean peninsula was suddenly forced to face the following tragic event.

Birth of a Demon

The South Korean plane KAL 858, with 115 people on board, disappeared over the Andaman Sea on 29 November 1987. It had departed from Baghdad and was supposed to arrive in Seoul via Bangkok. Right after the disappearance, the South Korean government and Korean Air began to suspect that the plane had been sabotaged by a North Korean bomb. While the South Korean authorities were tracing two suspects, who were disguised as a Japanese father and daughter (Hachiya Shinichi and Hachiya Mayumi), the pair tried to kill themselves by taking poison pills on 1 December in Bahrain; the woman, however, survived because of a security guard's intervention. These suicide attempts convinced South Korea that the plane had been bombed by the suspects, and that North Korea might have been involved. The woman was brought to South Korea on 15 December, one day before the presidential election. She confessed to her crime a week later, on 23 December, saying that she was a secret agent from North Korea who had sabotaged KAL 858 and revealing her name as Kim Hyunhee. According to the suspect, the North Korean leadership (more specifically Kim Jong-il) had instructed her to bomb the plane in order to disrupt the 1988 Seoul Olympic Games. She confessed that she and her accomplice had begun their mission by first flying from Pyongyang to Moscow, and then travelling on to Budapest, Vienna, Belgrade and Baghdad, where they successfully boarded KAL 858.

According to the official account, Kim was born in 1962 as the first daughter of a North Korean diplomat. Her beauty had been praised since she was a child; Kim claimed that she appeared in several North Korean films while she was an elementary school girl. She enrolled at Kim Il-sung University, the most privileged educational institution in the country. She then transferred to Pyongyang University of Foreign Studies, where she majored in Japanese. Her life changed there when she was recruited as a secret agent thanks to, among other qualities, her intelligence and good looks. Her self-confession was made public at a press conference on 15 January 1988, when the South Korean government released the official findings of the case. This confession, or official result, was categorically rejected by the North. Indeed, as South Korea began to publicly link North Korea to the bombing in early December, North Korea strongly protested. For example, in his visit to the Swedish Ministry of Foreign Affairs, the North Korean Ambassador to Sweden claimed that 'the crash had probably been caused by orders from the South Korean government for the purpose of throwing suspicion on North Korea' (UD,[1] 1987). During a visit after the official findings were released, the Ambassador directly questioned the credibility of Kim's confession: if Kim was brought over to North Korea, 'she would most certainly give another version of the chain of events' (UD, 1988d). Additionally, North Korea released a series of statements in response to South Korea's continued accusations (UD, 1988a, 1988b).

Nonetheless, following the official result, several foreign governments (mainly South Korea's allies) imposed sanctions against North Korea. Most notably, the US placed the North on the list of state sponsors of terrorism on 20 January 1988 and Japan took similar measures. When it came to North Korea's allies, the Swedish Ambassador to North Korea documented his observation from Pyongyang that they were very reluctant to defend the North in public (UD, 1988c). One month later, the UN Security Council held emergency meetings on 16–17 February; the Security Council ended without an agreed resolution on the matter. Meanwhile, Kim was put

---

1. UD refers to the Swedish Ministry of Foreign Affairs.

on trial and sentenced to death in March 1990, after which she was granted a special pardon by the South Korean authorities about 15 days later. She was employed by the South Korean intelligence agency the following year and became actively involved in anti-North Korean campaigns. Kim published several books, delivered public lectures and appeared in various media coverage. Throughout her public engagements, Kim confirmed her crime and strongly criticized the North Korean regime. Her active campaigns nonetheless did not last long. Kim married a former South Korean secret agent and disappeared from the public eye in December 1997. This was when democratic opposition leader Kim Dae-jung was elected as the president, marking the first peaceful power shift in South Korean history.

The Mysterious Demon

At this point it must be noted that the official findings have faced three sets of challenges related to the search operations after the disappearance of the plane, the initial investigation conducted by the authorities and the official closure of the case.

First, the South Korean government did not make sufficient efforts in its search operations. Notably, the government's search operation continued for only ten days. No black box was recovered and neither were any dead bodies. Furthermore, the search team did not find any proper wreckage of the plane. Second, the official investigation relied almost entirely on Kim's statements. Technically speaking, there was no physical evidence to support Kim's confession. It is also important to note that Kim's statements contained substantial contradictions (I discuss some of them below). Third, for some reason, the government tried to close the case hurriedly. Almost all of the 115 people were unilaterally registered as dead by the government two months after the incident. According to the relevant law related to unconfirmed deaths, the deaths should have been registered by individual families at least one year after the event, because the people had only been *missing*. Also, compensation was forcefully distributed to families at the end of 1987, even before the official findings were released in 1988. With respect to Kim's trial, it was revealed that the government had planned to pardon her from the very beginning. All the above factors suggest that the government's treatment of the case was neither thorough nor fair.

More serious questions arose in relation to Kim's statements, which played a crucial role in establishing the official account and which contain substantial contradictions. These contradictions need to be taken seriously, because Kim's confession, from the government's point of view, functioned as the objective and absolute evidence of the truth. For instance, inexplicable discrepancies are observed in Kim's (1992) confession-oriented book and its English, translated version (1993). First, there are contradictory accounts of who activated the timer of the bomb. According to the Korean-language edition, Kim's accomplice had activated the time bomb. According to the English version, however, it was Kim herself. Kim states that her partner asked her to do it: 'You must take the bomb into the women's rest room and set it yourself' (1993, p. 104). This discrepancy is alarming in the sense that the bomb played a core part in the case. Second, we can observe different accounts of how she obtained an airline ticket in Vienna. According to the Korean edition, she bought the ticket with her accomplice. But according to the English version, the two agents met another secret agent woman in a park and secured the ticket by exchanging the code word 'Nakayama' (1993, p. 96). It is hard to understand how such a specific yet different account could be offered. Third, there are discrepancies in describing the flight from Pyongyang to Moscow. According to the Korean edition, it was difficult to obtain a ticket because this was the first flight on a newly launched route. The plane was full of German people, with very few Koreans. According to the English version, however, the flight 'was almost empty' (1993, p. 90). This part of the statement is important, as it is related to the beginning of Kim's operation. In addition, other discrepancies regarding how many South Korean embassy members visited her and whether she committed an act of violence during the interrogation are also observed.

In all, it is fair to say that valid questions surround the official findings. (Drawing upon these questions, there have been attempts to establish alternative scenarios, particularly in popular culture such as cartoons, television dramas, novels and films. The most popular theory is that the case was the then-South Korean military regime's own political plot.) Even an observer who firmly believes in the official narrative acknowledges that there are 'some internal inconsistencies' in the findings (Burmudez, 1998, p. 273). Of course, it would be dangerous to claim that the above questions automatically lead to the construction of an alternative truth, and I do not intend to do so. The point seems to be that these questions need to be answered in one way or another. For the families of KAL 858 victims, the unanswered questions were significant enough to lead them to organize reinvestigation campaigns. It was not easy to organize and start active campaigns until 2001, when the leading figures of the family association of KAL 858 changed. Before 2001, the leading members of the association were mostly concerned with getting proper compensation from the government; endorsing the official findings was in their interest, as was maintaining strong connections with anti-North Korean organisations, whose voice was close to the conservative government stance towards North Korea. In 2001, however, those leading members were replaced by families who wanted more than anything to learn what really had happened to their loved ones. Since this leadership change, the

KAL 858 association has launched several of reinvestigation campaigns intended to find answers to the still-unanswered questions. (There had been reinvestigation demands before the change, but they were not so well organized.)

Following the campaigns, the government launched two separate reinvestigations. First, the National Intelligence Service (NIS) reopened the case in 2005, when its internal commission was established to investigate some major misconduct during the past authoritarian regimes. The NIS released its findings in 2007, which basically endorsed the original official report; this result was criticized by many people, as the NIS had failed to investigate the most important figure in the case: the bomber. Second, at the request of the families of the passengers, the Truth and Reconciliation Commission launched another reinvestigation in 2007. Due to various limitations, however, it had to face substantial challenges including the continued failure to question Kim. In 2009, the families decided to withdraw their request for further reinvestigations; the Commission subsequently withdrew without producing any official result.

Meanwhile, Kim returned to the public stage in 2009, after a conservative president came to power, replacing the previous two liberal governments. Now, Kim claimed that the previous governments had pursued *pro-North Korean policies* that made her life very difficult; she even claimed that the governments tried to overturn the official result of her case for political reasons. This claim needs to be examined with caution. Most of all, given her active anti-North Korean campaigns, it is understandable that she was worried about the so-called pro-North Korean policies or more correctly, South Korea's engagement policy towards North Korea; her claim about pro-North Korean policies is highly controversial, as is the term itself. Moreover, it is not right to say that the government attempted to overturn the official findings. It did try to reinvestigate the case, but those efforts unearthed no reason to overturn the result. It seems that she might have expressed her uneasiness about the reinvestigation itself; after all, she had repeatedly and vehemently refused to cooperate with the reinvestigation (Unlike Police or Prosecution Service, those agencies in charge of reinvestigations did not have any authority to force her to testify.) In 2018, the case marked its 31st anniversary amidst ongoing controversies.

The One-Colour Rainbow

Leaving aside the controversies over truth, it is important to note that 115 innocent people disappeared and are believed to have died. This was a direct outcome of the divided situation on the Korean peninsula. The bodies of those 115 people have not been found and, consequently, their families have been haunted by the case for years without any sense of closure. The event happened in the mid-1980s, one of the most confrontational moments in Korea during the (conventional) Cold War era, but its context and unfinished process obviously went far beyond that. If one takes the case seriously, the world has not changed much before and since 1989, the year of the dominant narrative of the end of the Cold War. One might then hardly think that the case can be properly captured by European/Great-Power-oriented accounts of the Cold War. To put it another way, the case has been part of a Korean version of the Cold War, or what I would call *the (Too Hot To Be) Cold War* – Korea was never cold during and after the Cold War with ongoing actual and virtual military confrontations. Let me elaborate this point in terms of the demonization of North Korea.

The case of KAL 858 reinforced and reproduced anti-North Korean sentiment in many ways. Primarily, particularly during the authoritarian regimes, people who raised questions about the official account were arrested under the National Security

Law. For example, a college student was arrested because he displayed a poster about the unanswered questions on campus. The publisher of a book that questioned the official findings was arrested under the same law. The government's logic was not complicated: to question the official account was to benefit North Korea. This is because the official account made clear that the KAL 858 event was an act of North Korean terrorism, even though North Korea denied any responsibility for it. Therefore, anyone who questioned the official result was assumed to be agreeing with North Korea. In other words, to question South Korea's result was to support North Korea's claim. The National Security Law effectively blocked any challenging questions in the public domain, thereby strengthening the anti-North Korean stance in South Korea. In this context, those who posed questions about the official narrative were framed as North Korean sympathizers and, consequently, as a threat to national security. Even the legitimate questions of the families of the passengers were dismissed as politically motivated pro-North Korean claims. Furthermore, a human rights lawyer who represented the family members was accused in 2012, based on his public remarks made back in 2003; this was part of a negative election campaign against his wife, who was running in the general election as the chairperson of a progressive political party. Its purpose was to label his partner, through him, as a North Korean sympathizer.

Operation Rainbow

The powerful anti-North Korean mechanism was actively deployed and consolidated even before the official findings were released. The then-military regime in South Korea initiated *Operation Rainbow* on 2 December 1987, in the run-up to the presidential election; its purpose was to take advantage of the case to generate a favourable political climate for the ruling party candidate by launching a comprehensive campaign against North Korea (Kim, 2007; NIS, 2007). The South Korean intelligence agency aimed to 'wither the North Korean puppet regime and to enhance alertness against North Korea by exposing that the case is the North Korean puppet regime's terrorist bombing' (ANSP, 1987, p. 1). The agency and the Chun-led military regime had specific operation plans at various levels. According to the document, it was likely that 'the North Korean puppet regime was preparing' another attack. The agency planned to 'expose' this possibility to the general public in South Korea (ANSP, 1987, p. 4).

The purpose of this exposure was winning the election. The government first stoked fears and then played on them in order to win votes, saying for example that opposition presidential candidates who 'ignore our security reality and promote a dangerous discourse on unification [with the North]' should be condemned (Ibid.). By doing so, conservative leaders believed, the victory of the ruling party's candidate would be secured. Therefore it was vital for the South Korean government to publicize the case of KAL 858 at the maximum level. As part of this campaign, mass anti-North Korean rallies were organized, where the north was blamed for the KAL 858 tragedy. Around 100,000 people attended an anti-North Korean rally in Seoul on 14 December 1987 (Choi, 1990), two days prior to the presidential election. It was even before Kim made her self-confession on 23 December.

One important question can be raised: how did South Korea know that 'the North Korean puppet regime' was behind the case? The plane disappeared on 29 November. As of 2 December, nothing had been recovered from the sea. Kim, the suspect, made a self-confession only on 23 December. Without any physical evidence, without any statement, the intelligence agency already claimed to know what had happened (and even what would happen). It must be noted that the agency mentioned some circumstantial evidence, such as Kim's suicide attempt. From the government's point of view, Kim tried to kill herself because she had not wanted to reveal her real identity. In addition, the agency obtained information on the fake Japanese passports possessed by Kim's accomplice. Based on this assessment, they could 'assume' that both Kim and her partner were 'related to the North Korean puppet regime' (ANSP, 1987, p. 2). Parts of the document in question are blacked out, which means there might be more conclusive evidence somewhere. But in any case, it remains a mystery how the intelligence agency knew what had happened with no smoking gun.

Meanwhile, to maximize the effect of the anti-North Korean campaign, the intelligence agency envisaged 'total mobilization' of media outlets and people, including the family members of the passengers (ANSP, 1987, p. 4). Furthermore, the government planned to encourage 'countries across the world and international organisations such as the International Committee of the Red Cross, the UN and the IOC' to publicly condemn 'the North Korean puppet regime' (ANSP, 1987, p. 5). The South Korean government's anti-North Korean campaign was in full swing. The elements of demonization were well outlined in the agency's 'psychological warfare guidelines' regarding the case. I filed a Freedom of Information Act request to the National Archives of Korea and accessed classified documents. One aim of this psychological warfare was to 're-highlight the North Korean puppet regime as a terrorist group' by condemning the brutality of the North as much as possible (TRC, 2011, p. 164). That way, the agency would, it hoped, 'deprive' North Korea of 'the value of existence' (Ibid.).

It appears that Operation Rainbow was carried out relatively successfully. Most of all, as the agency designed, the ruling party's candidate won the presidential election. Although it is difficult to calculate how much the operation contributed to this victory, it is widely believed that the case of KAL 858 heightened 'people's sense of national security and anti-communist sentiment', which helped the conservative candidate Roh Tae-woo get elected (Lee, 2002, p. 106; see also Jung, 1998, pp. 124–125). The operation lasted until 31 May 1988, and another significant political event, a general election, was held on 26 April the same year. That means there is a possibility that the then-military regime, or at least the intelligence agency, planned to influence the general election as well. This is partly evidenced by a document from the Ministry of Foreign Affairs (1988, p. 118). To continue the discussion, the Ministry of Foreign Affairs was one of the central government organisations that was deeply involved in Operation Rainbow. The Foreign Minister, according to the plan, was expected to issue a statement suggesting the assumed connection between the case and North Korea around 5 December 1987. The government planned to 'guide the domestic and international media to give prominent coverage to' this announcement (ANSP, 1987, p. 3). The statement did not come out as planned, but the Ministry of Foreign Affairs (1988) aggressively carried out the anti-North Korean campaign abroad. In general and unsurprisingly, the South Korean media supported the government's effort to demonize North Korea.

Along with the above, Kim Hyunhee's direct engagements contributed to the spread of anti-North Korean sentiments. She blamed North Korea in several books and public lectures. Her confession, which she wrote in great detail, confirmed that she had carried out the bombing at the instruction of the North Korean leadership (Kim, 1991). She went on to say she realized South Korea's superiority to North Korea and criticized North Korea as a strict communist society where freedom was not permitted. Her books were translated into foreign languages including English, Japanese, German, Swedish, Czech and Finnish. It was later revealed that even the original Korean-language edition was actually written by a ghost-writer commissioned by the South Korean intelligence agency.

The Cold War Rainbow

The case also had some conventional components of Cold War bloc politics. Conventional Cold War politics are well-evidenced throughout the UN Security Council meetings (it is worth remembering that the government, from the very beginning, planned to use the UN platform to pursue Operation Rainbow). When South Korea filed a request for the emergency meeting, the US strongly supported the move. The Soviet Union, however, opposed South Korea's request, apparently on behalf of North Korea. Once the Security Council meetings started, Cold War bloc politics were almost exactly replicated at the UN. The South Korea–US-led factions, including Japan, clashed with the North Korea–Soviet-led factions, including China. On the one hand, the South Korean side made clear that the issue was North Korea's terrorist bombing and urged other member states to join the South in blaming the North. The US strongly supported South Korea: 'We think it especially important that all civilized countries make it clear to North Korea that this uncivilized behaviour must not be repeated' (UNSC, 1988b, p. 67). On the other hand, the North Korean side questioned the validity of the official findings and pointed out that the meetings had been initiated by a politically motivated South Korea. For example, North Korea claimed that the case was a 'smear campaign ... a campaign linking the KAL incident with us from the beginning of the new year without any scientific ground' (UNSC, 1988a, p. 55). The Soviet Union stated at the beginning of the meeting: 'Because of its tendentiousness and the groundless nature of its assertions ... the document submitted by South Korea cannot serve as a point of reference for the Council's debate' (UNSC, 1988a, pp. 3–5).

The UN Security Council meeting ended without adopting a resolution against North Korea. Instead, a Presidential statement was adopted; this statement was somewhat vague and general in its contents (it basically says that tragedies such as the case of KAL 858 should not be repeated). I would say that South Korea did not actively pursue the adoption of a resolution. In the light of the power dynamics within the UN Security Council (with strong opposition from the Soviet Union and China who could exercise their veto rights), the South might have just wanted to use the meeting as an opportunity to criticize North Korea. This point has been confirmed by Park Keun, the then-South Korean ambassador to the UN (interview, 9 August 2011): the South did not plan to pursue the adoption of any particular resolution. Rather, the government was much more interested in making the most of the chance to blame North Korea on the international stage. In other words, South and North Korea had to fiercely defend their claims to get support from international audiences. It is not surprising, therefore, that an Australian diplomat offered the following observation on the meeting: it 'degenerated into a rather tiresome slanging match' between the two related parties (DFAT, 1988, p. 406).

As such, regarding the case of KAL 858, the South Korean government had begun the demonization of North Korea without knowing who the demon was. The comprehensive campaign against the North, without any physical evidence except for Kim's confession, continued on the international stage. The magic of the rainbow prevailed.

A Land of Sad Twins

In many ways, the case of KAL 858 reminds me of the South Korean naval ship that was sunk on 26 March 2010: the case of Cheonan, in which 46 sailors were killed. There are several similarities. Right after the incident, the South Korean authorities suspected North Korean involvement; the official findings confirmed this initial speculation and North Korea immediately denied any responsibility. In addition, many unanswered questions were raised, the case happened before an important political election, and people demanded a reinvestigation. As with the KAL 858 case and in spite of the government's official findings, the families of the passengers, their supporters and human rights activists continue to demand a full-scale reinvestigation. The issue of the truth has not been settled yet. The official findings could be proven true. But whatever the truth of this case, the extraordinary and vicious nature of Operation Rainbow should be critically examined.

In 2002, George W. Bush described North Korea, Iran and Iraq as 'an Axis of Evil.' It would be fair to say that North Korea has never been an easy issue for anyone to address. Although North Korea for some might be part of an axis of evil, it could also be in an axis of unification. In a way, Korea is a twin – that of North and South. The pair are twins not only in the sense that they share one language and one history, but also in that they share one peninsula or social body; their fates have been deeply entangled from the very beginning. But they are sad twins. Despite the dramatic

In a way, Korea is a twin – that of North and South. The pair are twins not only in the sense that they share one language and one history, but also in that they share one peninsula or social body; their fates have been deeply entangled from the very beginning. But they are sad twins.

improvement of inter-Korean relations in 2018, a permanent peace treaty remains elusive and the possibility of war in Korea continues to persist. Any type of attack on either side could easily escalate into a peninsula-engulfing war. This tiny land already suffered devastating war a few decades ago. As with any war, people were killed, buildings were gone and lives were destroyed – more than destroyed, as the war consolidated the division between the North and South. A land of sad twins, that is the Korean peninsula. The demonization of North Korea (and counter-demonization of South Korea) only makes these sad twins even sadder.

Author's Note

I would like to express my deepest appreciation to Geir Helgesen for inviting me to join this project. I must also thank my colleagues in Finland, my second home: Lauri Paltemaa, Outi Luova, Katri Kauhanen and Sabine Burghart, among others. Rachel Harrison, Gerald Jackson, David Stuligross and an anonymous reviewer also deserve credit. My special gratitude extends to Christine Sylvester, Cynthia Enloe, Stephen Chan and Cecilia Milwertz for their continued support.

Many parts of this chapter are drawn and revised from Park-Kang (2014).

Sungju Park-Kang

Sources of particular relevance

ANSP (1987) Operation Rainbow. 2 December. Seoul: Agency for National Security Planning (in Korean).

Burmudez, J. S. (1998) *North Korean Special Forces* (2nd ed.). Annapolis: Naval Institute Press.

Choi, J. (1990) 'Kim Hyunhee and Mystery of KAL858', *Mal*, 50 (in Korean).

DFAT (1988) UN43603, 406. 17 February. Canberra: Department of Foreign Affairs and Trade.

Jung, J. (1998) 'The Politics of Northern Wind: Elections and Northern Wind', *Korea and World Politics*, 14(1), 101–113 (in Korean).

Kim, C. (2007, April 4) 'Operation Rainbow', *Tongilnews* (in Korean).

Kim, H. (1991) *Now I Want to be a Woman 1*. Seoul: Koryowon (in Korean).

———(1992) *I Cry When I Feel Love*. Seoul: Koryowon (in Korean).

———(1993) *The Tears of My Soul*. New York: William Morrow & Company.

Lee, J. (2002) 'Presidential Elections and Inter-Korean Hostile Interdependence', *Critical Review of History*, 60, 111–151 (in Korean).

Ministry of Foreign Affairs (1988) KAL 858 Archives: 2017060056. Seoul: Ministry of Foreign Affairs (in Korean).

NIS (2007) *A Conversation with the Past, A Reflection of the Future.* Seoul: National Intelligence Service (in Korean).

Park-Kang, S. (2014) *Fictional International Relations: Gender, Pain and Truth.* London: Routledge.

TRC (2011) KAL 858 Archives: DA0799654. Seoul: Truth and Reconciliation Commission (in Korean).

UD (1987) Anklagelser Nord-Sydkorea. 16 December. Stockholm: Utrikesdepartementet (Ministry for Foreign Affairs).

———— (1988a) KCNA Statement. 26 January [15 January]. Stockholm: Utrikesdepartementet (Ministry for Foreign Affairs).

———— (1988b) Statement of DPRK Foreign Ministry Spokesman. 26 January [25 January]. Stockholm: Utrikesdepartementet (Ministry for Foreign Affairs).

———— (1988c) Det försvunna KAL-flygplanet. 22 January. Stockholm: Utrikesdepartementet (Ministry for Foreign Affairs).

———— (1988d) Samtal med Nordkoreas ambassadör. 10 February. Stockholm: Utrikesdepartementet (Ministry for Foreign Affairs).

UNSC (1988a) S/PV. 2791. 16 February. New York: United Nations Security Council.

———— (1988b) S/PV. 2792. 17 February. New York: United Nations Security Council.

Demonization Turned Inwards

IN THIS CHAPTER, WERTSCH AND FINKE outline the sources and power of views in the US that assume North Korea must be understood in terms of aggressive intentions and actions. These views are shared by many of the voters who elected the current US president, yet they run counter to the opinion of most experts in foreign affairs. From the latter perspective, the media in America are exacerbating a problematic and dangerous state of affairs and are part of a picture of demonization turned inwards in the context of domestic politics. After outlining how mainstream media and social media have depicted North Korea in negative terms and supported ideas about violent 'solutions', the authors consider the case of a scholar nominated to become US ambassador to South Korea as an illustration. When he publicly expressed the need to entertain 'a more nuanced approach to the North Korean issue', the White House withdrew his nomination, providing a clear example of demonization turned inwards. This is a fragment of a larger mosaic of international demonization directed toward North Korea.

About the Authors: James V. Wertsch studies language, thought and culture, with a special focus on national memory and narratives. His publications include *Vygotsky and the Social Formation of Mind* (1985), *Voices of the Mind* (1991), *Mind as Action* (1998) and *Voices of Collective Remembering* (2002). After finishing his PhD at the University of Chicago, Wertsch studied with neuropsychologist Alexander R. Luria. He is a fellow in the American Academy of Arts and Sciences and the Russian Academy of Education. He is a non-resident Senior Fellow at the Brookings Institution and has served as a guest professor at the University of Oslo, Tsinghua University in Beijing and Fudan University in Shanghai.

Jacob Finke is a student at Washington University in St. Louis, where he studies International Affairs and Chinese Language & Culture. Jacob's research interests include China's Century of Humiliation, perceptions of the One Belt, One Road initiative in American media, and American foreign direct investment (FDI) restrictions. His senior honors thesis will analyze the United States' failed attempt to mediate peace between the KMT and CCP in China 1946 before the resurgence of civil war in 1947.

CHAPTER ELEVEN

The Dangers of Demonization: An American Perspective

Introduction

*T*he media matter. Even as America's media focus moves away from traditional print outlets and into more unregulated means, such as cable news, streaming news, and social media, viewership remains high. As the news has become more polarized, its influence has grown; viewers can tune into their Twitter feed or cable news network and see exactly what they want. And, with the reality TV president Donald Trump, these media have the ability to directly inform policy, not just the general population.

Social media have the fewest barriers to entry of any major news source and are extremely popular. In 2016, 62 per cent of Americans took at least some news from social media like Facebook and Twitter (Mitchell & Holcomb: 6). But even with the rise of social media news, the most formidable news source remains cable television. The 'big three' networks in the US – *CNN, Fox News* and *MSNBC* – are polarized and partisan, but they inform millions of Americans every single day, making their content extremely important.

Cable news outlets do not inform only the general public; they also inform policy. President Trump's obsession with cable television has been well-documented: one report estimates that he watches five hours of television per day, far more than previous presidents (Godfrey 2017). Understandably, this has led to the public perception that what the president watches informs his policy positions. The president routinely tweets about Fox News shows, and advertisers understand that 'ads on his favourite networks' provide an opening to 'try to influence Trump' (*Ibid.*). Even if the broadcasts do not directly influence Trump's policy positions, his tweets are quite often 'provoke[d]' by what he sees on television (VandeHei & Allen 2017); these tweets go on to be analyzed as policy positions or personal beliefs held by the president.

This is all to say that the media matter, including in some unusual ways during the Trump administration. With that in mind, it is important that news – especially cable news, with its wide and unchallenged reach – remains open to nuanced opinions from experts, academics and government officials, especially on a topic as sensitive and complex as the Korean Peninsula. It is the responsibility of the mass media to bring rational viewpoints to the American people. But in reality, the American media have increasingly embraced sensationalism and turned away from presenting nuanced policy positions. Academics who do present such measured positions risk fierce blowback from popular political opinion. As a result, academic commentators have retreated to academic settings where their research and positions can be respectfully debated, but without the wide exposure that the public so desperately needs. This means that, while there is a large variety of policy positions about the North Korea issue, the most popular and widespread ones are increasingly sensationalist and interventionist.

Friendships and firings: Extreme positions on North Korea

During early stages of the Trump administration, US–DPRK relations were tense. People close to the president were advocating a 'bloody nose' attack, and it was unclear to what extent the president was considering that option and others like it. After multiple summits with Kim Jong-Un, President Trump changed his approach from one of 'fire and fury' to one of mutual admiration and almost friendship. Partisan supporters and detractors of President Trump were quick to analyse the summits in positive and negative lights, respectively. However, experts cautioned restraint, advocating that partisanship should be kept from diplomacy on issues as important as denuclearisation (DePetris 2019b). Unfortunately, that was not the case, and social media – as well as partisan cable news – enabled political pundits to shape narratives on the summits. Even with the benefit of hindsight, many pundits have not changed their views and view the summits in all-or-nothing ways. Policy experts have taken more nuanced approaches, and some have changed their views after seeing the lack of progress after the summits (DePetris 2019a).

On 30 January 2018 Victor Cha, the Trump administration's nominee for US ambassador to the Republic of Korea, published an op-ed in the *Washington Post* decrying the 'huge risk' that a 'preventive military strike' on North Korea would present to the American people. Cha is a widely respected expert on North Korea; he currently teaches at Georgetown University and previously served in the George W. Bush administration. His ambassadorial nomination was widely supported, given his experience, conservative credentials and lack of any 'never Trump' comments. In his op-ed, however, Cha argued for a more nuanced approach to the North Korean issue. He challenged the idea of a preventive strike, noting that any North Korean missiles not immediately destroyed could be used in retaliation, putting hundreds of thousands of American servicemen, servicewomen, their families and Koreans at risk. This sort of escalation, he argued, would be difficult for the United States to control and could lead to mass casualties on the Korean Peninsula.

Cha instead asserted that a three-pronged approach would best counter the North Korean threat: strengthen the UN coalition, enhance alliances with South Korea and Japan, and build a maritime coalition surrounding North Korea. Cha even acknowledged that a strike might be necessary if North Korea were ever to attack first – something that he maintains is a distinct, though unlikely, possibility. This op-ed that Victor Cha wrote for the *Washington Post* was a respectful, nuanced and rational disagreement with 'bloody nose' proposals emanating from the White House at the time. Cha even sympathized with the White House's concerns, stating that the threats facing the US were 'real and unprecedented', and that it was not wholly unreasonable for the administration to struggle with deciding how to deal with them. Cha's op-ed should have been read and debated widely.

The response from the White House was far less nuanced. Just a few days later, officials announced that Victor Cha was 'no longer nominated' for the position of US ambassador to South Korea (Labott 2018). Reports soon circulated that a 'policy difference over a pre-emptive strike' led to Cha's removal. The episode serves as a good example of American discourse regarding North Korea today. There is a wide range of opinions and stances regarding how the United States should interact with North Korea. However, the continued loud talk about the 'bloody nose' proposal continues to have great sway. To be sure, there is uncertainty in all of this, with alternatives ranging all the way to direct negotiations between the leaders of the DPRK and the US, which have in fact taken place. Nevertheless, the belligerent option of a military attack continues to be present in the background.

To understand how this discourse plays out in America, we turn to a popular news outlet and to examples from social media, as well as comments on online media websites, to outline some of the most popular positions. To fill out the picture, we turn to commentaries from the Brookings Institution, *Foreign Affairs* magazine and *Foreign Policy* magazine. As sensationalist tweets and positions have become more popular and gain more coverage, they have often come to be more commonly held. And as these positions become popular, pundits in major media outlets adopt them, hoping to receive approval – or any sort of reaction – from Trump to boost their ratings. These dynamics have led to a variety of positions in the United States and a growing concern that more rational and nuanced positions have taken a backseat to sensationalism.

Popular media

Consider an article from *Fox News*, a right-wing, often pugilistic television and online news outlet that claims to be America's 'Most Watched ... Most Trusted' news network. An article written by Gregory Keeley (2017) and published online argues that 'a naval blockade might work' in truly enforcing US and UN sanctions against North Korea. In his view, a full naval blockade by the United States, Japan, South Korea, India, Taiwan, Singapore, Australia and NATO forces constitutes a moderate position, juxtaposed against the 'two potential responses, both bad' of military intervention or complete failure to act (*Ibid.*). Keeley lambasts the United Nations as 'feckless', assumes that other Southeast Asian – and even NATO – allies would participate as 'key players' in this effort and asserts that his idea of a blockade is 'not only palatable... [but] may be the only alternative' to the United States' current policy options.

Keeley's argument overlooks more nuanced approaches and instead opts for an oversimplified, quick, quotable piece sure to get online views. Whereas Cha advocated for a three-pronged, multilateral approach with safeguards and contingency measures, Keeley advocated a United States-centred, bombastic approach. This sort of firebrand journalism is common in online news sites. Media figures have sensed that there is a more jingoist, interventionist sentiment in America today, and in this case feed into it by authoring pieces that present a full naval blockade as the defensive approach. One of the comments on this *Fox News* article states that Keeley was a 'Leader' and goes on to ask 'are we really prepared to do this' and suggests that this blockade could be a good idea. The same commentator moves on to the idea of attacking Russian and Chinese ships that cross the American blockade (note that Russia and China were two of the parties at the Six-Party Talks). 'Can we [disable Russian and Chinese ships] with EMPs [EMPs are pulses of energy that can be emitted from the blast of a nuclear weapon]? If we cannot, then we have to be prepared to shoot', he opines in the same comment. Later on, this commentator postulates 'can we take out Kim Jong-Un?' (*Ibid.*).

In another article advocating for a naval blockade of North Korea, a commentator proposed an attack of Russian and Chinese ships and the assassination of Kim Jong-Un. This is why Keeley outlined such aggressive proposals, namely, if he could attract comments like this, he would be likely to attract more views. This does not mean that Donald Trump will begin making assassination plans or sending the Pacific Fleet to blockade North Korea. However, it does mean that these ideas are out there, circulating on America's 'Most Trusted' news network, garnering views on a news article with over one thousand comments, which placed it close to the top at that time.

It seems as if these ideas have made their way into the White House. On 14 January 2018, the *New York Times* reported that the United States military was 'quietly preparing for a war' with North Korea on orders from Secretary of Defense James Mattis (Cooper et al. 2018). However, news reports from around the same time reported that Mattis 'express[ed] concern about the prospect' of a military engagement with North

Korea (Labott 2018). The orders themselves may reflect the wish of the president at the time. Even as experts – not only the Secretary of Defense, but also the Chairman of the Joint Chiefs of Staff and the Secretary of State – express doubts about the feasibility of military intervention and call for more diplomacy, the administration has ordered troops to make preparations for war.

Since President Trump changed his perspective on Kim Jong-Un, *Fox News* also has changed its editorial bent on the issue. Articles on the network's website no longer advocate decapitation attacks or naval blockades. Instead, they published a review of a book claiming that Kim Jong-Un sees President Trump 'like a new father figure' (Dorman 2019). Some of the most-liked comments compare Obama's and Trump's different North Korea policies, lauding Trump for 'at least trying to bring an end to the Korean War' and 'engaging him [Kim] in conversation' because Trump 'sees the world as it truly is' (*Ibid.*). These commentators are drawn from the same pool as those who read and commented on Trump's fire and fury policies just two years eatlier.

Social media

These trends are often carried to an extreme in the president's use of social media to make insults such as calling Kim Jong-Un 'Little Rocket Man'. Instead of measured, diplomatic communication, the president has communicated through social media platforms to insult and to brag about things such as the size of his nuclear button. The first tweet in which Donald Trump referred to Kim Jong-Un as Little Rocket Man received 36,000 retweets and 42,000 replies; presumably, all 47.8 million of his Twitter followers saw that tweet. Possibly even more dangerous than the pedantic insult of Kim Jong-Un is the threat that '[North Korea] won't be around much longer!' (*Ibid*) What, exactly, might this mean? Could it be an assassination, as #sailingnewyork, *Fox News*' leading commenter, suggested? Or perhaps it was the war that Defense Secretary Mattis was preparing for? Messages of this sort from President Trump do not reflect a one-off lapse in judgement; he has spoken of 'Little Rocket Man' numerous times to describe Kim Jong-Un.

These insulting and bombastic tweets are not only distressing for the United States and the rest of the world. They could also be dangerous. In November 2017, the North Koreans launched a nuclear missile that demonstrated its capability to hit the United States (Pak 2018). The threat of a nuclear attack at the hands of North Korea does not seem imminent, but it can no longer be ignored as impossible: North Korea apparently has developed the technical capability to hit the entire continental United States with a nuclear weapon. In this state of affairs, Trump's language can only exacerbate the situation. And while it may be humorous to watch two of the world's leaders trade insults such as 'Little Rocket Man' and 'dotard', it does nothing to minimize the threats and counterthreats. It can only serve to incite followers of both leaders, pushing the American public toward yet further demonization of North Korea.

Trump's bombastic tweets are reinforced by his supporters, many of whom post encouraging internet memes. One such account posted a meme accusing Bill Clinton, Barack Obama and Hillary Clinton of giving nuclear weapons or materials to North Korea, Iran and Russia, respectively ('Nuclear Transfers'). That tweet was retweeted by 1,500 people and was presumably seen by all 33,000 followers of the account (*Ibid.*). This account was found quickly by just searching using the hashtag '#NorthKorea'. (A hashtag is a means by which tweets are linked together quickly.) There are undoubtedly thousands more tweets from Trump supporters excusing his behaviour and encouraging Trump to 'clean up' the 'mess' he inherited from his predecessors, with little or no concern over the way Trump manages this *(Ibid)*. These tweets likely also garnered tens or hundreds of thousands of retweets and views, further popularizing a narrative that President Trump is right in pursuing any manner of military options against North Korea, regardless of what expert commentators say.

Social media are designed to impose no barriers to entering a conversation. This means that anybody can post anything with virtually no validity requirements or ramifications for spreading false information. The result is an environment where Twitter users – including the president and others noted above – can popularize fringe opinions based solely on the users' popularity, with no regard to validity or rationality. This influences popular opinion, making the idea – no matter how fringe or unrealistic – seem mainstream as it racks up more retweets, favourites and views. In principle, rather than conspiracy theories and fringe opinions, social media could be used to promote well-rounded and better-conceived arguments, such as those outlined below, but this seems to be the exception rather than the rule.

The academic approach

Tweets from Donald Trump and his followers may receive millions of views and hundreds of thousands of affirmations in retweets and likes, but that is not to say there is not a more balanced and professional contingent of the American media and American thinkers on the topic of North Korea. Serious analysts have written countless pieces advocating rational approaches to North Korea. Victor Cha himself is one example; Dr. Jung H. Pak another. Many of these sources propose strengthened alliances, the de-escalation of tensions and a gradual ratcheting up of sanctions on the North Korean regime, to encourage it to conform to international norms. Along with this, many experts warn against the impossibility of success in the kind of 'bloody nose' attack that Donald Trump has been suggesting.

An attempt to assassinate Kim Jong-Un would be a 'gamble of epic proportions' (Sagan 2017: 78). The United States has a sorry history of failed execution attempts throughout the twentieth and twenty-first centuries, many of them in countries more open and easy to infiltrate than North Korea. Surely a failed assassination attempt on Kim Jong-Un would enrage him, pushing him toward retaliatory action. Even if North Korea did not go nuclear, a cyberattack, military strike against North Korea or some other type of armed action could be devastating for the United States' reputation and for the damage it causes. Even in the unlikely event that Kim Jong-Un were to be successfully assassinated, there is a possibility that he already has an order in place for a military strike in the event of his death; given his cult of personality, there is 'no reason' to believe that the North Korean military would fail to attack the United States in that event (*Ibid.*). The answer to #sailingnewyork's question 'can we take out Kim Jong-Un?' is a swift and resounding 'no' (Keeley 2017).

Several policy analysts have pointed to the near impossibility of a successful 'bloody nose' first strike by the United States. Indeed, the possibility that a first strike could deter Kim Jong-Un from retaliating is, in and of itself, irrational. If Kim Jong-Un is so irrational that he might launch a strike unprovoked, how could we assume that a first strike by the United States would bring him to the rational conclusion to de-escalate (Sagan 2017:78; Cha 2018) Kim Jong-Un is unlikely to be simultaneously irrational and rational; to assume otherwise is a deep failing in the logic of those who believe that a first strike could deter him.

Furthermore, such a strike would probably not even be successful in disarming North Korea. North Korea is notoriously difficult to analyze and has been described as 'the hardest of targets' for American intelligence analysts (Pak 2018). With this in mind, a first strike by the United States probably would not be successful in destroying all of North Korea's weapons since we probably do not know where most of them are located. The ones we could find are 'buried in deep places, impenetrable' by even very high-capacity weapons (Cha 2018); and the weapons that we know about are likely to be the ones we could not destroy. With that in mind, is such a first strike worth the risk? Probably not. Given the tension of the situation and the opaqueness of the North Korean regime, it is likely that the a US 'bloody nose' attack could be perceived as the beginning of an offensive against the North Korean regime, leading to catastrophic retaliation.

Instead of 'bloody nose' strikes, the articles by academic experts and policy analysts cited here all advocate similar strategies: strengthened alliances with current allies in the area, de-escalation and a long-term approach to controlling and combatting the Kim regime.

US alliances in the region are extremely important to furthering the American interests of containing the North Korean regime and leading it back from its aggressive stance. This point is argued most explicitly in academic articles, but Gregory Keeley also hints at the importance of 'US allies support[ing]' American initiatives, in his case, a naval blockade. More importantly, the strengthening of alliances would project to North Korea that major players in the region – South Korea and Japan – would be 'in lockstep' with American goals and would present a unified front (Pak 2018). These strengthened alliances could also send a message of support to our allies, easing fears that they must increase their own military capacities or acquire nuclear weapons. By keeping Japan and South Korea under the US 'nuclear umbrella', we reduce incentives for those nations to pursue nuclear weapons themselves (Sagan 2017: 82).

Also important is understanding that a new approach to North Korea might be necessary. As some experts have pointed out, the rise of China has given North Korea a more powerful ally in East Asia to balance against US interests. American policies and practices will have to adapt to this new balance of power in the near future. This will not defuse a national security threat that has existed for over half a century. Instead, a more nuanced approach is more likely to succeed, and it will take time. The 'mutual hostility and alienation will take decades to solve' (Delury 2018: 26). This might require US military leaders to 'pour cold water on the idea of a US first strike' through public discussions that are straightforward and honest about the costs of a war with North Korea (Sagan 2017: 77).

This could take many forms and reach many outlets and facets of society in America. Military leaders should be honest about the 'catastrophic' consequences of a war with North Korea. Up to one million people could die *in one day* of all-out conflict with North Korea, if a combination of conventional, biological and nuclear weapons are launched (*Ibid.*: 79, 80). Military leaders could make it publicly known that a long-term war would end in victory for the United States, but this rhetoric should not be overblown and turned into jingoism. Instead of echoing statements from Donald Trump about 'fire and fury' or 'falling in love' with Kim Jong-Un, American leaders would be well-served to tell the truth: 'it would be a disaster' if the United States and North Korea went to war (*Ibid.*: 67). This sort of rational, calculated thinking – rather than fire and fury sensationalism or apologism – is all too often lacking in the social and popular media.

American perspectives in conclusion

To understand the American stance on North Korea and where it might head, it is essential to appreciate that multiple voices are involved in the debate. Policy analyses from experts and scholars are important, but they constitute only one of these voices, and sometimes not even the most crucial one when it comes to decisions made by US leaders. The Brookings Institution reports that its most-read article in 2017 had 560,000 unique page views (Broadie 2017: 48). Likewise, *Foreign Affairs* magazine reportedly has around 200,000 subscribers (Grinapol 2017). Readership for *Foreign Policy* magazine is not readily available, but we can assume it is similar to that of *Foreign Affairs*. Combined, all three of these outlets may have a readership of about one million. This is assuming that every subscriber reads every edition of *Foreign Policy* and *Foreign Affairs*. In contrast, Donald Trump has 48 million Twitter followers. *Fox News, CNN* and other popular media outlets have millions of viewers, and Keeley's article alone attracted over one thousand comments. Compared to popular media and the president of the United States, scholarly articles – even those published in popular academic settings – attract much smaller numbers of views.

The Victor Cha incident serves as one example of how this plays out when it comes to American demonization of North Korea. While Cha's thoughtful analysis in the *Washington Post* was consistent with what many scholars of North Korea say, instead of being lauded for his ability to bring nuanced and complex policy to the forefront of the popular debate about North Korea, he was essentially

> Academics write for forums where their opinions will be read and critiqued closely and thoughtfully, but without full exposure in the popular media, which seeks out attention-grabbing headlines and positions. Instead of nuance, the American people are left with diatribes ...

fired from a position for which he was extremely well qualified. The upshot is that academics' voices tend to remain within the academic sphere. Academics write for forums where their opinions will be read and critiqued closely and thoughtfully, but without full exposure in the popular media, which seeks out attention-grabbing headlines and positions. Instead of nuance, the American people are left with diatribes about a 'feckless UN', with people asking if we can take Kim Jong-Un out?' (Keeley 2017). The American people are left with the president hurling insults, and his supporters urging him to 'clean up' the mess he inherited from past administrations.

By the middle of 2020, US–DPRK relations have fallen from the forefront of many Americans' minds as news of COVID-19, an extended trade war with China and the 2020 election consumed news cycles. However, North Korea's missile tests continued, and US–DPRK relations are likely to return to the headlines one day. There are many perspectives in American discourse about North Korea. Some are apologist, some are moderate, and some are jingoist and interventionist. The latter perspective demonizes North Korea by portraying Kim Jong-Un as a madman and moving the United States ever closer to a war that nobody wants. They are also the perspectives that receive the most media coverage, the most retweets, the most 'likes' on Facebook.

In order to understand the role of domestic political forces on decisions about foreign affairs, including the use of military force, it is important to appreciate the voices that compete for space in the broad media context in today's world. This media context has evolved rapidly over the past decades with the rise of the internet, and it is transforming political discourse in ways no one had anticipated. Among other things, this means that it is important not to pick out only one media source, be it the *Washington Post* or Twitter, as indicating the mood in America or the White House. As we have noted, the media in today's world range from nuanced, rational analysis to simple jingoist calls to war. No one should doubt the power of voices calling for the latter or how easily conspiratorial views can go viral in this new media context, but we should not be overly pessimistic that they are the *only* voice at work. This calls for an appreciation of how forces of demonization can operate within as well as between countries, when it comes to North Korea.

James V. Wertsch and Jacob Finke

Sources of particular relevance

'@BillClinton Gave Nukes to #NorthKorea, @BarackObama Gave Nukes to #Iran @HillaryClinton Gave Uranium to Russia Now They Want Me to Believe Trump Is Dangerous? @realDonaldTrump Inherited This Mess & Now He's Cleaning It up While They Lie about Him #MAGApic.Twitter.Com/HraANnUUG7'. *@jcpenni7maga*, 5 Feb. 2018, https://twitter.com/jcpenni7maga/media.

Broadie, Valerie T. (2017) *Brookings: 2017 Annual Report.* Annual Report, The Brookings Institution: https://www.brookings.edu/wp-content/uploads/2017/12/2017-annual-report.pdf.

Cha, Victor (2018) 'Victor Cha: Giving North Korea a 'Bloody Nose' Carries a Huge Risk to Americans', *The Washington Post,* online edition (30 Jan): https://www.washingtonpost.com/opinions/victor-cha-giving-north-korea-a-bloody-nose-carries-a-huge-risk-to-americans/2018/01/30/43981c94-05f7-11e8-8777-2a059f168dd2_story.html?utm_term=.edc17dd4fc6d.

Cooper, Helene et al. (2018) 'Military Quietly Prepares for a Last Resort: War with North Korea'. *The New York Times* (14 Jan.): https://www.nytimes.com/2018/01/14/us/politics/military-exercises-north-korea-pentagon.html.

Delury, John (2018) 'Normalize the Hermit Kingdom' *Foreign Policy* 227 (Jan.): 26–27.

DePetris, Daniel (2019) 'One Year After the Singapore Summit: Lessons Learned', *38 North* (13 June): https://www.38north.org/2019/06/ddepetris061319/.

———— (2019) 'When Partisanship Gets in the Way: Giving Negotiations a Chance', *38 North* (1 July): https://www.38north.org/2019/07/ddepetris070119/.

Dorman, Sam (2019) 'Kim Jong Un Is 'fascinated' by Trump, Views Him as Father Figure, New Book Claims'. *Fox News* (2 Nov.): https://www.foxnews.com/media/kim-jong-un-trump-doug-wead.

Godfrey, Elaine (2017) 'Trump's TV Obsession Is a First', *The Atlantic* (April): https://www.theatlantic.com/politics/archive/2017/04/donald-trump-americas-first-tv-president/521640/.

Grinapol, Corinne (2017) 'Foreign Affairs Magazine Passes the 200,000 Paid Circulation Mark', *Adweek* (23 Feb.): http://www.adweek.com/digital/foreign-affairs-magazine-passes-the-200000-paid-circulation-mark/.

Keeley, Gregory (2017) 'North Korea Sanctions Are Not Working - a Naval Blockade Might'. *Fox News* (31 Dec.): http://www.foxnews.com/opinion/2017/12/31/north-korea-sanctions-are-not-working-naval-blockade-might.html.

Labott, Elise (2018) 'Ambassador Candidate Victor Cha Dropped over Stark Warning on North Korea', *CNNPolitics* (30 Jan.): https://www.cnn.com/2018/01/30/politics/victor-cha-ambassador-to-south-korea/index.html.

Mitchell, Amy and Jesse Holcomb (2016) *State of the News Media 2016*. Annual Report, Pew Research Center, 15 June): http://assets.pewresearch.org/wp-content/uploads/sites/13/2016/06/30143308/state-of-the-news-media-report-2016-final.pdf.

Pak, Jung (2018) 'The Education of Kim Jong-Un', *The Brookings Institution* (6 Feb.): https://www.brookings.edu/essay/the-education-of-kim-jong-un/.

Rodrigo, Chris Mills (2018) 'Trump: Kim Jong Un and I "Fell in Love"', *The Hill* (29 Sept.): https://thehill.com/blogs/ballot-box/409104-trump-kim-jong-un-and-i-fell-in-love.

Sagan, Scott (2017) 'The Korean Missile Crisis', *Foreign Affairs* 96(6) (Dec.): 72–82.

Trump, Donald J. (2017) 'Just Heard Foreign Minister of North Korea Speak at UN If He Echoes Thoughts of Little Rocket

Man, They Won't Be around Much Longer!' *@realDonald Trump* (24 Sept.): https://twitter.com/realDonaldTrump/status/911789314169823232?ref_src=twsrc per cent5Etfw&ref_url=https per cent3A per cent2F per cent2Fwww.huffington-post.com per cent2Fentry per cent2Fold-trump-twiiter-kim-jong-un_us_5a07a7efe4b01d21c83ee7c4.

VandeHei, Jim and Mike Allen (2017) 'Trump 101: What He Reads and Watches'. *Axios* (24 Jan.): https://www.axios.com/trump-101-what-he-reads-and-watches-1513300066-41aaed6d-20e3-4022-acaa-f0099058d9e3.html.

Southeast Asian Pragmatism

IT IS WELL KNOWN THAT NORTH KOREA is being punished by 'the international community' via the UN, for its testing of nuclear devices and missiles. In this chapter, Mobrand and Kim present a more nuanced picture, showing states beyond North Korea's traditional friends, in particular China, hold different views on this. The authors review relations between Southeast Asia and the Koreas, historically and from the current perspective. They find that the views promoted by the USA and supported by Western countries – that the North must be punished, which includes exclusion and isolation – have weak support in Southeast Asia. Apparently, only arm-twisting by Washington can make these countries compromise their common principle, which is: dialogue does not presuppose agreement. These countries are also less convinced that what are termed 'universal values' by the West are truly universal. They conclude by suggesting that the ways countries in this region deal with international affairs might well be effective in resolving disagreements and conflicts worldwide. An international order that fosters open dialogue and promotes interaction seems needed, globally. This chapter draws from and builds on the article, Erik Mobrand and Hyejin Kim, Southeast Asia's Roles in Inter-Korean Affairs, *East Asian Policy*, Vol. 11, No. 3 (July–Sept. 2019): 50–58.

About the Authors: Erik Mobrand teaches in the Graduate School of International Studies at Seoul National University. He is the author of *Top-Down Democracy in South Korea* (2019), as well as several articles on Korean and East Asian affairs.

Hyejin Kim teaches in Political Science and Global Studies at the National University of Singapore. She is the author of six books, including the fieldwork-based novel, *Jia: A Novel of North Korea* (2007).

CHAPTER TWELVE

Beyond Binaries: Southeast Asian Relations with North Korea

Introduction

*I*n English-language news reports, North Korea is often presented as exceptional and as a 'pariah.' Washington has tended to promote such a view, as have conservative administrations in Seoul. However, in Southeast Asia, the depiction of North Korea as exceptional is far less common. Southeast Asia largely rejects a dichotomous view of international politics. As a region seeking to navigate between competing larger powers, its governments have long espoused an openness to dialogue without judgment. This openness extends to North Korea. Southeast Asia thus offers an example of engagement with North Korea, an engagement that comes without 'demonizing' the country. There is a material basis to this neutrality on Korean affairs. To many in Southeast Asia, North Korea is a regional neighbour, a trading partner, a source of opportunities, a source of danger to be watched, or possibly an old friend. The region's approach holds potential for efforts to help improve inter-Korean relations and North Korea's international standing. In this chapter, we point to the ways this region has approached North Korea as a 'normal' country.

The development of relationships between Southeast Asia and Korea

Although the Korean peninsula's external ties to its immediate neighbours and to the United States overshadow any other foreign relations, its connections to Southeast Asia are not insignificant. For North Korea, three of its top ten trading partners are in the region. One-fifth of the foreign embassies in Pyongyang are Southeast Asian missions. South Korea's economic and aid relations with the region have expanded greatly and the Moon administration has proposed a renewal of links with Southeast Asia: in November 2017, the South Korean government announced a 'New Southern Policy' aimed at strengthening ties and economic cooperation in the region. Moon called for the Association of South-East Asian Nations (ASEAN) to receive the same treatment as the four major powers most relevant to South Korea – the United States, China, Japan, and Russia. This move points to the region's significance for the two Koreas.

Southeast Asian neutrality on Korean peninsula issues is grounded in history. Most countries in the region have maintained continuous diplomatic relations with North Korea since the 1960s or 1970s, that is, relations were established at the height of the Cold War. While South Korea had relations with much of the region in this period, ties with the socialist bloc of Vietnam, Cambodia, and Laos were not established until the 1990s.[1] The socialist countries have their own particular historic ties with Pyongyang. Many other Southeast Asian nations were part of the non-aligned movement, which was touched off with the conference in Bandung, Indonesia in 1955. In keeping with the mission of that movement, Southeast Asian governments sought to maintain a position between the Soviet and American spheres of influence. On the Korean peninsula, this approach meant recognizing both North Korea (DPRK) and the Republic of Korea (ROK).

This history set the basis for today's diplomatic relationships. All ten ASEAN member countries now have diplomatic relations with both North Korea and South Korea. There are DPRK

---

1. South Korea did have relations with South Vietnam and, briefly, with Laos in 1974–75. Seoul's relations with this sub-region were established or re-established in 1992 (Vietnam), 1995 (Laos), and 1997 (Cambodia).

embassies in Cambodia, Indonesia, Laos, Malaysia, Myanmar, Singapore, Thailand and Vietnam. Only Brunei and the Philippines do not host DPRK missions. Five countries maintain embassies in Pyongyang: Cambodia, Indonesia, Laos, Malaysia (closed from 2017) and Vietnam. Southeast Asian representation in Pyongyang is significant when compared with other regions. In Europe, large countries such as France do not recognize the DPRK. Further, many European states have a single ambassador for the Korean peninsula; that person tends to stay in Seoul. Southeast Asian foreign ministries have thus become valuable zones where the paths of North and South Korean representatives can intersect.

> Southeast Asian foreign ministries have … become valuable zones where the paths of North and South Korean representatives can intersect.

South Korean ties with Southeast Asia have expanded rapidly in the past two decades. These ties have numerous dimensions, from development assistance and foreign direct investment to tourism, labour migration and popular culture. South Korea has emerged as a major economic player in the region. Besides tens of billions of US dollars in annual trade, the ROK has some USD 5 billion in foreign direct investment in the region. Indonesia, Vietnam and Cambodia are the biggest targets of South Korean investment in Southeast Asia. Overseas development assistance has also put the region into focus. In recent years, the Korea International Cooperation Agency (KOICA) has directed USD 400–500 million in annual development assistance to the region, with Vietnam as the largest single recipient. Seoul's economic influence appears to give the government advantage in its diplomatic relations with regional states. The conservative ROK administrations of Lee Myung Bak and Park Geun Hye, aware of Southeast Asian dependence on economic ties with South Korea, pushed governments to take a tough stance on Pyongyang in international organizations, such as in condemning missile tests or supporting sanctions.

In Southeast Asia, several linkages make North Korea familiar to ordinary people. One example is the chain of 'Pyongyang restaurants.' Several major cities in Southeast Asia, as well as in China, host a branch of this government-operated chain. North Koreans serve the food and the servers also put on musical performances. Such displays make this North Korean institution a familiar sight in cities such as Jakarta, Bangkok, Kuala Lumpur, Ho Chi Minh City, Phnom Penh and Siem Reap. While this venture attracts criticism as a method of foreign currency accumulation by the regime and for the strict rules presumably placed on staff, it also gives Southeast Asians greater exposure to North Korea. Perhaps just as important, South Korean tourists are among the most numerous patrons. They watch the performances, take photographs and chat with the women who work there. In a third country, South Koreans can interact – even if superficially – with North Koreans. Performances often include renditions of the well-known Korean folk song *Arirang*, and South Korean visitors often join in with the North Korean staff. Given that many South Koreans grew up thinking about North Korea as an abstract, distant idea, meeting points such as these afford opportunities to see and speak with North Koreans in person.

The role of ASEAN

As a regional organization, ASEAN has characteristics that make it useful for engaging North Korea. ASEAN adheres strictly to the principle of non-interference. The body is quite sensitive to ensure that decisions do not infringe on the sovereignty of its members. The 'ASEAN way' allows for cordial meetings, but it also makes solving collective problems difficult. States are reluctant to criticize each other, and the body is unable to make effective decisions on problems such as refugees. While ASEAN efforts to coordinate the actions of member states may have limits, the body's unwillingness to pass judgment on particular countries turns into a refusal to 'demonize' North

Korea. For this reason, the organization can assume neutrality on Korean peninsula issues.

ASEAN neutrality on inter-Korean affairs is on display at annual ASEAN Regional Forum (ARF) meetings. Both North and South Korea are invited. North Korea was first invited in 2000, immediately after the historic summit between then-president of South Korea Kim Dae Jung and North Korean leader Kim Jong Il. Representatives of both states have opportunities to give speeches. Since these speeches do not entail commitments from ASEAN, the body is willing to hear any invited party speak. This attitude makes the event an inclusive one in which North Korea is an ordinary member. Representatives of the DPRK, for their part, are pleased to have a public platform for stating their views. This form of engagement reflects ARF's goals, which are 'to foster constructive dialogue and consultation on political and security issues' and 'to make significant contributions to efforts towards confidence-building and preventive diplomacy in the Asia-Pacific region.' While the meetings do not directly resolve tensions, they allow North Korea to be heard and to engage the international community.

The ARF is also important as the only major annual meeting where representatives from both North Korea and the United States are regularly present. It affords an opportunity to hold talks without extensive planning. Former US Secretary of State Colin Powell seized this opportunity in 2002, when he held a discussion with North Korean foreign minister Paek Nam-sun. In most years, though, the opportunity has been left unavailed. In 2017, in light of Pyongyang's missile and nuclear bomb tests, Washington sought to suspend North Korea from the ARF. ASEAN opposed the move, since the body's aim is to foster dialogue that might help manage conflicts. This episode highlights the contrast between the ASEAN view and the perspective is regularly displayed by the United States. While Washington warns that discussion with North Korea is tantamount to friendship or capitulation, ASEAN treats dialogue as unrelated to friendship because the very purpose of admitting North Korea to the ARF was to foster dialogue and promote interaction, rather than encourage isolation; expelling the country would go against ASEAN's basic approach to addressing international problems in the region.

Bilateral relationships with North Korea

Media reports on bilateral relations between North Korea and several Southeast Asian countries routinely note the 'special' nature of those relations. On closer inspection, very little that is 'special' can be seen in these sets of ties; rather, North Korea maintains ordinary relations with most Southeast Asian countries. In a few cases, former leaders maintained good personal ties, but for the most part the relationships appear 'normal.' A discussion of a set of these relationships establish this point.

Kim Il Sung, the first supreme leader of North Korea, and Indonesian president Sukarno formed a relationship in the 1960s. Relations between the two countries continued, despite periods of tumult in each place. Indonesia's president Megawati, and also Sukarno's daughter, visited Pyongyang in 2002 and there have since been further high-level exchanges. As some observers have pointed out, it can seem inconsistent that Southeast Asia's largest democracy insists on maintaining a relationship with a state that departs so greatly from democratic values. Indonesia does not promote a Manichean view of the world, even while espousing democratic values and urging democracy in its home region. As a result of this relationship, Indonesia provides North Korean an opening through which to engage the international community. Such openings are crucial for enmeshing North Korea in positive international networks and for reinforcing any moves to reform. For example, in 2013, in response to an announcement that new special economic zones were to be created, Indonesia's foreign minister made a trip to Pyongyang to seek business opportunities. Such moves send a signal to the DPRK leadership about the benefits of opening.

North Korea and Singapore cooperate in a range of areas. Travel between the two countries is relatively easy: Singaporean tourists visit North Korea and North Koreans could enter Singapore without a visa until 2016. Also, Singapore (along with Thailand) is consistently among the DPRK's top ten trading partners. Singapore has several areas of business cooperation. Singaporean firms run shopping and fast food outlets in Pyongyang. The city-state also hosts North Korean ventures. One such venture came to light in 2013, when a North Korean ship carrying missiles was found in Cuba. That ship belonged to a firm called Chinpo Shipping, which was based in Singapore. Singapore authorities penalized Chinpo for the incident. Singapore is also the home of a non-governmental organization focused on North Korea: the Choson Exchange offers business training to North Korean officials through courses run in both North Korea and Singapore. This program exposes North Koreans to new ways of operating. An initiative such as Choson Exchange can help make the most of reform moments. In 2017 however, in response to missile and nuclear tests, as well as United Nations sanctions, Singapore suspended business relations with North Korea.

The Singapore government prides itself on its pragmatism. While this position may sound like an excuse for refusing to commit to any ideals, it is also critical of discourses that place political systems in 'normal' and 'abnormal' categories. Former Prime Minister Lee Kuan Yew was directly critical of claims that certain modes of politics were normal and should be universal aspirations. It was in the context of this criticism that, in the mid-1990s, discussion of 'Asian values' emerged. While such language may aim to defend illiberal politics, it also means that 'democracy' and 'human rights' cannot be used as excuses for intervening in other countries' politics or economies. Singapore does not promote a vision of the world.

It does not belong to the OECD and it does not even have an aid agency. Instead, Singapore is direct about its interests. Insofar as North Korea represents an opportunity, then there is reason to engage the country. This is a self-serving attitude, but it is also one that eschews the demonizing frame.

Relations between Cambodia and North Korea were strengthened by a personal friendship between Kim Il Sung and King Sihanouk. The pair had met in the 1960s at a non-aligned countries' meeting. In the 1970s, Sihanouk left the violence of Cambodia to stay with Kim Il Sung near Pyongyang; he resided there for two months a year until the early 1990s. He reportedly returned to his country with North Korean bodyguards. In 2015, a North Korea-funded museum, the Angkor Panorama Museum, opened near Angkor Wat. North Korean staff work at the museum. Cambodia has supported North Korea in certain situations. The country banned the Hollywood film *The Interview*, which spoofed the leadership in Pyongyang. North Korea, for its part, backed up the Cambodian leadership against UN charges of human rights violations. A recipient of aid and investment from South Korea, Cambodia works with both Korean governments. The country needs Seoul's financial support, but it also attempts to retain neutrality – a principle that is enshrined in the constitution.

Vietnam has a rather more complex relationship with the Korean peninsula than other Southeast Asian nations. South Korea participated alongside the United States in the Vietnam War, and the number of its troops there was second only to the Americans. Further, South Korean soldiers were known for their cruelty in the war. War memories have raised challenges to building ties between South Korea and Vietnam. Diplomatic relations were established in 1992 and South Korea has gone on to invest heavily in the country.

Meanwhile, North Korea and Vietnam share revolutionary histories. The DPRK was the third country to recognize North

Vietnam, after China and the Soviet Union. Ho Chi Minh visited Pyongyang in 1957. However, when conflict between China and Vietnam emerged in the late 1970s, Vietnam shifted closer to the USSR while Pyongyang remained allied to Beijing. Thus, despite a shared socialist background, the countries were not the closest of comrades.

North Korea and Vietnam have areas of muted cooperation. The DPRK maintains six trading companies in Vietnam. Until recently, four Pyongyang restaurants and one health products store operated; the number of restaurants has now dropped to two. Tension on the Korean peninsula also puts stress on relations with Hanoi. Vietnam states that it supports stability on the peninsula and does not approve of North Korea's weapons development. On the other hand, on Vietnam has occasionally supported the country when the international community has not. In late 2017, for example, the North Korean national football team was denied visas to Australia, where matches were scheduled to be played, because of the United Nations embargo. Vietnam agreed to host the matches.

Malaysia and North Korea have maintained relations since 1973. Several different types of ties have developed between the countries. East Malaysia took in labourers from North Korea, who earned cash for the nation. The North Korean airline, Air Koryo, operated flights from Kuala Lumpur. Kim Jong Un, the Supreme Leader of North Korea since 2011, was given an honorary doctorate from Malaysia's Help University. However, the killing of Kim Jong Il's son – and Kim Jong Un's half-brother – Kim Jong Nam at Kuala Lumpur airport in 2017 caused relations to sour. The two countries took turns expelling nationals of the other country. Time will be needed for bilateral relations to recover from the assassination episode.

Each of these relationships has been called 'special' in news reports on the DPRK's dealings with Southeast Asia. If all of these relationships are 'special,' then it is difficult to grasp what a relationship that is not special would be. No country in the region is an especially close ally of North Korea. Southeast Asian governments take the view that diplomacy entails speaking with everyone, not just friends. Dialogue does not presuppose agreement. Long wedged between great powers, Southeast Asian countries know that it is necessary to talk with all parties. These relationships are simply 'normal' country-to-country relationships. It is the way North Korea is often interpreted that leads to labelling the relationships as special. The demonizing frame casts any normal relationship with Pyongyang as abnormal, and therefore stories of special relationships with Southeast Asian nations abound.

Grounds for hope

A sceptic might suggest that ties between Southeast Asia and North Korea are little more than artifacts of friendliness among authoritarian regimes. The region is home to undemocratic governments and several regimes have recently seen their democratic processes and protections decline. The military in Thailand has curtailed freedoms in order to remain in control under a civilian regime, the government in Cambodia has sidelined the opposition, and there are massive questions about the rule of law in the Philippines. ASEAN, too, does not espouse universal values in the way the European Union does, and the body can be charged with doing little to deal effectively with regional problems such as refugee flows, territorial disputes and transnational pollution. Yet it would be incorrect to understand Southeast Asian views of North Korea as merely the reflection of a willingness to overlook the abuses of a fellow dictatorial regime. The region avoids moralizing, which is precisely the sort of attitude that makes many other governments, as well as the media, unwilling to actually engage the country. Southeast Asia provides North Korea with an approach to the international community. It is also worth stressing that working relations with North Korea are established not just in those countries that are skeptical – or outright critical – of liberal democracy. Indonesia's continuing relationship with the DPRK demonstrates this point.

Multiple pillars anchor Southeast Asian engagement with North Korea. One is the long-standing commitment to the non-aligned movement. This commitment is a core feature of Southeast Asia's relationship with the global political order. A history of resisting assimilation into Cold War binaries, exemplified best by Indonesia, created an openness to dialogue. This spirit held that dialogue without judgment is a key component of international relations. Countries in this movement actively sought to avoid the black-and-white views of international relations that were generated by the Cold War and by later 'axis-of-evil' style categories. North Korea's involvement in the non-aligned movement also created opportunities for relations with the country to begin early and on a positive note. A second pillar is the enduring set of links with the region's reforming socialist states. While North Korea cannot be called a close ally of Vietnam, their ideological commitments have provided reason for continued cooperation and exchange. A third pillar is the more pragmatic attitude of regimes like those in Malaysia and Singapore, which are critical of liberal democracy. While these regimes are organized very differently from the DPRK, they share a rejection of external criticism of internal affairs. As we have emphasized, none of these pillars suggests that governments in Southeast Asia condone the way North Korea is ruled nor support the country's weapons-development programs. Rather, these countries are willing to interact and talk with the North Korean regime instead of chastise and isolate it. Such a position does not imply 'special relationships' but simply an embrace of diplomacy in a world that is more complicated than the dichotomy between friends and enemies.

ASEAN might be viewed as a zone where North and South Korean representatives can meet, and inter-Korean relations can be improved. The region's ties with both governments and the non-judgmental approach to external relationships provide opportunities for the DPRK and the ROK to intensify positive interactions and have quiet discussions about the future. Discussions in Southeast Asia takes place away from the influence of the United States or the other major powers. This feature can allow dialogues to be more independent. The administration in Seoul could consider understanding part of the value of Southeast Asia is its potential role in forging co-operation with Pyongyang. President Moon's 'New Southern Policy' could include inter-Korean relations as part of the agenda. Creative initiatives located in Southeast Asian spaces could attempt to foster collaboration in education, training, research and business, among other fields. If the two Korean governments make the most of the opportunities afforded by this region, which is both neutral and tied to the two sides of the peninsula, then the benefits for inter-Korean relations could be great.

From North Korea to China?

North Korea is not, of course, the only country that is demonized. As tension between the United States and China increases, the possibility of applying a similar frame to China emerges as well. Might demonization shift from North Korea to China? China differs in many ways from North Korea, which has been picked out as a pariah in part because it is not fully incorporated into the global capitalist system. China, though, is indisputably integrated into that system, so that basis for demonizing is largely absent. Subsequent chapters develop further ideas about this possibility. A comment is deserved here on where Southeast Asia might be positioned if China were so treated.

Unlike North Korea, the People's Republic of China (PRC) wields tremendous influence in parts of Southeast Asia. The PRC is a source of huge investment and loans in Southeast

Asia. Some of these have gained attention as parts of the Belt and Road (*yi dai yi lu*) initiative. Others are separate from that. Chinese firms have large infrastructure and housing development projects in Malaysia. Investments in Cambodia, Myanmar and Laos are also big. Numerous Chinese firms have moved into the areas immediately bordering China. A railway, built with Chinese money, was to cut through Thailand and all of Malaysia. China also plays host to negotiations between the Myanmar government and rebel groups.

The flow of resources has effects on diplomatic ties. Cambodia regularly supports Beijing. Even the Philippines, a staunch American ally, has under Duterte shifted away from the United States toward China. Laos and Myanmar are also wary of confronting China. Singapore has long positioned itself between major powers, but finds it increasingly difficult to play Beijing and Washington off one another.

Due to China's power and proximity, Southeast Asia – China relationships are quite different from those between Southeast Asia and North Korea. While ASEAN can be more or less united on the point of encouraging dialogue with North Korea, the PRC divides the regional organization. China has ongoing territorial disputes in the South China Sea with Southeast Asian countries. Vietnam and the Philippines oppose China's claims, but ASEAN members who are not directly affected by the disputes have little reason to support their Southeast Asian neighbours. ASEAN does not speak with a single voice on such issues.

For all of these reasons, it cannot be assumed that Southeast Asia's neutrality on North Korea would apply to China. North Korea is distant enough not to be caught up in problems with Southeast Asian countries, and it holds little power in the region. Those factors condition the role that the region can play in North Korea's external engagement.

Erik Mobrand and Hyejin Kim

Europe–China, partners–enemies?

IN THE FOLLOWING CHAPTER, Chunrong Liu takes a look at how his own country has been portrayed recently by the European mass media and, increasingly, also by the research community. It seems clear that one difficulty for observers of China is to locate the newly arrived great power on the global scene. Another is that this power is governed by a political system not readily accepted by the West. And last, but certainly not least, that the political culture of that power in many ways seems difficult to comprehend, without opening up for the possibility that other, non-Western ways of organizing societies might have 'local' legitimacy. The author surveys China–Europe relations, and looks into one particular Chinese infrastructure project, the so-called Belt and Road Initiative (BRI), to see how European nations and Europe as such has received this colossal project. Two perspectives are prevalent: the project exemplifies how increasingly China is seen to constitute a geopolitical threat; and the other focus lies on the impossibility of the project. This obviously differs from how China depicts its international engagements. In his discussion of Chinese–European relations, Liu suggests that both parties have work to do in the sphere of cross-cultural relations in order to attain a better mutual normative resonance.

About the Author: Dr Chunrong Liu is associate professor at the School of International Relations and Public Affairs, Fudan University. He is co-director of the Fudan–European Centre for China Studies at the University of Copenhagen and a researcher at the Nordic Institute for Asian Studies. His research interests are in the areas of political sociology and comparative political studies. Dr Liu has published widely on China's state–society relations and he is currently working on a project about Sino–Nordic cooperation.

CHAPTER THIRTEEN

A Systemic Rival on the Doorstep? The Politics of Politicizing Chinese Regional Influence in Europe

Introduction

*W*hile the emotional cocktail of fear, hatred and compassion is an enduring element in political life, the vilification of others (either a political leader or a political system) has appeared to be a rather pronounced cognitive framework in some media and policy narratives. As implied elsewhere in this book, such a demonization exercise takes various forms and tends to be reinforced in a confrontational political climate. Its manifestations can be easily felt: image distortion, perception gap, blame game, etc. In one way or another, demonization handicaps constructive dialogue and trust-building. More often than not, it leads to a process of normative exclusion and a growing readiness to engage in escalating conflict.

Reading the dynamics of Chinese politics as well as China–EU engagement over the last few years, one can be easily impressed by the contestation of China's presence in Europe both in media discourse and within the research community. Increasingly, Chinese investments and acquisitions in the framework of the Belt and Road Initiative (BRI) are perceived as threatening the competitiveness, strength and unity of

Europe. China's cultural engagement and image promotion programmes, which present the country as an alternative to the Western democratic model, often tend to be identified as a kind of information warfare, a form of 'charm offensive' or 'sharp power'.[1]

In particular, with China's growing presence in Europe's periphery zones through sub-regional initiatives such as the China–CEEC (Central and Eastern European Countries) cooperation, media and scholarly communities are now canvassing and crystalizing a 'divide and rule' discourse on China. While this cooperation plan has nurtured a flourishing interconnectivity and generated new sources of growth in the region, China is seen as a geopolitical player exploiting Europe's 'soft underbelly' to create new fault lines within the EU. As one commentator warned: 'There is an attempt by China to divide the EU at various levels'; as a result, 'a large number of smaller countries will take a separate approach from the rest of Europe when dealing with China.'[2]

This article looks into the politically volatile divide-and-rule discourse produced by European stakeholders – a phenomenon of perception gap that sometimes features a quality of demonization or what we call 'normative differentiation'. Our assumption is that a strategic frame is maintained and reproduced through interplay of actors attached in different institutions and norms. Framing is a deliberate process that

1. Christopher Walker and Jessica Ludwig, 'The Meaning of Sharp Power: How Authoritarian States Project Influence', *Foreign Affairs* (16 November 2017): https://www.foreignaffairs.com/articles/china/2017-11-16/meaning-sharp-power; see also: 'Sunlight v subversion: What to do about China's "sharp power"', *The Economist* (14 December 2017).

2. Andrew Browne, 'China's Offensive in Europe: Is There a Master Plan in Beijing?' *The Wall Street Journal* (22 June 2016): https://blogs.wsj.com/chinarealtime/2016/06/22/chinas-offensive-in-europe-is-there-a-master-plan-in-beijing/.

comes as a result of the media and policy actor's *identity crisis*; the way the EU actors view and make sense of Chinese footprints in geopolitical terms hence can be viewed as a struggle to reclaim European normative influence.

An Imperfect Strategic Partnership

Since the establishment of diplomatic relations in 1975, China and the EU have been going through a bumpy process of mutual adaptation. Over time, a fruitful network of dialogues has been developed in the framework of strategic partnership, which was formally established in 2003. China is now the EU's second-biggest trading partner behind the United States, and the EU is China's biggest trading partner. Both sides have attempted to promote effective multilateralism and worked together through mechanisms including the G20 and World Trade Organization to address financial and economic challenges. They have actively supported the 2030 Agenda for Sustainable Development and have played a leading role in international development cooperation and coordinated actions for climate change, energy and resource efficiency.

The much-celebrated strategic partnership is not without problems, ranging from textile disputes and an arms embargo to the refusal of the EU to give Market Economy Status (MES) to the PRC. Compounding these issues is China's presence in Europe through regionalized interconnectivity initiatives. In 2012, the '16+1' mechanism between China and CEEC was established, and China announced a policy package with 12 measures for promoting friendly cooperation with CEEC. This includes a USD 10 billion special line of credit for projects on the development of infrastructure, high-tech industry and the green economy. The '16+1' constitutes a cluster of bilateral and multilateral initiatives concentrated in trade, investment and transportation networks, and is an important building block of China's Belt and Road Initiative (BRI). Of the 16 CEEC members, 11 are EU member states, four are EU candidate countries, and one is a potential candidate state. Clearly, the 16+1 mechanism involves a quite hybrid group of countries, and the cooperation it generates and facilitates appears to be driven by this diversity.

In Europe's southern belt, where the sovereign debt crisis erupted in 2009, China has become more visible by actively purchasing public debts and exploring industrial capacity cooperation between the CEEC and the other parts of the Mediterranean states. In December 2014, China and four Mediterranean countries (Hungary, Serbia, Macedonia and Greece) decided to build the 'China–Europe Continental and Ocean Expressway'. In April 2016, China Ocean Shipping Company (COSCO) acquired a controlling stake in the Greek port of Piraeus, which was widely viewed as an important piece in the complex BRI jigsaw. In April 2019, Greece formally joined China–CEEC cooperation and the '16+1' became '17+1', signifying China's extended commitment to connectivity in this regional context.

China sees these regions primarily as gateways into the more developed European market, and frames its regional activism as a balanced engagement with the EU. As explained by China's Premier Li Keqiang in his speech at the Riga Summit in 2016, the '16+1' Cooperation should be positioned as a functional ingredient of China–EU partnerships, and it will contribute to a more dynamical development across Europe and European integration.[3] This was also emphasized by President Xi Jinping in his visit to Finland in April 2017. Addressing the importance and potential of China–Nordic

---

3. SC-PRC (State Council of People's Republic of China). 2016. Speech by H.E. Premier Li Keqiang At the Fifth Summit of China and Central and Eastern European Countries, Riga, 5 November 2016: http://english. gov.cn/premier/speeches/2016/11/06/content_281475484622881. htm.

cooperation, he suggested that 'sub-regional cooperation is a useful complement to China–Europe relations.'[4]

Indeed, China's regional interconnectivity has been fruitfully practised in its cooperation with ASEAN, with the flagship scheme of The Greater Mekong Sub-Region Economic Cooperation Program (GMS-ECP). It has also been promoted as a viable platform to cooperate with other regional bodies including the African Union and the Community of Latin American and Caribbean States. Multilateral cooperation, which provides an inclusive pragmatic platform for multiple actors, has been driven by many bottom-up initiatives.[5] Moreover, it has been framed as a tool for building a 'community of common destiny' by upholding China's norm of international relations, namely the Five Principles of Peaceful Coexistence: mutual respect for sovereignty and territorial integrity, mutual non-aggression, non-interference in each other's internal affairs, equality and mutual benefit, and peaceful coexistence.[6]

> **For many Western observers and stakeholders, ... it is tempting to investigate the 'political risks' associated with China's trade and connectivity plans.**

For many Western observers and stakeholders, however, it is tempting to investigate the 'political risks' associated with China's trade and connectivity plans. Accordingly, China's BRI is identified either as an over-ambitious endeavour doomed to failure or a master plan to gain geopolitical leverage. As a German analyst claimed, the BRI will not only cause 'a huge financial burden' for many Asian countries; it will also 'trigger

---

4. Jinping Xi, 'Our Enduring Friendship', *The Helsinki Times* (3 April 2017).

5. In the case of 17+1, the 'local leaders forum' offers such a consultation platform, thereby boosting interconnectivity in a decentralized manner.

6. These principles were first codified in 1954 and have been enunciated in many international treaties since then.

serious domestic and geopolitical conflicts'.[7] In the European context, China's regionalized infrastructure financing and investments are likely to weaken the EU's competitiveness and unity. It seems that China is practising a 'pick and choose' strategy, 'focusing on its direct interests, and often ignoring EU norms in its proposals', and China has 'seized the opportunity of the euro crisis for massive takeovers in southern Europe'.[8]

Moreover, as realist theories would predict, this kind of regional activism will enable China to boost its political influence and even encourage the spreading of illiberal norms in Europe. Increasingly, China is portrayed as an opportunistic geopolitical player in Europe: regional engagement may provide China with the strategic means to encourage or pressure its regional partners to act according to China's interests, thus weakening the EU's voice on human rights and other politically sensitive issues.

The Politics of Politicization

What, then, causes such a politicized discourse? China can easily be blamed for inducing such an image for many reasons, including the deficit of transparency regarding the role of the Chinese government behind private Chinese investors. Arguably, it also reflects a long-standing ideological bias – the default mode for some Western observers when it comes to the nature of the China model. This is well-illuminated in a recent think-tank report that explicitly defines the presence of China in Europe as 'authoritarian advance':

---

7. Shamil Shams, '"New Silk Road" and China's hegemonic ambitions', (15 May 2017): https://www.dw.com/en/new-silk-road-and-chinas-hegemonic-ambitions/a-38843212

8. François Godement and Abigaël Vasselier, 'China at the Gates: A New Power Audit of the EU-China Relations', European Council on Foreign Relations (December 2017), p. 1: http://www.ecfr.eu/page/-/China_Power_Audit.pdf.

China's political model is based on an authoritarian regime intent on strengthening a deeply illiberal surveillance state at home while also exporting – or at least trying to popularize – its political and economic development model abroad ... China's rapidly increasing political influencing efforts in Europe and the self-confident promotion of its authoritarian ideals pose a significant challenge to liberal democracy as well as Europe's values and interests.[9]

This augmentation seems to be powered by a moral attachment to a liberal-capitalist order. More than an economic giant, the EU is an exceptional global actor. Unlike other powers, the EU's foreign relations are ordered by a set of exceptional values, including 'core norms' – peace, liberty, democracy, rule of law and human rights – and four 'minor norms': social solidarity, anti-discrimination, sustainable development and good governance.[10] These norms are well articulated in the EU's new Global Strategy on Foreign and Security Policy (EUGS), entitled 'Shared Vision, Common Action: A Stronger Europe', which was presented to the European Council on 28 June 2016. In her foreword to EUGS, Federica Mogherini, the Vice President of the European Council, justifies a stronger and unified EU to 'promote the common interests of our citizens, as well as our principles and values.'[11]

For some years now, however, the EU moral stance has been facing a number of serious challenges: the financial and

9. Thorsten Benner et al., 'Authoritarian advance: responding to China's growing political influence in Europe', Global Public Policy Institute and the Mercator Institute for China Studies, 2018: https://www.merics.org/sites/default/files/2018-02/GPPi_MERICS_Authoritarian_Advance_2018_1.pdf.

10. Ian Manners, 'Normative Power Europe: A Contradiction in Terms?' *Journal of Common Market Studies* 40(2), pp. 235–258.

11. EEAS (European External Action Service), *Shared Vision, Common Action: A Stronger Europe. A Global Strategy for the European Union's Foreign and Security Policy*, (28 June 2016): https://europa.eu/global-strategy/sites/globalstrategy/files/eugs_review_web.

debt crisis, refugee crisis and the accompanying resurgence of nationalism. From Hungary to Italy, Austria, France and the Netherlands, there has been a significant revival of populism as well as economic and cultural protectionism.[12] Apparently, an identity crisis has occurred in the continent and would undermine the EU as the modern world's greatest 'convergence machine'.[13]

Entangled in such an identity crisis, it would be tempting for some European political actors to portray the actions of China and many other issues as a common challenge to its internal solidarity and cohesion. In a speech in Paris in August 2017, German Foreign Minister Sigmar Gabriel warned against Beijing's attempt to 'divide Europe, declaring that 'If we do not succeed in developing a single strategy towards China, then China will succeed in dividing Europe', and that 'setting up parallel networks such as China and Eastern Europe or China and Southern Europe are somewhat inconsistent with a commitment to a coherent and strong EU.'[14] In March 2019, the EU's released a new strategic outlook paper with revised assumptions about Sino-European relationships. While both sides will continue to share commitment and strengthen cooperation on many areas, China is now perceived by the EU as a 'systemic rival' promoting alternative models of governance. This leads the EU to call for 'a flexible and pragmatic whole-

---

12. Thierry Chopin, 'The Populist Moment: are we moving toward a post-liberal Europe?' *European Issues* no. 414, Robert Schuman Foundation (December 2016).

13. Ridao-Cano, C. and C. Bodewig, 'Growing United: Upgrading Europe's Convergence Machine', *World Bank Report on the European Union* (2018) Washington, DC.

14. Wendy Wu, 'Berlin Uneasy about Beijing's Growing Clout in Eastern, Southern Europe', *South China Morning Post* (18 February 2017): http://www.scmp.com/news/china/diplomacy-defence/article/2072046/berlin-uneasy-about-beijings-growing-clout-eastern.

of-EU approach enabling a principled defence of interests and values.'[15]

Every 'in-group' often needs an 'out-group' in order to be morally justified. The EU's hardening political stance on China as well as the framing of China's regional activism as an 'authoritarian advance' and a 'divide-and-rule' project, arguably reflect a dynamic of identity mobilization. China is therefore perceived as a 'systemic rival' much as the way immigration is securitized as an existential threat in Europe, which is largely 'motivated by the need for national governments to control influxes, placate media pressures and comfort public opinion against the fear of being swamped by foreigners'.[16]

Paradoxically, as often revealed in cases of group conflicts, internal cohesion may not increase as a result of external tension if the group lacks a strong and centralized leadership.[17] While China's pragmatic presence in Europe may entail urgency for internal coordination within the EU, the Union's capacity to do so is limited by an institutional configuration that already has been undermined by intra-competition, the rise of populist political parties as well as Eurosceptic sentiment. As a research report recognized, 'it is intra-European competition and lack of coordination over China that makes Europe vulnerable. In other words, China does not need to divide Europe because Europe is already divided.'[18]

---

15. See: https://ec.europa.eu/commission/sites/beta-political/files/communication-eu-china-a-strategic-outlook.pdf

16. Alessandra Buonfino, 'Between Unity and Plurality: the Politicization and Securitization of the Discourse of Immigration in Europe', *New Political Science*, 26:1 (2004), p. 24.

17. A. Arthur Stein, 'Conflict and Cohesion: A Review of the Literature', *Journal of Conflict Resolution* 20(1) (1976), pp. 143–172.

18. Mikko Houtari, et al. (eds), *Mapping Europe-China Relations: A Bottom-up Approach*, European Think-tank Network on China (ETNC) (October 2015).

In Search of a New Schemata

Political entities of all kinds struggle for mutual recognition. It would be naïve to deny that China has refrained from attempting ·to increase its visibility and attraction on the global stage. However, it would be equally misleading to assume China's economic and diplomatic activism in Europe's periphery zones is a subversive geopolitical game. For China, an integrated Europe and a strategic China–EU partnership serves its own domestic agenda of developing a more balanced, more sustainable quality of economic growth. Furthermore, the decentralized approach of cooperation in Europe exhibits what Brantly Womack called the 'logic of relationship', which prescribes practical cooperation and peaceful coexistence between countries despite differences in ideologies and disparity of capacity and power. It differs greatly from the normative power of the EU, which is driven by 'the logic of appropriateness'.[19]

Carl Schmitt famously explained the political distinction between friend and enemy, which denotes 'the utmost degree of intensity of a union or separation, of an association or dissociation.' He further specified that 'the political enemy needs not be morally evil or aesthetically ugly … he is, nevertheless, the Other, the stranger'.[20] Given that differences of normative stances often produce structural misperceptions of the Other's intentions, one may wonder how China and the EU can avoid a vicious circle of systemic misperception. In particular, how can the EU live and prosper with China as a 'strategic partner'? Do the Europeans have to treat China as a 'good enemy' whose

19. Brantly Womack, 'China as a Normative Foreign Policy Actor', in Nathalie Tocci (ed.) *Who is a Normative Foreign Policy Actor? The European Union and its Global Partners.* Brussels: Centre for European Policy Studies (2008), pp. 265–298.

20. Carl Schmitt, *The Concept of the Political.* Chicago: University of Chicago Press (2008), pp. 26–27.

very presence necessarily helps to promote EU solidarity and defend EU moral standards?

In any case, a deeper and healthy engagement between China and Europe is expected by those who are able to move out of the boxes of Sino-centric and Eurocentric perspectives. On the one hand, China has a lot of homework to do in order to improve its domestic governance and reach moral resonance with its European partners. On the other hand, Europe may embrace China with a more pragmatic attitude and reclaim its solidarity and unity by addressing the root cause of its identity crisis, instead of engaging in blame games fuelled by an unsubstantiated fear of normative differences.

As the theme of this book – *de-demonization* – suggests, it is both necessary and possible to develop a balanced schemata of framing in a world of increasing political and cultural diversities. This can be instructed by Max Weber's idea of 'empathetic understanding' (*Eklarendes Verstehen*). Weber maintained that human beings have a 'reflexive nature' which makes it possible to understand and explain social action, social relationships, cultural significance and historical causes of events, and connections among events. In this line of *reflective dialogue*, one may be further inspired by the wisdom of Mencius, who said that 'If a man loves others, and no responsive attachment is shown to him, let him turn inwards and examine his own benevolence ... If he treats others politely, and they do not return his politeness, let him turn inwards and examine his own feeling of respect.'[21]

Chunrong Liu

---

21. Mencius, *Chapter Li Lou* (part I).

US–China, partners–enemies?

DANIEL A. BELL HAS COME TO SEE CHINA as the main target of demonization today. After reminding us that this process places the demonized in a position of complete evil, Bell points to the absurdity of demonizing large groups of people, not to mention whole populations, arguing that this may in part be motivated by racism. While some of the most dedicated US 'China-bashers' are plainly also racists, Bell also questions the more 'nuanced' ones, those who see the Chinese communists as evil, despite the fact that a group consisting of 90 million people hardly can ALL be evil, without exception. The author provides indisputable evidence about present-day China and its government's policies to substantiate his views. It moreover becomes clear that when the target of demonization is a major global power, the effect of the activity may be worse for the demonizer than for the demonized. This is certainly the case when even positive achievements are seen in a negative light, such as when high-tech developments are seen as a part of an aggressive Chinese global strategy. Or given that 'green' developments in China go almost unmentioned by the Western media. Both approaches hamper the global cooperation necessary to tackle current major challenges. Demonization may thus be nothing less than a serious threat to our common future.

About the Author: Daniel A. Bell, a Canadian scholar living and working in China, is Dean of the School of Political Science and Public Administration at Shandong University (Qingdao). His books include *The China Model, China's New Confucianism, Beyond Liberal Democracy, East Meets West,* and *The Spirit of Cities* (co-authored with Avner deShalit), all published by Princeton University Press. His latest book (co-authored with Wang Pei) *Just Hierarchy: Why Social Hierarchies Matter in China and the Rest of the World* was published by Princeton University Press in 2020. He is founding editor of the Princeton-China series. He writes frequently for leading media outlets in China and the West and his works have been translated into 23 languages. He has been interviewed in English, Chinese and French. In 2018, he was awarded the Huilin Prize and was honoured as a 'Cultural Leader' by the World Economic Forum. In 2019, he was awarded the Special Book Award of China.

CHAPTER FOURTEEN

Demonizing China: A Diagnosis with No Cure in Sight

*T*o demonize, according to the Cambridge Dictionary, is 'to try to make someone or a group of people seem completely evil.'[1] Perhaps some people are completely evil – Hitler comes to mind. But no group of people can be completely evil. Most people are mixtures of good and bad and there are always some good and bad people in large groups. So when a group of people is demonized, it means that the 'demonizer' is lying, whether consciously or not. The act of demonizing a group of people says more about the demonizer than the demonized: either the demonizer has an ugly agenda – he or she seeks to whip up irrational hatred against another people – or the demonizer suffers from a serious case of false consciousness.

Today, China is the main victim of global demonization. The demonizers are mainly government officials and mainstream media organizations in the United States. The Trump administration seems to be doing all it can to curb China's economic rise and global influence, with the support of the Democrats and leading media organizations. It's the one policy area where just about everybody in the United States speaks with one voice: they don't like China. What motivates this attitude? At times, the underlying racism is barely concealed: as the director of policy planning at the State Deparment Kiron Skinner puts it,

---

1. https://dictionary.cambridge.org/dictionary/english/demonize.

the United States is now locked in 'a fight with a really different civilization and a different ideology … [with] a great power competitor that is not Causasian.'[2] On a popular late-night American television program, CNN's chief national security correspondent, Jim Sciutto, said the Chinese are 'subtly evil … like the mob' and he approvingly quoted the FBI's former head of counter-intelligence: 'No one is more vicious than the Chinese, they will kill you, they will kill your families.'[3] No wonder the American people largely endorse Trump's hard line policies against China.[4]

But the more nuanced demonizers (if that's not an oxymoron) usually distinguish between the 'good' Chinese people – who would want an American-style democracy and way of life if they could get it – and the 'evil' Chinese Communist Party, which allegedly suppresses the Chinese people.[5] As Stephen Bannon, former chief strategist for Donald Trump, puts it, 'China has emerged as the greatest economic and national security threat the United States has ever faced … the United States' fight is not with the Chinese people but with the CCP. The Chinese people are the first and continuous victims of this barbarous regime.'[6] In the same vein, media organizations such as the *New York*

---

2. Quoted in Peter T.C. Chang, 'To avoid a clash of flawed but great civilizations, the US and China must address their own deficiencies and hubris', *SCMP*, May 31, 2019.

3. https://www.youtube.com/watch?v=59VJzrxxdE8.

4. Faucheux China Poll (results discussed in The Nelson Report, June 4, 2019).

5. The policies of the US government, however, do not always neatly distinguish between the CCP and the Chinese people: tariffs against Chinese exports, for example, are more likely to harm ordinary Chinese workers than China's political elites.

6. https://www.washingtonpost.com/opinions/steve-bannon-were-in-an-economic-war-with-china-its-futile-to-compromise/2019/05/06/0055af36-7014-11e9-9eb4-0828f5389013_story.html?utm_term=.487664ad56eb

Times and the *Washington Post* are generally careful to portray the Chinese people in a sympathetic light, but news reports about the Chinese Communist Party are almost invariably negative. The demonization of the CCP has exploded in the past few years, with even previously balanced China specialists endorsing a document that warns, with hardly a shred of evidence, against a sinister Chinese government that seeks to 'exploit the openness of our democratic society to challenge, and sometimes even undermine, core American freedoms, norms and laws.' Here too, the authors are careful to distinguish between the Chinese people and the rulers: 'Throughout the report, "China" refers to the Chinese Communist Party and the government apparatus of the People's Republic of China, and not to Chinese society at large or the Chinese people as a whole.'[7]

The more balanced China experts recognize that the CCP has widespread support among the people and that there is substantial diversity in the ruling organization. Rather than seeking to overthrow the CCP, the United States should seek to engage with more moderate forces. But even here, the underlying point is to limit China's rise. An influential group of China experts signed a letter that denounces China's 'greater domestic repression' and its 'more assertive international role'. Instead of working alone to deter China from its evil-doing, however, 'a successful US approach to China must focus on creating enduring coalitions with other countries in support of economic and security objectives.' The United States needs to 'work with allies to maintain deterrence.'[8] What is missing here is any mention of the possibility that China and the United States can work together to deal with global problems such as climate change and

---

7. https://www.hoover.org/research/chinas-influence-american-interests-promoting-constructive-vigilance

8. https://www.washingtonpost.com/opinions/making-china-a-us-enemy-is-counterproductive/2019/07/02/647d49d0-9bfa-11e9-b27f-ed2942f73d70_story.html?utm_term=.4f568789a758

regulation of nuclear weapons, not to mention the possibility that the United States might have anything to learn from China.

In sum, the dominant view in the United States – shared by intellectual and political elites with otherwise radically different outlooks – is that China's rise, led by the Chinese Communist Party, needs to be challenged and resisted. The not-so-underlying hope is that China institutes multi-party elections and that the Chinese Communist Party makes room for alternative rulers, especially rulers who are more sympathetic to liberal democracy and capitalist economics. It may take a long time and, meanwhile, the United States government should try to distinguish between the (bad) ruling party and the (good) Chinese people.

For the sake of argument, let's assume that anti-CCP voices are sincerely committed to fighting against the Chinese Communist Party rather than the Chinese people and that it's possible to neatly distinguish between the two. Is the CCP as 'evil' as advertised? The ninety-million-strong Chinese Communist Party includes millions of farmers, workers, entrepreneurs and intellectuals; as one might expect of any large organization, some members are good people, some are bad people, with most people in between, with a mixture of motives. In my own experience, most CCP members are talented and hard-working: many of my dearest friends in China are members of the CCP. As far as I'm concerned, demonization of the CCP is patently absurd. I'm employed as dean at a large Chinese university, and most of the senior scholars and administrators are members of the Chinese Communist Party who work hard for the good of our students and teachers.[9] 'Evil' is the last word I'd use to describe my friends and colleagues.

9. A friend of mine – a leading liberal thinker at a prestigious American university – recently asked if I am a member of the CCP. For the record, I am not, and have never been, a member of (any) communist party. As far as I know, no foreigner has joined the CCP in the last few decades (some did join in the pre-1949 years when China was at war against Japan and the KMT).

Perhaps the 'evil' nature of the CCP is more the apparent if we shift the focus to the top policy makers in Beijing. No doubt there are worrying trends. The end of term limits for China's top leader leaves open the possibility of a return to Maoist-style personal dictatorship. Increased censorship demoralizes intellectuals and artists. The mass incarceration of Uyghurs in Xinjiang seems like a gross overreaction to the threat of religious extremism. But why should these worrisome developments in China threaten the United States? How can China pose a greater existential threat to the United States than the former Soviet Union, which threatened to annihilate the United States in a nuclear war? China hasn't gone to war with anybody since 1979 and even the most hawkish voices in the Chinese military establishment do not threaten nuclear war with the United States. The idea that China would seek to go to war against the United States anywhere near its territory is crazy (on the other hand, China is surrounded by US military bases, and it's not absurd for Chinese policy-makers to think the US might go to war with 'allies' near Chinese territory). Here's the big picture: China has never been so open to the world: it is largest trading country in the world, over 130 million Chinese tourists go abroad every year, and one third of the more than one million foreign students in the United States come from China. At home, the CCP has presided over the most spectacular economic growth story in global history, with over 800 million people lifted out of poverty. Arguably, it is the freest period in China's history: more than ever before, ordinary Chinese have the freedoms to make money and to decide where to live, where to work and who to marry. How can the CCP be so fundamentally at odds with its 'slave-like' people?

Overall, then, recent developments in China cannot explain why demonization of the CCP has gone from bad to worse in the United States. Demonization of ninety million people says more about the demonizer than the demonized; as Stephen

Wertheim puts it, 'the anti-China turn of the past year has been triggered more by American anxieties than by Chinese actions.'[10] It's worth asking why American elites have become so obsessed with the 'China threat'. In my view, the demonization of China's political elite stems from the sudden realization that 'they' won't be like 'us': us meaning the US. This reaction is grounded in a form of self-love. It was perfectly fine to support China's economic and political development so long as 'they' were viewed as a somewhat inferior civilization that would eventually learn the truth about the superiority of American-style capitalism and liberal democracy. But those hopes have faded. For one thing, China has (re)discovered its own past. For most of the twentieth century, Chinese liberals and Marxists looked to the West for inspiration. It may have been flattering for Westerners – look, they want to be just like us! – but there is less sympathy now that Chinese are taking pride their own heritage and turning to their own traditions, such as Confucianism, for thinking economic, social and political reform.

The real worry, however, is that 'they' will surpass us/the US. The flaws of American-style democracy are becoming increasingly evident. Populist leaders with no political experience can get elected by lying on a daily basis and appealing to the people's worst emotions. There is political gridlock at home and the country as a whole is losing its economic dominance. Whereas once China was denounced for churning out uncreative copycats, today companies such as Huawei are feared because they are more innovative than American competitors. Not to mention that the United States has almost completely abandoned its global responsibilities. Partly, the problems are rooted in the democratic system itself. Global challenges like climate change require concern for future generations in the

10. https://www.nytimes.com/2019/06/08/opinion/sunday/trump-china-cold-war.html?action=click&module=Opinion&pgtype=Homepage

whole world. But political equality in electoral democracies ends at the boundaries of the political community: those outside the community are neglected, especially if their interests conflict with those of the voting community. The national, this-generational focus of the democratically elected leaders is part of the system, so to speak: they are meant to serve the community of voters, not future generations, and even

> Whereas once China was denounced for churning out uncreative copycats, today companies such as Huawei are feared because they are more innovative than American competitors. Not to mention that the United States has almost completely abandoned its global responsibilities.

less foreigners living outside the political community. Even democracies that work well tend to focus on the interests of citizens and neglect the interests of foreigners and future generations. But political leaders, especially of big countries like China and the United States, make decisions that affect future generations and the rest of the world and they need to consider their interests when they make decisions. Nobody, unfortunately, formally represents the interests of future generations and foreigners in democratic systems.

The Chinese political system, whatever its flaws, does allow for more serious consideration of the needs of future generations and foreigners, and it's not surprising that the country has been taking the lead on dealing with climate change. Global challenges also require long term planning. Consider the development of artificial intelligence (AI): nobody can predict the future in any detail, but we can be sure that AI will radically upend the way we lead our lives in a few decades time. Hence, the Chinese government has been developing and implementing strategies for putting AI to socially desirable uses in the future. China's leaders are also aware that China cannot thrive unless its neighbors also thrive: the Belt and Road initiative is meant to support infrastructure in surrounding countries that provides the foundation for economic development. Large Chinese state-owned enterprises are prepared to take short term losses for the sake of long term gains. Political leaders in the United States and other electoral democracies, meanwhile, tend to worry about the next elections, and find it difficult to plan beyond four or five years.

What can be done to reduce demonization of the CCP? First, there is a need to break out of the democracy/authoritarian political dichotomy. Packaging the debate in terms of 'democracy' versus 'authoritarianism' is not helpful for understanding China's political system. It is wrong to think that all countries that do not use democratic elections to select leaders share the same authoritarian nature. China is not run by a family or by the military. In principle, it is a political meritocracy, meaning equality of opportunity in education and government, with positions of leadership being distributed to relatively virtuous and qualified members of the political community. The idea here is that everybody has the potential to become an exemplary person, but in real life the capacity to make competent and morally justifiable political judgments varies between people and an important task of the political system is to identify those with above-average capacity. Hence, China has been building up a complex bureaucratic system over the last few decades that is designed to select and promote public officials with political experience and above average ability and virtue. Of course, there is a large gap between the ideal and the reality.

China is a highly imperfect meritocracy, just as the United States is a highly imperfect democracy. But political meritocracy can and should serve as the moral standard for improvement in China, just as democracy can and should serve as the moral standard for improvement in the United States. The point here is not to deny the validity of universal political values. All countries need to respect basic human rights – 'negative rights' not to be killed, tortured, enslaved, as well as 'positive rights' to a decent level of material well-being – but we do need to allow for diverse ways of selecting and promoting political leaders.

Why should all countries use the same mechanisms to select leaders? Surely what's appropriate depends on the history and culture and size and current needs of a country. What works in the United States won't necessarily work in China. Few Chinese intellectuals and political reformers in China would dispute this point, but in the United States it seems almost impossible to shake dogmatic attachment to the idea that one person, one vote is the only morally legitimate way of selecting political leaders.

A change of perception won't be enough, however. If it does turn out that the Chinese political system has some advantages, then the United States needs to make more room for China's participation at the global level. The days of unilateral economic, political and cultural dominance by the United States are over. Rather than fighting every step of the way whenever China seeks to have greater input on the world stage – opposing all its initiatives, such as the Asian Infrastructure Investment Bank and Belt and Road – why not step back a bit and let China try to improve the world? In fifty years time, is it possible to imagine that the United States will still be the dominant hegemonic power in the East Asian region? Instead of bellicose rhetoric and provocative military action on China's shores, why not propose, say, joint military patrols in the Asia Pacific region? Or why not allow for the possibility of an EU-style regional organization in East Asia, with East Asian countries forging an alliance on security and trade issues. As the largest power, China would have the most say (just as Germany has the most say in the EU), but it would be bound by the need for consensus and by the moral imperative to favour win–win policies for all sides, including weaker powers.[11] It may sound utopian now, but it would have sounded

---

11. For a systematic defense of the idea that hierarchical relations between countries should be 'win-win', with the example of an East Asian

even more utopian to advocate an EU-style organization at the height of World War II. Stranger things have happened.

That's not to deny that China cannot do more to improve its global image. Most obviously, increasing repression at home sends the wrong message about its intentions abroad. A more open political system would help to alleviate concerns. Electoral democracy at the top would undermine the advantages of Chinese-style political meritocracy – all leaders have political experience at lower levels of government and they can plan for the long term – but the Chinese political system can and should allow for open recognition of diversity within the CCP and increased consultation and deliberation and democratic practices such as sortition at lower levels of government. The problem, however, is that China's leaders are not about to take serious political risks and promote further democratic experimentation when they feel the whole political establishment of the world's most powerful country seems united in its fight against them. Chinese leaders may be paranoid, but their paranoia is well-founded.[12] So both sides are locked in a vicious political cycle, with the United States growing more antagonistic and war-like, and China reinforcing its walls and repressing alternative political voices.

In principle, it's not hard to imagine more optimistic scenarios. The American people would realize that they cannot be the world's number one economic, military and political

---

regional order led by China that also benefits weaker countries, see Daniel A. Bell and Wang Pei, *Just Hierarchy: Why Social Hierarchies Matter in China and the Rest of the World* (Princeton: Princeton University Press, 2020), ch. 3.

12. I do not mean to imply that US hostility to China is the only source of paranoia. The Legalist-inspired anti-corruption drive has created many political enemies, and the leaders have good reasons to fear backlash from hundreds of thousands of purged cadres and their supporters (see Bell and Wang, *Just Hierarchy*, ch. 2). Now that the campaign seems to be winding down, such pressure will likely diminish over the years.

power forever. They would recognize that China is not 'evil' just because it doesn't use electoral democracy to select top leaders, that both the American and Chinese political systems have advantages and disadvantages, and that both systems can learn from each other and learn to live with differences. Then, a new American government would (re)engage with China on equal and respectful terms. The Chinese government could relax somewhat and allow for more political openness and democratic experimentation at home. It would be the start of a virtuous cycle. China and the United States would exchange scholars, scientists and entrepreneurs, who would learn from each other's best practices and work together on common global challenges. At the moment, however, it's hard to be optimistic. An external threat might push the United States to reengage with China – another massive terrorist attack, a global pandemic, climate disasters that kill millions, a war with aliens or AIs who threaten the human species – but no sensible person would wish for those eventualities. Meanwhile, all we can do is put forward the blind hope that the demonizing of China will cool off before the vicious cycle leads to catastrophic war.

Postscript

I wrote these words in late 2019. It's now March 2020. I'm saddened to report that the demonization of China, especially in the United States, has only intensified the last few months. What happened? A coronavirus epidemic seems to have originated in Wuhan, China and spread to the rest of the world, spawning a global pandemic with thousands of deaths. China's response to the crisis sheds light on the both advantages and the disadvantages of its political system. In the early days of the epidemic, political overlords in Wuhan shut down the warnings of conscientious health professionals, allowing the epidemic to spread to the rest of China and eventually, the rest of the world. The central government finally took draconian measures to contain the crisis on 23 January 2020. Wuhan and other cities in Hubei province were locked down, and most schools and workplaces were shut down in the rest of the country. The containment measures were rigorously enforced at all levels of government and the dutiful citizenry largely complied with measures designed to contain the epidemic. In late March 2020, such measures seem to have contained the epidemic in China, just as the crisis seems to be getting out of control in other countries. I certainly hope that the rest of the world can contain the epidemic, but it may be more difficult without a strong central government and citizens willing to engage in collective sacrifice in extreme circumstances.[13] China obviously bears some responsibility for the epidemic and the government has been helping countries in great need, such as Italy and Iran. The help seems to be driven by a mixture of motives: the desire to help countries that helped China when it was in the midst of its public health crisis; the need to improve China's image abroad; and commitment to the ideal that large countries bear special responsibility to improve our world. Whatever the motive(s), the effort to help other countries and to promote international collaboration for global challenges such as pandemics is obviously a good thing.

Unfortunately, the United States government showed a distinct lack of sympathy for China's plight in its moment of crisis. In the early days of the epidemic, US Commerce secretary Wilbur Ross could barely conceal his joy at China's predicament, saying the crisis would 'help to accelerate the return of jobs to North America.'[14] President Trump minimized the

---

13. See my comments, co-authored with Wang Pei: https://www.scmp. com/comment/opinion/article/3074850/chinas-coronavirus- response-and-italys-struggles-show-benefits; https://www.scmp.com/ comment/opinion/article/3051402/coronavirus-holds-mirror-chinas- problems-and-nation-will-be-better.

14. https://www.bbc.com/news/business-51276323.

impact on the crisis on the United States until it it was too late, then chose to label the coronavirus the 'Chinese virus'. Gone are the 'fine' distinctions between the 'evil' Chinese government and the 'good' Chinese people, and now the demonization seems firmly tied to race, with Asian Americans reporting incidents of racial abuse and physical attacks.[15] Meanwhile, officials from the Chinese government float conspiracy theories that the virus originated from the American military and journalists from leading US media organizations are expelled from China.[16] The tit-for-tat seems endless, with both sides trying outdo each other in jingoistic stupidity. That said, there are tiny glimmers of hope. China's ambassador to the United States openly broke with his own foreign ministry and reaffirmed his opposition to the view that the virus originated in an American lab.[17] But such voices are few and far between. Perhaps I'm too pessimistic, but the main 'hope' is that the two countries plunge into such deep crisis that their leaders come to the realization that only collective sympathy and action between the two great powers can bring us back to 'normal' life. For the moment, however, it looks like we need to brace for deep, dark and terrifying times.

Author's Note

I am grateful for helpful comments by John Delury, Rachel Harrison, Geir Helgesen, Wang Pei, and an anonymous reviewer.

Daniel A. Bell

15. https://www.nytimes.com/2020/03/18/us/politics/china-virus.html?action=click&module=Spotlight&pgtype=Homepage

16. https://www.buzzfeednews.com/article/ryanhatesthis/chinese-diplomats-are-pushing-conspiracy-theories-that-the; https://www.bbc.com/news/world-asia-51938035

17. https://www.bloomberg.com/news/articles/2020-03-23/china-s-top-envoy-to-u-s-breaks-with-foreign-ministry-on-virus

Enemy Images in Peacebuilding

THE FOLLOWING CHAPTER FOCUSES ON THE ROLE played by enemy images in the peacebuilding process, a largely neglected theme. The author, Steinar Bryn, is an experienced Norwegian peacebuilder with extensive field involvement in war-torn former Yugoslavia and its successor states. We believe that his exceptional insights are extremely relevant to the subject matter of this book, and that the experience he shares with us here underlines the main message of the previous chapters: demonizing the enemy Other promotes reasons for conflict and further complicates dialogue and mutual understanding. Dialogue is necessary in order to prevent a conflict from erupting, as well as to build trust in the aftermath of a conflict. To this, Bryn adds something that is mostly overlooked in theorizing about peacebuilding as well as in practical efforts in the field: the upbringing and education of children. In this way, he underlines that successful peacebuilding requires a long-term commitment to the process, and is necessarily time-consuming. More than anything else, it is about people, relations between people, empathy, and mutual understanding. The act of demonizing the enemy Other is to pour poison in the water that both parties in a conflict need to sustain them. This chapter is based on an article first published in Norwegian in *Arr*, 2019 (3), pp. 29–38. *Arr* is Norway's only scientific journal of the history of ideas.

About the Author: Steinar Bryn was educated in United States. He wrote his dissertation on 'The Americanization of Norway' at the University of Minnesota (1993) with a strong focus on how countries create images of each other. This thorough study of cultural perceptions was his background when he started dialogue work at the Nansen Academy in Lillehammer in 1995. Between then and 2003 he facilitated 15 three-month dialogue seminars. In addition, he has facilitated close to 300 seminars of shorter length in Lillehammer and in the Western Balkans. He has invested much energy in sharing these experiences with civil society in Ukraine after war started there in 2014. He received the Bridge-builder prize from the Norwegian Church Academy in 2004 and the Danish Livia Prize in 2010 for his committed struggle to rebuild communication and cooperation in the most war-torn areas in Europe after WWII.

CHAPTER FIFTEEN

Why Images of the Enemy are Neglected in Conflict Analyses and Peacebuilding Processes

*D*ecision-makers – and indeed most people – feel frustrated by the huge effort going into peacebuilding in war zones and conflict areas around the world, and the often limited peace growing out of it. There is a serious discrepancy between the human and financial resources going into areas such as the Middle East, Bosnia-Herzegovina, Kosovo, Iraq, Afghanistan and Libya and the impact that this has had. This discrepancy is so wide that it gives good reason to ask: is there something wrong with the very way we try to rebuild states after they have been ripped apart by war?

Images of the enemy play an important role in this process. After 25 years of dialogue work in some of Europe's most war-torn areas, it is my experience that the reproduction of extreme enemy images provides a major explanation as to why these conflicts are so hard to solve, passed down as they are from one generation to the next. It is difficult to imagine how such enemy images can be kept alive when the UN, EU, OSCE[1] and multiple humanitarian organizations are moving in with full force to build peace and functional states. The reason for this is that the international community focuses mainly on strong institutions and infrastructure: the rule of

1. Organization for Security and Cooperation in Europe, a 57-state institution that engages in a wide range of pan-European issues.

law, democratization, public administration, fighting corruption and integrating states into international organizations. Of course, strong institutions are important. However, when, consequently, soft institutions like homes and schools are neglected – and this is where much of the production of enemy images takes place – the conflict is sustained, and the effects of peacebuilding efforts are diluted.

At the Nansen Academy in Lillehammer, Norway, we started our dialogue work in 1995 because of Olympic twinning. Lillehammer, the previous year's host, was paired with Sarajevo, the city that hosted the Games in 1984. Members of several ethnic groups from former Yugoslavia were invited to three-month-long stays in Lillehammer, and this chapter builds on my first-hand experience of dialogue between people in extreme conflict. My assumption is that there are certain repeating patterns in the production of enemy images, whether the conflict is between ethnic or religious groups, or simply people fighting to control the same territory. It is further my conviction that the dialogue experience at the Nansen Academy, rebuilding trust and cooperation in countries ripped apart by war, has relevance for the ongoing dialogue between North and South Korea.

Moral compasses

In his research on morality, Jonathan Haidt (2012) concludes that human beings are self-righteous by nature. This seems to be a characteristic shared by human beings the world over. To divide people into the categories of *us* and *them* is not necessarily harmful, whether we live in a village in India, a working-class neighbourhood in Philadelphia, a fishing community in northern Norway or in urban Pyongyang; we all do it: we separate people into *us* and *them* groups. This division is not in itself conflict-inducing, but when a conflict is developing, we think that *we* are right, and *they* are wrong. In such a situation, we avoid taking our own self-righteousness into the equation and instead see they/the Others as the ones who are mainly responsible for the causes of the conflict, not we/us.

Jonathan Haidt argues that this can be explained by the fact that we operate according to different moral compasses. He mentions at least six of them. One is 'Do no harm, care for others' and another is 'fight for liberation against oppression'. Here we can see that these two compasses might collide: the struggle for liberation might lead a person to harm the oppressor. Haidt argues that we often enter into conflicts judging our enemy according to our own moral compass and unaware of which moral compass our opponents operate from. According to Haidt this can explain why good people are divided by politics and religion. Had we understood their moral compasses better, we would perhaps have been kinder in our judgements.

The development of these compasses might happen in a moment of transformation. Most often, however, it is developed over longer periods and ends up consisting of childhood memories, memorable sentences uttered by grandparents, the stories we love to hear over and over again because they made *us* the heroes and demonized the Others, turning it into an exciting tale of good versus evil. These stories gather strength when they travel to schools where we are gathered among our own. One's own story becomes repeated so often that it becomes accepted as normal, as the true interpretation of what happened. It becomes a collective truth.

My first realization was that, in conflicts where enemy images play an important role in mobilization in the lead up to and during war, these enemy images must be taken seriously in the dialogue and reconciliation work that follows after the shooting has stopped. This is where the international community failed in Kosovo. Support for education was defined as the physical rebuilding of schools, not as changes in the curriculum. Donors, including Norway, spent millions on high quality school buildings. The finished and furnished buildings became a sign of success. The curriculum was defined and decided separately, by local authorities. The schools were then completely segregated, and the teaching of language, literature and history became an important force in shaping the different (often contradictory) narratives. The children were not exposed to any 'modifying' voice and learned one of the two completely different narratives about what happened and why.

A child does not learn who the enemy is from political speeches or journalistic reports. Enemy images are learned at a very early age. The side of the mountain, the island or the side of the border you are born on will determine not only your language, but also your narratives and moral evaluations. I was once teaching my grandchild the difference between lies and truths. When she finally got it, because you need to understand both simultaneously, her comment was 'grandpa never lies'. I wouldn't say that. That would be a lie. It is the small child who connects grandpa and truth, most likely out of love and respect.

In conflict areas, enemies live in relative isolation from each other, even if they live only a few kilometres apart. Day-care and schools are segregated, there are no joint parks or playgrounds, sports clubs are divided, and few cafes or other meeting grounds are frequented by members of both groups. In this way, children grow up without correctives to all the stories they are told about others. The stories – often brutal – about what *they* did to *us* go unchallenged and legitimize aggression toward the perpetrators, and often also their children. In Norway, for example, it is a well-known fact that the children of German soldiers and Norwegian women experienced serious discrimination and were regularly beaten up.

Understanding the Other[2]

My work on a book project called 'Understanding the Other' is designed not to produce an efficient ten-step programme, but

2. http://www.peace.no/nb/download/understanding-the-other/

rather will be an analysis of how difficult it is to understand the Other.[3] Understanding the Other is often misunderstood as showing respect and tolerance toward people you strongly disagree with or even feel you should show zero tolerance toward. My perspective is different. Through dialogue work, I have learned the importance of understanding enemy images and the role they play in conflicts: to understand these enemy images is an absolute prerequisite to solving conflicts. The first question one must ask is not the objective one: who is the real enemy here? It is a more subjective one: who do you think the enemy is and what do you think the enemy is capable of?

If you have received a solid enemy image shaped in your home and strengthened by your school, you will be very resistant toward arguments that your understanding of history is not correct. That your ancestors were not heroic, that your people have not suffered as much as you think they have, and that you are not as unique as you believe.

Acknowledging the difficulties of understanding the Other

Most conflicts emerge over contested interests and how assets are distributed across a society: clashes over land, natural resources or simply the control of territory or political power. One assumes that the parties know what they are fighting about. But it is my experience that demonization is underestimated or neglected in these analyses, and that de-demonization is therefore not sufficiently integrated into peacebuilding processes. One of my colleagues argued that the frontline is basically a mirror. The two soldiers who have reached the frontline have both been exposed to a demonization process so strong that it has strengthened their self-righteousness and demonization of the Other in such a way that both feel licensed to kill.

---

3. Supported by the Norwegian Non-fiction Writers and Translators Association.

How, then, can we develop reconciliation strategies that interrupt this continuous demonization of the Other as the enemy? How can we break this spiral of passing on the conflict to the next generation? How can we de-demonize the Other? My argument is that we need to take the soft institutions of home and school much more seriously. One often-mentioned example of this is the South African Truth and Reconciliation Commission, although criticisms have grown in its aftermath. To admit to wrongdoing became a way to avoid accusations and to get amnesty. The process was, to a larger degree controlled from above and many victims have not yet received the compensation they were promised.

A more successful intervention took place before our very eyes in Europe, though we rarely mention it – and that is the reconciliation process between France and Germany after WWII.[4] It must be termed a success, considering the two countries' leading positions in the region today. Important components of the reconciliation process and the de-demonization of the Other were the cooperation between historians in writing a joint history, in face-to-face student exchanges, through town twinning and by regular meetings between ministers, even if they had 'nothing to talk about'. By the turn of the century (2000), millions of students had participated in student exchange programmes and close to 70 per cent of the towns and cities were involved in 'sister-town' projects. This process was very horizontal and was built on a unique historical condition: Germany accepted much of the blame for starting WWII, which is not common in most peace agreements following violent conflicts.

---

4. Valerie Rosoux is a senior researcher at the Belgian National Fund for Scientific Research (FNRS). She teaches international negotiation, and transitional justice at the University of Louvain (UCL). She has written several articles about the difficult reconciliation, with examples from both South Africa and Germany/France.

The unification of East and West Germany can hardly be seen as equally successful. Part of the reason for this is the undermining of the Eastern industry and the lack of equivalent reconciliation initiatives in the same proportions. Cooperation over the writing of history was also undertaken by Sweden and Norway after 1905, and 'Historians without Borders' are currently engaged in the same collaborative process between historians in Ukraine and Russia.[5] But, historians work in higher education, and what is also needed are fundamental changes to school curricula. When peace agreements are forced upon the parties, and one party is made to feel like a winner and the other a loser, such changes are difficult to implement.

The Nansen Academy Dialogue Project

In 1995 the Nansen Academy began to host dialogue seminars for participants from war-torn Yugoslavia, a state that was ripped apart and no longer exists. This was a new experience and a difficult challenge both for the participants and for us. This work has further developed over the past 25 years, both in form and content. An early realization was the necessity to build confidence, both between the participants and us and among the participants themselves. Without fundamental respect, there can hardly be any will towards honest dialogue. Attempting bridge-building was simply not enough. We needed to lie down and be that very bridge ourselves.

In these dialogue seminars, we spent a lot of time on sharing ideas about the people, events and experiences that shaped us and formed our positions. We shared how the conflicts affected our lives in a variety of different ways: living conditions, work/life, raising children and hopes for the future. In these kinds of conversations, it became possible to see that if *I* had been *you*, I would have been thinking like *you*, a relatively logical conclusion. If *I* had been *you*, I would have been *my*

---

5. www.historianswithoutborders.fi/en/.

own enemy. The communication technique we used the most was questions and answers. One simply asks the most direct questions one wants to hear the answer to. This often leads to a very intense conversation.

It is relatively easy to argue why dialogue is necessary. The obvious contact hypothesis is proven over and over again. When people communicate with each other, they develop better contact with each other. Personal conversations about what happened, and why, improves understanding between people and contributes to reconciliation. The main challenge is how to recruit: how to convince people in conflict that it is worth their time to engage in dialogue with the enemy. In addition, they perceive the dialogue itself as a show of respect for the enemy, which they do not in fact have.

In the dialogue project at the Nansen Academy, the participants lived together for three months in an extreme communal and intimate environment. They stayed in a dormitory where there were queues for the shower, and they all had kitchen duties. Education filled part of the day, but socializing was also important. Back in the 1990s, the smoking room was also an important conversation room across ethnic division. The participants came from segregated societies into a life where they shared everyday experiences. This living experience became an integral component of the process of understanding the Other. The discovery of the literal humanness of the Other contributed to the de-demonization process and to building confidence between the participants. Through living together, they discovered that we humans are not only ethnic or religious categories; we are also music lovers, basketball players, dancers, teachers, lawyers, parents and politicians.

It was easier to build confidence and trust in these other life arenas, but this respect could be brought back into the dialogue room to strengthen the conversation. For some it became a source of inspiration they took with them back to work in one of the ten Nansen Dialogue Centres that were established in the Western Balkans.

One challenge in particular remained: since it was a rather exclusive experience to have lived in Norway for three months, how could this experience be shared among friends, colleagues, neighbours and family members back home? How could one change enemy images held by people who had already integrated these images as true descriptions of the Other?

Pedagogical breakthrough in Macedonia

In the aftermath of the Kosovo war 1997–99 there was an outbreak of violence in Macedonia in 2001 between Macedonians and Albanians. Although the Ohrid agreement (2001) stopped a potential war, the years that followed witnessed the increased segregation between the parties in conflict. Schools became more mono-ethnic. Skopje developed into a more divided city. But at the Nansen Dialogue Centre (NDC) in Skopje, established in 2000, the staff became deeply engaged with community peace-building and began to develop the Nansen Model of Inter-Cultural education in the municipality of Jegunovce.[6]

The starting point was rebuilding confidence and trust, which could only be achieved by getting directly involved ourselves. The Nansen workers are not a third party, but represent and identify with the parties in the conflict, and they know it will be a long-term process. Reconciliation is not a project, but a process where mobilization is needed on many different levels in society. The first stage was marked by visits and conversations over coffee, with parents, teachers and local politicians. NDC registered 260 visits in Jegunovce in 2006. To build confidence, the organization started with very basic projects such as fixing the toilets in some schools and handing out model globes to classrooms. The next step was to conduct

---

6. https://ndc.org.mk/.

a needs assessment among the parents to ensure that the NDC staff understood the parents' perceived needs. Little could be done about the majority of those needs, but when the parents expressed worries over, for example, shortcomings in IT and English education, NDC Skopje could offer courses in these topics at both the basic and advanced levels.

NDC Skopje followed with a smart move. Most villages were perceived as either 'Albanian' or 'Macedonian'. Since they could not offer courses in each village, they had to collect the children and bus them safely to a shared area. The basic course in IT took place in one village, while the advanced course was held in a second village. The basic course in English was in a third village, and the advanced course in the fourth. In this way, the students got to travel to each other's villages and the parents were consulted and involved all along the way. It was the children themselves who expressed confusion regarding why they did not understand each other's languages. As a result, NDC Skopje began to offer language classes in Macedonian and Albanian. The parents were again consulted, and they, too, were offered language courses, an activity which prepared the ground for opening the first Nansen school in Macedonia in Jegunovce on 1 September 2008. A new curriculum was piloted for five years, and a sophisticated programme of ex-tracurricular activities was developed.

The students still received their basic education in their own mother tongue, but all extracurricular activities focused on learning each other's language and culture through games and interaction, rather than through formal teaching. The evalua-tion was positive, and the school drew international attention. NDC Skopje received a Max van der Stoehl Prize of 50,000 Euros from the High Commissioner of National Minorities (HCNM), which inspired NDC Skopje to develop the Nansen Model for Inter-Cultural Education. The respect shown by both the Council of Europe and HCNM led some members of the

Ministry of Education to understand that they had cracked the code, not only for Macedonia but also for segregated schools in many places throughout Europe.

Having developed a curriculum during 2008–2013, NDC Skopje went from operating one pioneer school to introducing the model in multiple schools. They hired scholars to analyse all the textbooks used in Macedonia. Their conclusion, based on solid research, was unsurprising in that they found the three most dominant cultures – Macedonian, Albanian and Turkish – all promoted their own culture and tended to stereotype that of the others. In some cases, they even made them invisible.

While the texts did not demonize the Other as such, they did strengthen a feeling of superiority of their own culture and inferiority of the others. The curriculum prepared a ground that was receptive to demonization should a conflict erupt. When a culture already feels superior, demonization meets less resistance. In 2016 NDC Skopje was asked by the Ministry of Education to write a new curriculum for grades 1–9. So far, they have completed the first three school years.

> **Although these are experiences from an ethnic conflict, they are relevant elsewhere. We have found dialogue has proven particularly useful when the participants have different perceptions of reality and the recent conflict.**

Although these are experiences from an ethnic conflict, they are relevant elsewhere. We have found dialogue has proven particularly useful when the participants have different perceptions of reality and the recent conflict. The Nansen school in Macedonia started to cooperate closely with Northern Ireland, Israel and Turkey. In Northern Ireland this was not an ethnic conflict but a one partly between rich and poor, partly between Catholics and Protestants and partly of territorial belonging. OSCE's keen interest in the Nansen model led to an invitation to Kiev, where NDC Skopje presented the Nansen

Model to the OSCE delegation in Ukraine and the Ministry of Education in Ukraine. I assume this because Ukraine is going through a period of division, from being a two-language country (Russian and Ukrainian) to becoming a more mono-language country. In April 2019 representatives from NDC Skopje visited Moldova for the same reason. Support from the HCNM lies behind these invitations.

Directors of Norwegian schools have travelled to Macedonia to see and learn. A group of fifty teachers from the Lillehammer Learning Center visited the Training Center in Skopje in November 2018. This work is still in its early stages, the Nansen Dialogue Centre having existed for only 20 years. One important discovery was the lack of multicultural training in the faculty for teacher education. NDC Skopje, therefore, opened a Nansen Training Centre for teachers and, at the time of writing, 750 have passed through this post faculty training.

Perhaps the most important learning experience came from the inclusion and continuous cooperation with the parents. When this educational experiment met obstacles or resistance, it was so crucial to have the parents on our side. On one occasion, parents demonstrated their commitment through resistance during a confrontation with a guerrilla leader who had just been released from prison. As the self-proclaimed leader of the village, he had strongly objected to Albanian children attending school with Slavic children, his group even putting up roadblocks to prevent parents from driving their children to school. The parents countered this by demanding a village council election to test the depth of his support. This demand was accepted and, after the new election, it became clear that the guerrilla leader did not have the support he had taken for granted. The school survived.

To work for intercultural coexistence is a very delicate job since it is so easy to be perceived as a traitor. We therefore held numerous dialogue meetings and gatherings for parents, teachers, school administrators and people from the local environment around the school, particularly village leaders. The Nansen Model pays particular attention to this larger context. Everybody must be included to make this work.

The Ohrid agreement, which brought a halt to the violent uprising in Macedonia, is built on establishing equality between conflicting groups within various structures of society. The work of NDC Skopje is a direct attempt to create equality in a school system deeply divided by national ethnicities by renewing the whole school curriculum, not simply the teaching of history and literature. It is an example of a concrete pedagogical attempt to overcome the power of the enemy images that are the foundation of continuous conflict between the different ethnic groups in Macedonia; and to break down self-righteousness and the feeling of ethnic superiority that is the foundation of a mono-ethnic curriculum.

The Model has also been tested in Kosovo, South Serbia and Herzegovina. There is a substantial political resistance against intercultural curricula. Do we have any choice? Do we have other alternatives? If the goal is to prepare our children for a multicultural coexistence in Europe and to make it possible for them to make educated decisions in life, they need to know the people they will coexist with. In 2018, in recognition of their fight against segregation, the students at Jajce High School in Bosnia-Herzegovina also received a 50,000 Euro Max van der Stoehl prize.[7] Specifically, municipal authorities had decided to build a new school for Muslim youth who hitherto had attended a mixed school. The students protested against this, with support from many of the teachers, and the plan was cancelled. Jajce is one of the municipalities where Nansen has been particularly active. Ethnically mixed female Nansen Volleyball teams from Jajce achieved success in both the under-18 and under-16 categories, meaning that their

---

7. https://www.osce.org/hcnm/402620.

parents, who perhaps would not otherwise have interacted within the community, instead united around the team and learned more about each other's different identities.

There is an ongoing discourse about the very usefulness of the concept of ethnicity. In Bosnia-Herzegovina the argument has been made that demonization itself has brought form and content to this concept, which in turn leads to the wrong conclusion that ethnic conflicts caused the war, while it is actually the other way around: the emphasis on ethnic differences is a result of the war.

In summary, in conflict areas, it is particularly difficult to foster an understanding of the Other. Reconciliation is a very difficult and challenging process. There are no shortcuts to this, but roads do exist. A dialogue seminar is not enough to make the necessary connections and to experience transformative moments; it is also necessary to implement structural changes that create new meeting grounds. Nansen Dialogue is therefore a long-term engagement. The main work is to move these processes forward.

I have argued that when people work for many decades for peace, with little or no success, it can be related to the role of demonization and the need for de-demonization in the peace process. This explains the current growing interest in the Nansen Model. In order to avoid the ethnic confusion, we have changed the name to the Nansen Model of Inter-Cultural Education. NDC Skopje will in 2020 have responsibility for the educational component within the 'One Society for All' programme initiated by ex-Prime Minister Zoran Zaev. The results so far indicate that there are ways to counter the process of demonization in the educational system.[8] In other words, there is hope.

Steinar Bryn

---

8. https://www.norway.no/en/serbia/norway-serbia/news-events/news2/torwards-integrated-education/

Sources of particular relevance

Bryn, Steinar (2011) 'Inter-ethnic Dialogue between Serbs and Albanians in Serbia/Kosovo, 1996–2008', in Ola Listhaug, Sabrina P. Ramet and Dragana Dulić (eds), *Civic and Uncivic Values: Serbia in the post-Milošević era*. Budapest and New York: Central European University Press: 369–397.

Daltveit, Egil (2007) 'The March 2004 Riots in Kosovo: A Failure of the International Community', Master of Military Arts and Science Thesis, Fort Leavenworth: US Army Command and General Staff College, 2007.

Feller, Amanda E. and Kelly R. Ryan (2002) 'Definition, necessity, and Nansen: Efficacy of Dialogue in Peacebuilding', *Conflict Resolution Quarterly* 29(4) (Summer): 351–380. DOI: 10.1002/crq.21049.

Haidt, Jonathan (2012) *The Righteous Mind: Why Good People are Divided By Politics and Religion*. New York: Pantheon Books.

Kelleher, Ann and Kelly Ryan (2012) 'Successful Local Peacebuilding in Macedonia: Sustained Peacebuilding in Practice', *Peace Research – The Canadian Journal of Peace and Conflict Studies* 44(1): 63–94.

King Iain and Whit Mason (2006) *Peace at Any Price: How the World Failed Kosovo*. Ithaca, NY: Cornell University Press.

Mertus, Julie (1999) *Kosovo. How Myths and Truths Started a War*. Berkeley, University of California Press.

Sørlie Røhr, Heidrun (ed., 2005) *Dialog – mer enn ord*. Lillehammer: Nansenskolen.

Toumani, Meline (2014) *There Was and There Was Not: A Journey Through Hate and Possibility in Turkey, Armenia, and Beyond*. New York: Metropolitan Books.

Korean leaders Kim Jong-un and Moon Jae-in cross the Military Demarcation Line together ahead of the Inter-Korean Summit in Panmunjeom in April 2018.

'Seventy years have passed since the Korean War began, and that sad war is still not over. We have yet to find an exit from what is probably the longest-running war in the world. ... If peace means restraint and compromise, arrogance and self-righteousness are the biggest obstacles to peace. That's why I'm worried by blinkered and binary viewpoints that ignore the fact that when the other side doesn't have peace, we don't either. If we want peace, we should prepare for peace – because we'll never achieve true peace if we only prepare for war.' – Moon Chung-in, column in *Hankyoreh* newspaper, 13 July 2020

(Moon Chung-in is Professor Emeritus at Yonsei University, Seoul, and currently serving as Special Advisor to President Moon Jae-in for Foreign Affairs and National Security.)

Editors' Afterthoughts

*W*hen people from different parts of the world feel, think and act in particular ways, quite differently from people from other parts of the world, we call this pattern their *culture*. This word has so many definitions that some people, often professionals within the social sciences and humanities, have stopped using it altogether. They may say that, since it encompasses almost everything, it has no explanatory power. We believe otherwise, and our belief has recently been supported by new research in social psychology dealing with cross-cultural studies, as well as in research within neuroscience, or brain studies, so to speak.

Cultural differences are often seen as an exotic aspect of entertainment, experienced, for example, during travel and on vacations. By contrast, however, when such differences are experienced on the home front, they can easily be viewed as 'disturbing' to the familiarities of our own daily life. In this case, they are often viewed more negatively. People may feel uncomfortable when others do not follow 'normal' procedures or generally accepted rules.

In societies where people stay put and remain where they are, and where travel to foreign destinations is rare, culture remains as invisible as the air one breathes and what scholars may refer to as cultural is, for the locals, simply natural.

Globalization, used here to underline the fact that connections between institutions and people from all over the world have grown tremendously, has changed all this. Digitalization has, moreover, made such connections easily accessible, while affordable (but unsustainable) air traffic has made intercontinental travel all too easy (but irresponsible). During the last 30 years, the private and public sectors have utilized these opportunities and new technologies to 'go global'. For a short while, this was seen as 'the end of history' meaning that there were no more stages left, nothing more to strive for, or to achieve.

Yet, things took a different direction. Globalization did not, in fact, level cultural differences. On the contrary. Exposure to such differences on a grand scale meant that more and more people became aware of culture. In the first instance, their attention was drawn to the *difference* of others. Now, however, we are approaching a time where people have become aware of their *own differences*. We are different, too.

That Asia and the West are characterized by different basic and historically rooted cultural values and norms is common knowledge. That both also are affected by similar influences in the modern world is equally obvious. The problem is that in social studies, most people have been convinced that the second influence would eventually overtake the first and basic one, which rightly belonged to the past. This is a typical Western mode of thinking – of either/or – and a typical Western perspective on development: as a movement towards Western ways that is largely identical with 'universalism'. These views are widespread in Asia as well, mainly due to the dominant position of Western academic institutions and the great number of Asian scholars with a Western academic degree, mainly obtained in the USA.

Western established and governed institutions advised the non-West to follow their lead. Although accepting some of their own peculiarities (exotic differences), they had to acknowledge and respect a few basic 'universal' truths, in particular: the supreme importance of the market economy, free trade, individually based human rights and liberal democracy (political representation based on one person, one vote). Local or indigenous culture, with its 'exotic' features, should not be allowed to hinder these universals. After all, these local traits would evaporate as economic and political development eventually caught up with the 'highest developed level of the West'. It was a matter of course, that if the culture of the Other was backward (and the West was certain that it was), then it would change with economic and political development. The end of history was nigh. Whoever (in the West) attempted to argue otherwise was told that such thinking was merely narrow-minded and egotistical, and was criticised for not granting other people the benefits that we enjoyed for ourselves – namely, freedom, rights, and happiness, not to mention the beauty of Western civilization. By contrast, those in the East who maintained the relevance of 'home-grown' ways were simply seen as parochial and nativist. Those of us who have questioned 'universalism' all along can confirm: it has been an uphill struggle.

In international relations, this difficulty in dealing with different cultural values and norms plays an increasingly negative role, and one reason for that is the inability – or unwillingness – to accept the Other's differences as legitimate. The often-misrepresented US political scientist, Samuel P. Huntington, aptly points to this problem when he writes that: 'In the emerging world of ethnic conflict and civilizational clash, Western

> **'In the emerging world of ethnic conflict and civilizational clash, Western belief in the universality of Western culture suffers three problems: it is false; it is immoral; and it is dangerous.'**

belief in the universality of Western culture suffers three problems: it is false; it is immoral; and it is dangerous.' He goes on to provide the eye-opening formulation: 'The non-Wests see as Western what the West sees as universal'.[1] It seems as though the West has for too long ignored its own weak spots and rejected

---

1. Samuel P. Huntington, *The Clash of Civilizations and the Remaking of World Order*. New York: Simon & Schuster, 1996, pp. 310 and 68.

possibly useful and transferable features derived from non-Western systems.

In the introduction to his exploration of the origins and early development of political organization, Elman R. Service writes:

> The human achievement was the creation of culture, the means by which societies tame and govern their members and create and maintain their complex social organization. Culture also has technological, economic, religious, artistic and recreational functions, among others. All of these depend on the ability of the political aspect of the culture to integrate and protect the society. The gravest problems, aside from sheer subsistence, are political, and all societies must be able to solve them in order to perpetuate themselves.[2]

Published some 45 years ago, before the end of the Cold War and before the word 'globalization' became a household expression characterising the present time, is this depiction of civilization(s) state(s), and culture(s) still relevant? We believe it is more relevant now than ever before. One of the things that the consequences of the Coronavirus pandemic has brought back to the international agenda is that the nation-state is as alive and kicking as the cultures that sustain and maintain it. It is imperative, therefore, that we reconcile ourselves to the fact that there are different cultures and civilizations; and that these need to co-exist, if the world and all its inhabitants are to survive. In order for us to effectively achieve this, it is imperative that we collaborate across cultures, and to do so with an appreciation of and deep respect for difference.

In the opening to this piece, we make reference to recent findings in psychology and neuroscience we see as relevant to understanding Others. Let us linger on this for a short while, in an effort to point out what we see as interesting and impor-

---

2. Elman R. Service, *Origins of the State and Civilization: The Process of Cultural Evolution*. New York: W.W. Norton, p. 3.

tant insights that should, or even must, influence our general understanding of the world in its given complexity.

Social science studies have repeatedly found that Asians and Westerners (Europeans and North Americans) not only have different habits and material cultures for all to see; they also see the world differently, and think differently. What is more, the natural sciences add, what they (all of us) have learned to see, understand, appreciate or despise, has a biological component. The brain becomes wired (shaped) according to our activities over time. In the field of neuroscience, one would probably say: *in cognitive neuroscience, we have provided evidence that sustained experience changes neural structures.* Hence, it has come as something of a surprise to neuroscientists as to how deeply culture (values and norms) shapes the brain. Equally, social scientists and other researchers need to rethink findings based solely on studies among Westerners (indeed, mainly among North American college students taking introductory psychology courses, who comprise the vast majority of study participants.)

Before returning to the specific focus of this book – the demonization of the (enemy) Other – let us quote one of the pioneers in cross-cultural psychology, Nalini Ambady, who states that: 'Both the structure and function of the human brain throughout its development are shaped by the environment. The social environment, in turn, is shaped by culture.'[3]

Important consequences arise from these *real-world implications*, and these need to be taken into serious consideration in a shrinking world where we all are – and will increasingly be – affected by events of various kinds, from terrifying pandemics to economic collapse over political conflicts to the ca-

---

3. Nalini Ambady, 'The Mind in the World: Culture and the Brain', Presidential Column, *Observer* magazine, Association for Psychological Science, May/June 2011 p. 1, https://www.psychologicalscience.org/observer/the-mind-in-the-world-culture-and-the-brain.

tastrophes wrought by accelerating climate change. In relation to the issue of demonization, can we, as citizens of the world, accept that a huge propaganda machinery produces fake news and lies as a part of political campaigns and ideological wars, all aimed at pointing people's minds and opinions in particular directions?

Let's take, as one example, the 'problem' of political leadership. Can it really be maintained that there is only one, universally acceptable form of political organization and governance? If we do maintain this, then we have to be prepared to falsify findings in the fields of social- and cross-cultural psychology as well as in biology and neuroscience in order to accommodate the reality that people in Asia feel deeply interconnected with each other in terms of their social relations. This is an important aspect of their worldview, and it differs from a typically Western self-construal that is individually independent. Broadly speaking, while a person from Asia emphasizes social harmony, conformity and adherence to group norms, a Westerner values autonomy, uniqueness, freedom and the right to self-expression. Will these two personae necessarily want exactly the same form of governance? Will they both feel comfortable in each other's ideal system? This is, as we see it and based on our experiences, not very likely.

The question is not whether we see the same thing, and like the same things, but whether or not we can understand the cultural particularities of the Other, accept and appreciate that these differences exist, and then communicate about how to deal with the world as it is. Importantly, this includes *agreeing to disagree*.

If the demonization of North Korea can be seen as an example of bad practice that is not to be repeated in our views and news about China, or Russia or Iran for that matter, then that negative experience will have contributed to an important positive mission.

Scholars and diplomats – from East and West alike – should, in the name of mutual interest in preserving peace and developing positive international relations with each other, engage in a collaborative de-demonization process. Key to this process is to identify and replace news that is biased and fake with news coverage and information about the Other *that consequently takes into account the impact on the real-world of culturally based world-views, values and norms, ideas about self and society, and understanding of power and authority.*

To provide governments with such knowledge and insights, and not least to provide news media with this, would be a very important international contribution.

This would obviously be a long and complicated process that must first be explored within the institution of academia itself. The implication for the social sciences and the humanities of the findings in the fields of psychology and neuroscience must be acknowledged, considered and taken into careful account. This means it must affect how we study and report our findings, and how we teach the next generation of academics in our disciplines. It seems obvious that changes must take place, and that cross- and interdisciplinary research must take root in the study of the Other. Moreover, this work must be undertaken comparatively and collaboratively.

The need for this adapted approach to learning and scholarship is acute and we cannot afford to wait; there is a critical need for this among practitioners in international affairs, among all those working internationally, and not least in the field of journalism. If we continue to accept news coverage that fails to take into account *the reality of cultural difference*, and if we fail to realise the dangers of demonization and fake news in a globalized world, the simmering animosities can easily erupt into full-blown conflicts.

In order to prepare this current volume of essays, we invited a group of 'like-minded' contributors, with no consideration of educational background, nationality, age, gender or political outlook. Since such characteristics undoubtedly affect all of us, as well as the wider population at large; we do not claim that it does not also colour our own different perspectives on the world. The term 'like-minded', however, holds another, much more important meaning: we are all concerned with the world we are living and working in, and we are particularly concerned with development in the present world, where differences often seem to be blown out of all proportion, and where differences are seen as problematic per se, even before they turn out to be so.

What unites the group of like-minded people who have collectively produced this work is our shared conviction that differences are here to stay and that although these differences may create difficulties, they are part and parcel of humanity. As a result, attempts to level the mindscape of humanities are absurd. On the contrary, it is extremely important to find ways to accommodate such differences, and learn to see them as what characterizes us as the species that we are. If we fail to achieve mutual understanding across cultures, then we can forget about visions of global cooperation to curb climate change, and all many of the other urgent tasks at hand, and just hope for miracles.

Index